Directory of Popular Culture Collections

by Christopher D. Geist
and Ray B. Browne
Michael T. Marsden
Carole Palmer

ORYX PRESS
1989

The rare Arabian Oryx is believed to have inspired the myth of the unicorn. This desert antelope became virtually extinct in the early 1960s. At that time several groups of international conservationists arranged to have 9 animals sent to the Phoenix Zoo to be the nucleus of a captive breeding herd. Today the Oryx population is nearly 800, and over 400 have been returned to reserves in the Middle East.

Copyright © 1989 by The Oryx Press
2214 North Central at Encanto
Phoenix, AZ 85004-1483

Published simultaneously in Canada

Printed and Bound in the United States of America

∞ The paper used in this publication meets the minimum requirements of American National Standard for Information Science—Permanence of Paper for Printed Library Materials, ANSI Z39.48, 1984.

Library of Congress Cataloging-in-Publication Data

Directory of popular culture collections / edited by Christopher D.
  Geist ... [et al.].
    p. cm.
  Includes indexes.
  ISBN 0-89774-351-2 (alk. paper)
  1. United States—Popular culture—Museums—Directories.
2. United States—Popular culture—Library resources—Directories.
3. Canada—Popular culture—Museums—Directories. 4. Canada-
-Popular culture—Library resources—Directories. I. Geist,
Christopher D.
E169.1.D54 1989
973'.025—dc19   88-28202

In Honor of
Russel B. Nye
Pioneer Scholar in Popular Culture Studies
and
The Hundreds of Dedicated, Visionary Librarians
Who Recognized the Importance of Preserving the Materials
Listed in This Volume

Contents

Acknowledgments

Numerous individuals assisted the editors in various ways throughout the two years during which this work was in preparation. Dr. Kendall Baker, former Dean of the College of Arts and Sciences at Bowling Green State University, provided generous financial assistance from the College. Christopher Geist was awarded a research leave through the Faculty Improvement Program at Bowling Green, during which the first draft of the manuscript was completed. Barbara Moran kindly shared her pilot study of popular literature collections in the southeastern United States with the editors, a study that provided more help and guidance than she might realize! Ms. Joyce Swope, the cheerful and devoted secretary of the Department of Popular Culture, took on the burden of coordinating the mailing of countless surveys and of filing the responses as they were returned. Dr. Madonna Marsden assisted by carefully proofreading substantial portions of the manuscript. Several individuals contributed valuable suggestions and located important collections, including Dr. Fred E.H. Schroeder, Dr. Dan Walden, and Ms. Brenda McCallum, Head of the Popular Culture Library at Bowling Green State University. Thanks, too, are due to the librarians and curators who responded to our surveys and who often devoted substantial time and effort to locating fugitive materials in which we were interested. Finally, we wish to thank John Wagner, our able editor at Oryx Press, who put up with numerous delays and changes and whose careful editing of the first draft has made this a much better book.

User's Guide

The entries in this volume have been grouped by state and city within the U.S. section, and by province and city within the Canadian section. Where a particular city has more than one entry, the collections are listed alphabetically by institution. Two indexes are provided: a complete and detailed subject index lists general categories (Blacks), subcategories (Black literature), and individuals by name (Dillinger, John); the second index lists institutions, individual collections, and sub-collections alphabetically. Thus, this volume can be used to browse for research collections within a given state, while at the same time scholars can use the subject index to search for specific and general references to materials related to their research topics and the collections index to find named collections of material in which they are interested.

Each entry includes the name of the institution, complete mailing address, names of the individuals responsible for the collections, phone number, days and hours of operation, special restrictions and access requirements, and a detailed listing of special collections in Popular Culture. In many cases the individual research collections will be organized and cataloged together, while in some instances research materials are scattered throughout an institution's collection. Many listings discuss several distinct collections housed within a single institution, while others describe only the general holdings of a library as a whole.

The editors have made every effort to check and double-check information within each listing. We advise that researchers attempt to contact the individuals responsible for these collections prior to visiting the institutions. This will help to avoid costly delays and disappointments. If you should discover information that is in error, please notify us so that we will be able to correct the listing in subsequent volumes.

Introduction

This finding guide to Popular Culture research collections has been evolving for more than 15 years. In the mid-1970s, Ray Browne and Michael Marsden discussed the potential usefulness of such a guide to facilitate their own research and that of scholars in the field throughout the United States and Canada. But the nature of Popular Culture Studies was already such that the scope of research and scholarship was vast, almost unlimited, with a myriad of both substantial and small research collections of possible interest to scholars scattered widely among academic, public, and industrial libraries and museums. Moreover, the subfields within Popular Culture were numerous but ill defined.

Nevertheless, Browne and Marsden attempted a modest experiment and mailed a questionnaire to a brief list of libraries where important collections were known to be stored. Marsden was able to compile and publish the results in the *Popular Culture Association Newsletter* (Vol. VI, March 1977). Occupying only 22 pages of the newsletter, the boldly titled "National Finding List of Popular Culture Holdings and Special Collections" attracted considerable interest and resulted in several updates in subsequent issues.

During the years between that modest beginning and the publication of the current volume, the field of Popular Culture Studies has broadened and become even more complex, and, even more exciting. Positive responses to the earlier guide and the maturation and general acceptance of research in Popular Culture have indicated that a reliable and extensive guide to archival collections in the discipline is overdue. This volume begins the task of organizing research access not only to major collections, but also to numerous smaller bodies of material.

It seems axiomatic that everyone collects something, for which we students of culture should be most thankful. No one library or museum could hope to collect and organize even representative samples of all the varied forms of artifacts that make up the width and breadth of our Popular Culture. Consider, for example, the inability of the Smithsonian Institution to accomplish that task, even with the advantage of its national mandate! Still, individuals and institutions can stake out their particular collecting claims and develop that most complete collection of _____ (fill in the blank!). Whatever their motivation, such collectors serve a crucial function in the future of Popular Culture scholarship.

The title of this work is somewhat pretentious. To assemble these entries the editors searched all standard library guides to special collections and research archives. They studied reference books and tour books for specialized museums that might house little-known archival collections. Letters of inquiry were mailed to all individual members and all institutional members of the Popular Culture Association and of the American Culture Association. Each institution listed in the earlier version of the guide published in the *Popular Culture Association Newsletter* also received our questionnaire. Individual responses to these questionnaires differed in depth of detail, and, in the case of some large institutions holding numerous collections of varied composition, in the respondent's selection of those holdings which seemed proper for inclusion. As responses were returned, many librarians generously suggested additional institutions and collections for our consideration. In this manner the entries in this volume were assembled. Even though these efforts were substantial, the editors realize that this volume remains incomplete. Later editions of our guide will attempt even broader coverage; we intend to contact *every* academic and public library in the United States and Canada. We also hope to add many collections from industrial archives (a few are included here) and to expand coverage of private collections, which are sometimes available to scholars.

Defining the field of Popular Culture is not easy and has fostered a healthy and extensive academic debate as scholars seek to develop disciplinary focus in the field. While no single definition has been received as totally satisfactory, the editors have been guided by several assumptions with which *most* scholars in the field would agree. In the simplest terms Popular Culture may be thought of as mainstream culture—the arts, artifacts, entertainments, fads, beliefs, and values shared by large segments (but not necessarily all segments) of the society. Much of this material is, of course, related to the mass media, but there are also numerous aspects of Popular Culture that are not mass-mediated, such as fast food restaurants, Little League Baseball, carnivals, amusement parks, board games, Tupperware parties, and scores of other categories. It is also true that we are not able to make a simple head count—i.e., do 51% of us like a given artifact?—to determine whether or not an item qualifies as Popular Culture. Indeed, many items we study may not be popular at all, but still fall under the rubric of Popular Culture Studies. A romance novel no one bought or a cheap space adventure film that was a financial failure may still be considered a part of the larger Popular Culture because both would be examples of attempts to imitate more successful works already in popular genres.

Ray Browne's own pioneering definition of the field insists that Popular Culture consists of all those aspects of our daily lives that are not narrowly academic and intellectual and that are free from the minority standards that commonly dominate the fine arts. Thus, Popular Culture tends to pay for itself in the marketplace and is rather more democratic than high art, which must always satisfy its learned and elite patrons. To be sure, other levels of culture often interact with Popular Culture. Folktales become episodes of television series and great paintings are transformed into advertising vehicles. Folklore in particular has always been closely related to Popular Culture. Some scholars argue that Popular Culture arose along with the mass media and became the functional replacement of folk culture in modern societies. While the editors do not fully accept this argument, we do view many aspects of folk culture as so closely related to the study of popular art that we have included several collections of folklore in our listings.

Other critics have asserted that Popular Culture consists of all those things people do to amuse themselves when they are not at work. Popular Culture could thus be viewed as what people in a culture do to play, to have fun, to divert themselves from the daily necessity of making a living. This idea has some merit, and many of the collections noted in this volume seem to have been developed with this definition in mind. Still, Popular Culture scholarship should not be limited in this fashion. We do not leave our Popular Culture behind when we punch the time clock. Popular Culture surrounds us and dominates our values, customs, modes of communication, and lifestyles even while we work.

With these sometimes conflicting definitions in mind, the editors have attempted to assemble entries that focus on mainstream culture and that center on a level of culture distinct and separate from the elite values espoused through high art. We realize that other scholars might quibble with some of our listings, but we are confident that all researchers in this vast field will find this volume a useful starting point for a wide array of projects. We would welcome comments and suggestions as we look toward later editions of this work.

HELP US FIND ADDITIONAL COLLECTIONS

Have we missed an imporant research collection? At the end of this book you will find a survey form similar to the one used to gather the information published here. Please photocopy and use it to report new entries. Perhaps your own institution has a collection that should be listed, or you might know of an appropriate archive or library from your research experiences. Feel free to solicit entries from colleagues. Although we will be able to extend our listings considerably in the next update, we need your help to insure that our coverage is as complete as possible. It is the users, after all, who are the best judges of the usefulness of a research guide such as this.

Popular Culture Collections in the United States

ALABAMA

Birmingham

1. Alabama Sports Hall of Fame and Museum

PO Box 10163
Birmingham, AL 35202

Contact: Dr Bob Willis
(205) 323-6665
Hours: Tues, 1-5; Wed-Sat, 10-5; Sun, 1-5
Accessible to Public: Yes
Accessible to Scholars: Yes
Special Considerations: Phone prior to visit

Collection consists of printed material, audiovisual material, and memorabilia related to almost 130 individuals whose athletic activities have brought fame and glory to Alabama.

2. Birmingham Public Library, Arts, Music and Recreation Department

2100 Park Pl
Birmingham, AL 35203

Contact: Anne F Knight, Head Librarian
(205) 226-3670
Hours: Mon-Tues, 9-8; Wed-Sat, 9-6; Sun, 2-6
Accessible to Public: Yes
Accessible to Scholars: Yes

Collins Collection of the Dance: Books, photographs, pamphlets, and memorabilia exploring the history and development of dance throughout the world with special emphasis on classical dance and ballet. The Collection contains 1,800 books and 1,000 photographs, programs, pamphlets, and other memorabilia.

Collections within the library also represent significant holdings in music, art, architecture, landscape architecture and gardening, sculpture, interior design, photography, film and television, recreation and sports.

3. Birmingham Public Library, Linn-Henley Research Library, Southern History Collection

2100 Park Pl
Birmingham, AL 35203

Contact: Mary Bess Paluzzi, Dept Head
(205) 226-3665
Hours: Mon-Tues, 9-8; Wed-Sat, 9-6; Sun, 2-6; closed holidays
Accessible to Public: Yes
Accessible to Scholars: Yes
Special Considerations: Hours by appointment for Hardie Collection and Agee Map Collection; Genealogical and Historical Collections open all hours Library is open

Hardie Collection of Children's Books: 19th century children's books, 850 titles.

Agee Map Collection: 2,500 maps, with books and atlases. Focus of the Collection is on the lower South.

Genealogical and Historical Collection: 50,000 printed volumes, 12,500 reels of microfilm, 6,000 pamphlets, 6,200 bound periodicals. Focus of the Collection is on the southern states.

Archives and Manuscripts Department: Material related to Birmingham and the state of Alabama; also a photograph collection.

The Tutwiler Collection of Southern History and Literature: One of the finest collections related to all aspects of southern U.S. history and literature, including 37,000 printed volumes, 1,600 volumes in microform, 5,300 volumes in bound periodicals, 8,500 reels of microfilm exclusive of newspaper and periodical holdings, 700 pamphlets, an extensive collection of scrapbooks on the political and cultural development of Birmingham, 36 cabinets of vertical file and clipping materials, and a large uncharted collection of rare books. Important areas of the Collection include genealogical materials, state and local histories, Civil War studies, Reconstruction studies, Black history studies, early Alabama rare book imprints, books on travel in the South and the Southeast from the 18th and 19th centuries, and materials relating to Indian affairs, including works by Henry Rowe Schoolcraft.

Montgomery

4. Alabama Public Library Service
6030 Monticello Dr
Montgomery, AL 36130

Contact: Alice Stephens
(205) 277-7330
Hours: Mon-Fri, 8-5
Accessible to Public: Yes
Accessible to Scholars: Yes

Alabama Authors Collection: Consists of books and manuscripts of various authors from Alabama.

University

5. University of Alabama, William Stanley Hoole Special Collections Library
PO Box S
University, AL 35486

Contact: Joyce H Lamont, Curator
(205) 348-5512
Hours: Mon-Fri, 8-5; Thur, 6-10
Accessible to Public: Yes
Accessible to Scholars: Yes
Special Considerations: Material does not circulate

Rare Book Collection: Several thousand early imprints from 1485, including Confederate imprints, first editions of Sir Walter Scott's works, the Robinson Jeffers Collection, the Lafcadio Hearn Collection, Armed Services Editions of paperback books designed for American servicemen during World War II, and Alabama and Rare Pamphlet Collections.

Alabama Collection: Vast collection of materials relating to all aspects of Alabama and University of Alabama history and culture. Materials include census records; family and local histories; all University of Alabama publications; a photograph collection related to people, places, and events in Alabama history; and 19th century newspapers from Alabama and throughout the South (special strength in Civil War era).

Manuscript Collection: 6,000 linear feet (10,000,000 items) in a collection devoted to all aspects of Alabama culture since territorial days. Special areas of strength include business and industry, agriculture, religion, social life and customs (journals, scrapbooks, photographs, and memorabilia), folklore (records and tapes of folksongs), political papers, Civil War and Reconstruction (letters, diaries, journals, accounts of battles, and 1,000 items in the papers of Jefferson Davis), transportation (railroad and steamboat company records and photographs, road construction, records of ferry operations), literary manuscripts (Alabama writers), and genealogy.

Archive of American Minority Cultures: Centers on the special subject areas of ethnic, folk, and minority and women's history and culture, and consists principally of original sound recordings and other materials that have been preserved on nonprint formats.

Map Collection: Maps contained in this Collection are primarily early Alabama and the southeastern region, including the 1585 Ortelius Map of the World that clearly outlines the southeastern portion of what is now the United States.

ALASKA

Anchorage

6. Anchorage Museum of History and Art
121 W 7th Ave
Anchorage, AK 99501

Contact: Collections Department
(907) 264-4326
Hours: Tues-Sat, 10-6; Sun, 1-5
(Winter); Mon-Sat, 10-6; Sun, 1-5
(Summer)
Accessible to Public: Yes
Accessible to Scholars: Yes
Special Considerations: Prior notification
necessary to view collections in
storage; collections on exhibit open at
all times listed above

Collections include 20th century material reflecting life in Anchorage and Alaska. 1,500 pieces, most mass produced.

Sitka

7. Sitka National Historical Park, National Park Service
PO Box 738
Sitka, AK 99835

Contact: Gary Candelaria, Chief Park
Ranger
(907) 747-6281
Hours: May-Sept, Daily, 8-5; Oct-Apr,
Mon-Fri, 8-5
Accessible to Public: Yes
Accessible to Scholars: Yes
Special Considerations: Request prior to
arrival

Collections of books, toys, buttons, coins, and ephemera from the Russian occupation of Alaska (1741-1867), relating to Sitka. Approximately 3,000 objects, including ceramic shards and 1,000 pre-1917 books in Russian.

Skagway

8. Days of '98 Museum
PO Box 415
Skagway, AK 99840

Contact: Contact City Manager
(907) 983-2297
Hours: May-September, 8-8
Accessible to Public: Yes
Accessible to Scholars: Yes

Large collection of late 1800s and early 1900s materials regarding the Klondike Gold Rush.

ARIZONA

Phoenix

9. National Historical Fire Foundation
6101 E Van Buren
Phoenix, AZ 85008

Contact: Dr Peter M Molloy
(602) 275-3473
Hours: Mon-Sat, 9-5
Accessible to Public: Yes
Accessible to Scholars: Yes

Collection consists of 2,000 artifacts relating to the history of firefighting in the United States, 1700-1950, and a 4,000 volume library.

Prescott

10. The Bead Museum
140 S Montezuma
Prescott, AZ 36301

Contact: Gabrielle Liese, Dir
(602) 445-2431
Hours: Mon-Sat, 9-4:30
Accessible to Public: Yes
Accessible to Scholars: Yes
Special Considerations: Displays open to
everyone, but archival materials and
the research library open only to
scholars and by prior arrangement

Displays offer a general survey of ancient, ethnic, and European jewelry and personal adornment items from cultures throughout the world. The 300 items on display date from 3,000 BC to the present. Study collection includes beads and ornaments from all continents, areas, and periods, and also includes a large collection of books, pamphlets, and handbooks relating to ethnological and cultural use of beads and jewelry.

11. Sharlot Hall Museum-Library/Archives

415 W Gurley
Prescott, AZ 86301

Contact: Sue Abbey, Archivist
(602) 445-3122
Hours: Tues-Fri, 9-5 (Summer); Tues-Fri, 10-4 (Winter)
Accessible to Public: Yes
Accessible to Scholars: Yes
Special Considerations: Noncirculating

Cowboy Folklore Oral History Project: Currently contains approximately 200 tapes of cowboy songs and folklore from Arizona and some from Texas.

Photo Collection: Approximately 50,000 images concerned with Arizona and Yavapai County history, 1860-1940. Includes many types of photo images and subjects, such as historic preservation, ranching, mining, etc.

***Yavapai Magazine* Collection:** Issues of the local magazine published from 1913 to 1940, with only scattered issues from the 1920s and 1930s. This Chamber of Commerce publication includes excellent information on mining and local events.

Tempe

12. Arizona State University, Hayden Library

Tempe, AZ 85287

Contact: Christine Marin, Asst Archivist
(602) 965-2594; 965-4932; 965-3145
Hours: Mon-Fri, 8-8; Sat, 9-12, Sat, 1-4; closed holidays
Accessible to Public: Yes
Accessible to Scholars: Yes
Special Considerations: Materials in the Southwestern Lore Collection must be used in the Arizona Collection Room

Chicano Studies Collection: Books, periodicals, serials, newspapers, and ephemera relating to the history and contributions of Mexican Americans, or Chicanos, in the Southwest. Special topics include 20th century history, Chicano literature, Chicano politics, bilingual education, Chicano social issues (1969-present), Mexican-American women, Chicano labor issues, and immigration. Emphasis is on Arizona.

Southwestern Lore Collection: Archival holdings are related to Arizona folklore and consist primarily of undergraduate papers developed as fieldwork projects in folklore courses.

13. Arizona State University, Music Library

Arizona State University
Tempe, AZ 85287

Contact: Contact Music Librarian
(602) 965-3513
Hours: Mon-Fri, 8-5; Sun, 2-10
Accessible to Public: Yes
Accessible to Scholars: Yes

Wayne King Collection: 117 kinescopes from the *Wayne King Show*, which ran from September 29, 1949, to June 26, 1952; orchestral library from the Wayne King Orchestra; recordings of the King orchestra.

Sheet Music Collection: Popular music from the late 19th century through the 1940s.

14. Arizona State University, World Humor and Irony Membership (WHIM)

Department of English
Tempe, AZ 85287

Contact: Don L F Nilsen
(602) 965-7592
Hours: Mon-Fri, 7:30-5:30 (but hours vary)
Accessible to Public: Yes
Accessible to Scholars: Yes

Names, addresses and phone numbers of comedy clubs, humor organizations, humor journals, humor newsletters, humor newspapers, humor scholars, and humor performers and comedians are available from every state and nearly 100 nations. The library consists of books, magazines, cassettes, and other materials related to the study of humor.

Tucson

15. University of Arizona, Music Collection
115 Music Building
Tucson, AZ 85721

Contact: Dorman H Smith, Head
(602) 621-7009
Hours: Mon-Fri, 8-5; Sat, 12-4
Accessible to Public: Yes
Accessible to Scholars: Yes

Grant Hill Collection: 150,000 popular songs from 1870 to the present in sheets and folios and on Tune-dex cards. Most accessible by title only.

16. University of Arizona Library, Special Collections
Special Collections
Tucson, AZ 85721

Contact: David P Robrock, Special
  Collections Librarian
(602) 621-6424
Hours: Mon-Fri, 9-5; Sat, 12-4 (during
  the regular school term)
Accessible to Public: Yes
Accessible to Scholars: Yes

Science Fiction Collection: Over 18,000 volumes and extensive runs of over 120 periodicals, 1920-present.

Picture Postcard Collection: 55 boxes of postcards, arranged geographically and by topic; most of the cards are pre-1950 and many date from the early 1900s.

17. Westerners International Foundation
PO Box 3485
Tucson, AZ 85722

Contact: W K Brown, Sec
Hours: By arrangement; inquire about
  specific holdings prior to visit
Accessible to Public: No
Accessible to Scholars: Yes

Library contains current books about the history of the Frontier West and serves the worldwide Westerner Corrals organization, which was begun in 1944 by Leland D. Case and Elmo Scott Watson.

ARKANSAS

Arkadelphia

18. Joint Educational Consortium
PO Box 499
Arkadelphia, AR 71923

Contact: Dolphus Whitten Jr, Dir
(501) 246-9283
Hours: Mon-Fri, 8-5
Accessible to Public: Yes
Accessible to Scholars: Yes

Oral History Collection: Approximately 400 taped interviews with people in southwest Arkansas, principally representing life in rural areas and small towns.

Photographic Collection: Negatives of photographs representing life in southwest Arkansas.

Eureka Springs

19. Elna M. Smith Foundation Sacred Projects
PO Box 471
Eureka Springs, AR 72632-0471

Contact: Marvin D Peterson
(501) 253-8559
Hours: Last Fri in Apr through Labor
  Day, 10-8; Labor Day through last Sat
  in Oct, 10-7; remainder of year by
  appointment
Accessible to Public: Yes
Accessible to Scholars: Yes

Bible Museum: Contains over 7,000 volumes in over 625 languages, as well as 3,000 primitive manuscripts and artifacts. Planning is currently underway to place parts of Bibles and related manuscripts on microforms. Additional collections include over 1,000 artifacts in a wide variety of art forms that relate to sacred art throughout the world.

Fayetteville

20. University of Arkansas Libraries, Special Collections
University of Arkansas
Fayetteville, AR 72701

Contact: Norma Oritz

(501) 575-5577
Hours: Mon-Fri, 8-5; Sat, 9-1
Accessible to Public: Yes
Accessible to Scholars: Yes
Special Considerations: Access and
registration form for manuscript
collections

Joseph Marsh Clark Liberty-Loan Posters: Consists of nine colored pictorial broadsides commissioned by the U.S. Treasury Department to promote the purchase of war loan certificates (1917-1918).

Faultless Starch Company Joke and Game Books: Consists of 36 volumes (8 x 13 cm) of joke and game books for children distributed with each package of Faultless Starch (c. 1900).

Gospel Songbooks, 1891-1973: Consists of 55 paperbound hymnals dealing with 19th and 20th century Southern Evangelical Christianity. Hymnals are arranged in three sections according to publisher and in alphabetical order by title.

Mary Dengler Hudgins Arkansas Traveller Scores, 1847-1971: Consists of eight items, five of which are printed scores of the "Arkansas Traveller," one version by Mose Case, another an unpublished score of "Hymn to Arkansas," and one mimeographed program.

Mary Dengler Hudgins Gospel Music Research Files and Songbooks, 1937-1974: Consists of 27 files of materials divided into the gospel music research files and the song book material in "shaped notes"; primarily published by Arkansas firms.

Gerald J. McIntosh Dime Novel Collection, 1879-1967: Correspondence, notes, memoranda, lists, printed matter, and other material relating to the history of American dime novels and also to Little Rock, Arkansas, dime novel collector G. J. McIntosh's interests and activities in the field.

World War I Collection: Consists of about 50 posters, 20 postal cards, and other materials concerning the U.S. Treasury Department's campaign for the sale of U.S. Savings Bonds and Thrift Stamps.

***Arkansas thomas cat* Collection:** Consists of 34 issues of the *Arkansas thomas cat*, which was published in Hot Springs, 1894-1949. Contains information about everyday life in Hot Springs.

Big Blue and Little Blue Books: Over 800 of the Big Blue Books and Little Blue Books edited by E. Haldeman-Julius in the People's Pocket Series.

Little Rock

21. University of Arkansas at Little Rock, Archives and Special Collections
33rd and University Ave
Little Rock, AR 72204

Contact: Bobby Roberts
(501) 569-3123
Hours: Mon, 8-9; Tues-Fri, 8-5; Sat, 11-3
Accessible to Public: Yes
Accessible to Scholars: Yes

Major holdings include the *J. N. Hershell Historical Collection* of 100 dime novels related to Arkansas and the Indian Territory; 2,500 postcards of Arkansas images (1900-present); 1,000 broadsides and campaign cards (palm cards) relative to Arkansas elections (1875-present); and 1,000 invitation cards, including dance cards, wedding invitations, funeral notices, and calling cards (1860-1910).

Bill Graham Cartoon Collection: Contains approximately 5,000 cartoons and 2,500 rough drawings from Graham's years as editorial cartoonist for the *Arkansas Gazette* (1950-1984).

Jan Kennedy Cartoon Collection: Contains approximately 2,400 cartoons from Kennedy's years as editorial cartoonist for the *Arkansas Democrat* (1948-present).

Pine Ridge

22. Lum and Abner Museum and Jot 'Em Down Store
PO Box 38
Pine Ridge, AR 71966

Contact: Kathryn Stucker
(501) 326-4442
Hours: Tues-Sat, 9-5; Sun, 11-5 (Mar 1-Dec 1); also by appointment
Accessible to Public: Yes
Accessible to Scholars: Yes

Special Considerations: Ramp for wheelchairs, but no handicapped restrooms

The museum is housed in original store buildings built between 1904 and 1909. Collections include *Lum and Abner* radio and movie memorabilia, general store merchandise and fixtures; farm and home tools, furniture, clothing, etc. *Lum and Abner* program cassettes available.

State University

23. Arkansas State University, Mid-South Center for Oral History

Box 143
State University, AR 72467

Contact: William M Clements; Larry D Ball
(501) 972-3043
Hours: By appointment
Accessible to Public: Yes
Accessible to Scholars: Yes

The collection includes about 200 tape recorded interviews with persons involved in farming, hunting, trapping, timber culture, education, and other aspects of northeast Arkansas culture.

CALIFORNIA

Bakersfield

24. California State College, Bakersfield Library

9001 Stockdale Hwy
Bakersfield, CA 93309

Contact: Jim Segesta
(805) 833-3172
Hours: Varies; make appointment
Accessible to Public: Yes
Accessible to Scholars: Yes
Special Considerations: Inquire in advance of visit

Contains taped oral history interviews with long term residents of Kern County and the *California Odyssey Project* of taped interviews, all transcribed, with several dozen individuals who participated in or were witnesses to the Dust Bowl migrations of the 1930s.

Berkeley

25. University of California at Berkeley, Bancroft Library

Bancroft Library
Berkeley, CA 94720

Contact: Peter E Hanff, Coord
Write for information
Hours: Regular Library hours
Accessible to Public: Yes
Accessible to Scholars: Yes
Special Considerations: Scholars should contact the Library prior to visit in order to ascertain which holdings are available; noncirculating

The Bancroft Library, the largest department of special collections at Berkeley, is so rich in collections that serve the scholars of popular culture that it is impossible to break the collection down into specific areas. A notable collection, the *Bancroft Collection of Western Americana,* might be viewed as one large collection to support popular culture research. Another area of special focus is the collection of early pictorial images of California and the American West. The *University Archives* document the history of the institution and include student papers, faculty papers, memorabilia, ephemera, handbills, photographs, etc.; the *Social Protest Project* collects leaflets, broadsides, and other ephemera documenting diverse socio-political activities in California during recent years; the *Mark Twain Project* houses the author's notebooks, correspondence, autobiography, other manuscripts, first editions, and additional special materials; the *Rare Books Collection* includes 400 incunabula along with rare European, English, U.S., and South American imprints, and also includes examples of fine printing of all periods and places, with an emphasis on American and English typography; and the *History of Science and Technology Program* includes manuscripts and rare books emphasizing 20th century American science and science-based technology and the physical sciences prior to 1800. The Library also houses the *Regional Oral History Office.*

26. University of California at Berkeley, Music Library

240 Morrison Hall
Berkeley, CA 94720

Contact: Contact Library reference staff
(415) 642-2623
Hours: Mon-Thur, 9-9; Fri-Sat, 9-5; Sun, 9-1; special hours in effect when classes not in session
Accessible to Public: Yes
Accessible to Scholars: Yes
Special Considerations: Archival collections used by appointment only

Collections include Sigmund Romberg autograph scores of musical shows; California folk music archive (field tapes and notes from 1930s); jazz music transcriptions, fakebooks, and sound recordings; monographs and sound recordings related to ethnomusicology; and vocal scores for musical shows (1920s-1940s).

Beverly Hills

27. Academy of Motion Picture Arts and Sciences, Margaret Herrick Library

8949 Wilshire Blvd
Beverly Hills, CA 90211

Contact: Linda Harris Mehr, Library Admin
(213) 278-8990
Hours: Mon-Tues, 9-5; Thur-Fri, 9-5; closed weekends and Wed
Accessible to Public: Yes
Accessible to Scholars: Yes
Special Considerations: Special collections are available by appointment only

The collections are vast and are related to the history and development of the motion picture as an art form and as an industry, including over 18,000 books and pamphlets (biographical, historical, analytical, and technical works), over 1,000 periodical titles (1906-present, including studio house organs, trade journals, fan magazines, and general film publications), 5,000,000 photographs, 5,000 screenplays, posters, lobby cards, and clipping files totalling over 1,100 file drawers (the latter related to production, biography, awards, festivals, publicity releases, actors, directors, writers, and the Academy of Motion Picture Arts and Sciences).

Poster Collection: Contains over 6,000 posters (primarily one-sheets) for films, 1911-present.

Special Collections: Consists of more than 200 manuscript, photograph, and scrapbook collections that document in depth the product and activities of major motion picture companies and organizations, as well as the careers of individual producers, directors, writers, actors, cinematographers, art directors, costume designers, and other artists who have made significant contributions to the motion picture industry. Among the collections are the MGM, RKO, and Paramount still archives; Thomas H. Ince and Cecil B. DeMille production stills; Paramount script files and pressbooks; MPAA Production Code Administration case files; and the personal papers, scripts, stills, and scrapbooks of Mary Pickford, Colleen Moore, Ray Milland, Alfred Hitchcock, George Stevens, George Cukor, John Huston, Fred Zinnemann, Lewis Milestone, Sam Peckinpah, Mack Sennett, Jules White, Hal Wallis, William Selig, Edith Head, Leah Rhodes, Louella Parsons, Hedda Hopper, Sidney Skolsky, Merle Oberon, Richard Barthelmess, Jean Hersholt, and Frank Borzage.

28. 20th Century Fox Film Corporation, Research Library

Box 900
Beverly Hills, CA 90213

Contact: Ken Kenyon, Dir
(213) 203-2782
Hours: Mon-Fri, 9-6
Accessible to Public: No
Accessible to Scholars: No
Special Considerations: Inhouse film and television productions and all studio departments can use services for a fee

Clippings Files: Includes newspaper and magazine clippings, photographs, pamphlets, etc. on a wide range of topics. Five folders contain material on Fox history (1916-present). There are also folders for such topics as cartoons, Disney, censorship, ratings, Keystone Cops, continuity sketches, and producers and directors.

Photograph Collection: Consists of pre-production research stills from about 38 films; World War II combat photographs (Europe) in the Wetzler and Tichy Collections.

Fox Films, 1920-1970: Contains about 400 films; also includes card file and four notebooks of indexes to contents of research books, plus films, books, and magazines.

Burbank

29. Burbank Central Library, Warner Research Collection

110 N Glenoaks
Burbank, CA 91502

Contact: Joan Michaels
(818) 953-9743
Hours: Mon-Fri, 9-5
Accessible to Public: Yes
Accessible to Scholars: Yes
Special Considerations: By appointment only; this is a fee-based service ($35 per hour, $15 per hour for students); closed stacks; research is completed by Warner's staff

Collections include older license plates from various states along with up-to-date files on each state's vehicle licensing policy; 135 Sears catalogs from 1894-present; 38,000 books on costume and architecture; 2,000,000 newspaper and magazine clippings and pamphlets related to costume, uniforms, and personalities; and an extensive collection of location photographs.

30. Walt Disney Archives, The Walt Disney Company

500 S Buena Vista St
Burbank, CA 91521

Contact: David R Smith, Archivist
(818) 840-5424
Hours: Mon-Fri, 8-5
Accessible to Public: Yes
Accessible to Scholars: Yes
Special Considerations: Use is limited to advance appointment and must involve specific research projects

A vast collection of material related to Disney and his work includes his office correspondence files (1930-1966) and assorted earlier files. Gifts to Disney are included, as well as personal memorabilia, recordings and transcripts of speeches, awards, 8,000 photographs of Disney, a Disney family history, and a collection of miniatures. Also includes 900 Disney books published in the U.S., a good representative collection of Disney books published in 35 languages, a complete collection of domestic Disney comic books and most foreign comics (1932-present), a nearly complete collection of phonograph records issued by the Walt Disney Music Company, several hundred singles and albums of Disney songs issued by other recording companies, tape recordings, sheet music of Disney titles, a vast clippings file dating from 1924, over 500,000 negatives of photographs related to Disney and his enterprises, thousands of merchandise items related to Mickey Mouse and other Disney characters (along with catalogs, correspondence files, photographs, and contracts), copies of Disney films (some on videotape for easy study), scripts for all Disney live action films (including cutting continuities and other production information), drafts and film sequence descriptions of animated Disney films, a large collection of movie props and artifacts, archival materials covering the history of Disney theme parks and Audio-Animatronics, most of Disney's original artwork and an excellent artwork collection from his animated films, and oral histories of Disney conducted with his key employees. All materials are organized, and key materials are indexed fully.

Carson

31. California State University at Dominguez Hills Library, Special Collections

800 E Victoria St
Carson, CA 90747

Contact: Contact Special Collections Librarian
(213) 516-3700
Hours: Open during regular library hours; these vary depending on school terms; inquire via telephone
Accessible to Public: Yes
Accessible to Scholars: Yes
Special Considerations: Closed stack

Claudia Buckner Collection of American Best Sellers: A group of 3,000 volumes, the collection represents

American popular taste in reading from the beginning of the country through 1980, and was developed using the major bibliographies in the field. Collection continues to grow and is being kept current.

Chula Vista

32. American Theatre Organ Society, Archives/Library
1393 Don Carlos Ct
Chula Vista, CA 92010

Contact: Vernon P Bickel
(619) 421-9629
Hours: By appointment
Accessible to Public: No
Accessible to Scholars: Yes
Special Considerations: Contact curator in advance of visit

Collections are extensive and include: piano/vocal music, 1,755 titles; piano accompaniment/conductor music, 1,199 titles; silent motion picture cue sheets and scores, 289 titles; organ sheet music, 96 titles; organ music books, 598 titles in 33 books; orchestral music, 259 titles; music books, 125 volumes; books, pamphlets, and booklets, 126 titles; 143 newspaper and magazine articles; periodicals, 589 issues; 21 organ contracts; 31 organ specifications; information on 1 organ builder and 53 organists; photographs of organs (22), individuals (34), residences (2), theaters (8); silent motion picture films (16mm), 5; reel-to-reel audiotapes, 164; cassette audiotapes, 135; 78 rpm phonograph records, 210; 45 rpm phonograph records, 2; 33 1/3 rpm phonograph records, 264 albums; Wurlitzer organ rolls, 490 titles on 288 rolls; glass song slides, 148 complete sets; and large archival files of miscellaneous items. Collection is related to the use of organ music in various theater settings, including early motion picture theaters.

City of Industry

33. Ralph W. Miller Golf Library and Museum
One Industry Hills Pkwy
City of Industry, CA 91744

Contact: Jean Bryant, Dir
(818) 965-0861

Hours: Mon-Sun, 8:30-5; closed Christmas
Accessible to Public: Yes
Accessible to Scholars: Yes
Special Considerations: Special considerations and requests are to be made directly to the Director

Collection includes 5,000 noncirculating reference and research books pertaining exclusively to golf, including its history, instruction, biographies of golfers, course architecture and design, course management, and golf-related fiction and humor. Also includes 1,200 bound periodicals dating from the 1870s and current subscriptions to 40 golf magazines; numerous guides, directories, club and course histories and yearbooks; 950 postcards dating from the early 1900s; 2,400 photographs of amateur, professional, celebrity, and historical men and women golfers; vast clipping file preserved on microfilm (an ongoing record of golf tournaments, personalities, and human interest stories and events); and over 1,000 museum items and an extensive art collection with worldwide representation.

Claremont

34. Claremont Colleges, The Ella Strong Denison Library
Scripps College
Claremont, CA 91711

Contact: Judy Harvey Sahak, Librarian; Susan M Allen, Reference Librarian
(714) 621-8000 Ext 3941
Hours: Mon-Fri, 8:30-5
Accessible to Public: Yes
Accessible to Scholars: Yes
Special Considerations: Identification required

Olive Percival Collection of Dolls, Toys, and Miniatures: Consists of assorted dolls (2 Kathe Kruse Dolls, 10 other dolls, assorted china head dolls, many doll babies, thousands of doll hats, doll furniture, and an extensive collection of doll clothing), large Valentine collection (1830-1960), tea sets, musical instruments, toy animals, and 80 framed Daguerreotypes.

Juvenalia Collection: Includes over 1,150 children's books, including horn books, primers, and American Tract Society pamphlets.

Balch Travel Films and Photo Album Collection: Includes 42 photo albums from the early 20th century (Europe, Middle East, Asia, South and Central America), 9 reels "European Trip" (1928-29), 8 reels "Trip to the Orient" (1929-30), and 3 reels Balch Personal (motion picture studio, picnic, etc., 1928-29), all of which are available in videotape format.

Hanna Cookbook Collection: Covers 1930-50s in 250 uncataloged pamphlets, 350 cataloged books, and 1,000 recipe cards.

Ida Rust Macpherson Collection: Consists of a collection of books, periodicals, and ephemera by and about women, including about 170 women's periodical titles from the late 18th century to the present with many titles from the 19th century (*Godey's Lady's Book* 1830-32, 1836-65, 1867-74, 1876-77, and 1879; *House Beautiful* 1928-36, 1953-68; and *Vogue* 1953-present are representative holdings). The collection is rich in the areas of domestic history, etiquette books, material on customs and manners, domestic employment including the education of children, and the history of dress.

Bookplate Collections: Includes the *Louise Seymour Jones Collection* of over 5,000 bookplates, mounted, indexed, and enclosed in special boxes, and the *Eleanor Homer Collection* of nearly 3,000 bookplates, mounted, arranged in categories, and enclosed in special boxes.

Holdings also include two cartons of uncataloged postcards, 270 travel guides (mostly Baedeker Guides), and 100 trade cards representing companies in San Francisco (late 19th century).

Culver City

35. Lorimar Research Library
10202 W Washington Blvd
Culver City, CA 90230

Contact: Barbara Ahmadzadeh
(213) 558-5518
Hours: Mon-Fri, 9-5
Accessible to Public: No
Accessible to Scholars: No

Special Considerations: Generally available to entertainment industry on a fee basis ($40 plus expenses)

Contains 35,000 books, 100 runs of magazines, and 250,000 photographs and clippings related to costume, U.S. cities, U.S. license plates, and individuals. Material gathered to provide visual references in the making of motion pictures and television programs.

Davis

36. Women's Resources and Research Center
University of California at Davis
Davis, CA 95616

Contact: Joy Fergoda
(916) 752-3372
Hours: Mon-Fri, 8-1, 2-5
Accessible to Public: Yes
Accessible to Scholars: Yes

The collection supports the study of women and includes over 3,000 books of nonfiction and fiction works by U.S. and foreign authors, many from feminist and small press publishers that are not generally available to researchers; over 130 periodical runs of women's studies journals, and women's newspapers, magazines, and newsletters; over 6,000 pamphlets, magazine and newspaper articles, reprints, student and faculty papers, reports, and leaflets; over 500 audiotapes of women's center programs and over 100 commercial audiotapes; 79 oral history audiotapes consisting of 14 autobiographies of Yolo and Solano County women; and a growing collection of research papers.

Fresno

37. California State University at Fresno, Henry Madden Library
California State University at Fresno
Fresno, CA 93740

Contact: Ronald J Mahoney, Head
(209) 294-2595
Hours: Mon-Fri, 10-5
Accessible to Public: Yes
Accessible to Scholars: Yes
Special Considerations: Closed stack

Donald G. Larson Collection of International Expositions and Fairs, 1851-1940: Contains 1,700 books, 1,240 pamphlets, 2,280 photographs, 1,060 postcards, 300 tickets, and assorted passes and souvenirs.

Glen Ellen

38. Jack London Research Center
Box 337
Glen Ellen, CA 95442

Contact: Russ Kingman; Winnie Kingman
(707) 996-2888
Hours: Daily, 11-5
Accessible to Public: Yes
Accessible to Scholars: Yes

Jack London Collection: Consists of four large filing cabinets of articles by or about London, 500 books that deal with London, 65,000 3 X 5 cards on Jack London and his friends (cross-indexed), bibliographic material on nearly everything written by or about London, unpublished manuscripts, theses, dissertations, scenarios, and other materials on London, as well as oral histories by people who knew London, microfilms of London's 27 scrapbooks, complete runs of *The Jack London Newsletter, Jack London Echoes, Wolf, Jack London Collector,* and *What's New About London, Jack?,* and hundreds of letters by Jack London.

Hollywood

39. Homosexual Information Center
6758 Hollywood Blvd, #208
Hollywood, CA 90028

Contact: Don Slater
(213) 464-8431
Hours: Mon-Fri, 12-5; Sat, by appointment
Accessible to Public: Yes
Accessible to Scholars: Yes

This large library was begun in the early 1950s and has expanded into a major research facility dealing with the homosexual movement.

40. Sherman Grinberg Film Libraries, Inc.
1040 N McCadden Pl
Hollywood, CA 90038-3787

Contact: Bill Brewington (New York Office: Nancy Casey, 630 Ninth Ave, New York, NY 10036-3787)
(213) 464-7491; (212) 765-5170
Hours: Mon-Fri, 9:30-5:30
Accessible to Public: Yes
Accessible to Scholars: Yes
Special Considerations: Facilities charge of $25 per hour with a $50 minimum; charge includes viewing, research, and computer printouts

This is the world's largest news and stock footage film and tape library covering the entire 20th century. Materials include collections related to ABC News (1963-present), Pathe News (1898-1957), Paramount News (1926-1957), Metro-Goldwyn-Mayer color and black-and-white features and television stock footage, Twentieth Century Fox color and black-and-white features and television stock footage, *Nova* and *Odyssey* television series stock footage, BBC Natural History "Wildstock" Collection (for U.S. and Canada), Fitzpatrick Short Subjects, and numerous other collections.

41. Western Costume Company Research Library
5335 Melrose Ave
Hollywood, CA 90038

Contact: Sally Nelson-Harb, Dir
(213) 469-1451
Hours: Mon-Fri, 9:30-5:30
Accessible to Public: Yes
Accessible to Scholars: Yes
Special Considerations: Fee is charged

Collection is devoted to costume research and is primarily for use in movie and television productions. Includes 15,000 books and bound periodicals, including *London Illustrated News* from 1844-present, and all issues of *Life* and *National Geographic* ever published. Also includes an extensive collection of books and periodicals on fashion and military uniforms (includes *Godey's Ladies Book* and similar titles), and 130 vertical file drawers of clippings and stills that contain information on fashion in numerous countries, military uniforms of all ages, and appropriate dress for most occupations and sports activities. Collection covers ancient through modern times.

La Jolla

42. University of California at San Diego Library

Department of Special Collections, C-075-S
La Jolla, CA 92093

Contact: Lynda Corey Claassen
(619) 534-2533
Hours: Mon-Fri, 8-5:30; Sat, 1-4
Accessible to Public: Yes
Accessible to Scholars: Yes
Special Considerations: Noncirculating collection for research only

Little Blue Book Collection: Approximately 5,000 Little Blue Books and other publications from E. Haldeman-Julius of Girard, Kansas, printed 1920s-1950s.

Los Angeles

43. California State University at Los Angeles, John F. Kennedy Memorial Library

5151 State University Dr
Los Angeles, CA 90032

Contact: Charles C Brinkley
(213) 224-2267
Hours: By appointment
Accessible to Public: Yes
Accessible to Scholars: Yes
Special Considerations: Must make advance appointment by mail or telephone

Leroy Ellsworth Harris Archive: Consists of 3,000 pages of original manuscripts and sketches, copies of published and unpublished works, correspondence, medals and other memorabilia, commercial and noncommercial recordings of the major portions of the works and the complete microfilm of the Library of Congress Harris Collection numbering over 2,000 pages, along with 15,000 uncataloged letters and musical sheets.

Stanley Newcomb Kenton Archive: Includes radio concerts and commercial recordings, reel-to-reel tapes, taped interviews, videotapes, honors and awards, scrapbooks, posters, cards, newspaper reviews, programs, ink sketches and photographs of Stan Kenton and his band dating from the early 1940s.

Anthony Quinn Collection of Film Scripts: Contains about 200 film scripts owned by the actor, some of which were realized with his participation and others which were never filmed.

Joseph Wambaugh Manuscripts: Consists of five manuscripts of Wambaugh's books: *The New Centurions, The Black Knight, The Onion Field, Choir Boys,* and *The Black Marble.*

Public Official Papers Collection: The collection consists of the papers of distinguished California public officials, including those of Congressman George Edward Brown, Jr., State Assemblyman and Los Angeles County official Ernest E. Debs, Congressman and Lieutenant Governor Mervyn Dymally, diplomat Julian C. Nava, and Congressman Edward R. Roybal.

Pollard Collection of Children's Books: About 2,000 titles make up this collection. Strengths include late 19th and early 20th century imprints, mainly American and English, including works of Horatio Alger, Jr., Victor Appleton, Willard Baker, Gerald Breckinridge, Thornton W. Duffield, Leo Edwards, Edward Ellis, Percy Keese Fitzhugh, Howard R. Garis, Lillian Garis, Fremont Deering, Zane Grey, I. Irving Hancock, William Heyliger, Laura Lee Hope, Howard Payson, and Harold Sherman.

Perry R. Long Collection of Books on Printing and Engraving: Contains 3,000 volumes, including printers' manuals, histories, works on the art and science of topography, paper making, color printing, graphic design, book design, book binding, uncataloged ephemera (keepsakes, announcements, broadsides), and other examples of fine printing.

44. Los Angeles Public Library, Social Sciences Department

650 W 5th St
Los Angeles, CA 90071

Contact: Marilyn Wherley
(213) 612-3242
Hours: Mon-Thur, 10-8; Fri-Sat, 10-5:30
Accessible to Public: Yes
Accessible to Scholars: Yes

Collections include published works in English about the various ethnic groups in the greater Los Angeles area. Includes approximately 350 volumes concerning Asian, European, Indian, Spanish, and West Indian immigrants to the area.

45. Louis B. Mayer Library, American Film Institute
2021 N Western Ave
Los Angeles, CA 90027

Contact: Anne G Schlosser, Library Dir
(213) 856-7655
Hours: Mon-Fri, 10:30-5:15
Accessible to Public: Yes
Accessible to Scholars: Yes

Collections are substantial and include 5,500 volumes of film and television scripts; *TV Guide* (1948-present); 44 volumes of oral history transcripts with pioneers of the motion picture industry; 7,500 books on all aspects of film, television, video, cable, satellite, and other technologies; books on photography, theater, costume design, stage plays, and short stories; 150 subscriptions to related periodicals; clipping files (over 30,000 individual entries), including pamphlets, reviews, and other ephemera related to the entertainment industry; film festival files with up-to-date information on all major U.S. and international festivals; transcripts from AFI seminars with professionals from the film and television industries (1969-1981) and audiotapes of seminars after 1981; numerous personal papers and manuscript collections of leading film figures; and the *Columbia Pictures Stills Collection* (1930-1950).

46. Music Center Operating Company Archives
135 N Grand Ave
Los Angeles, CA 90012

Contact: Contact Director
(213) 972-7499
Hours: Mon-Fri, 10-5
Accessible to Public: No
Accessible to Scholars: Yes

Collections document the 23-year history of the Los Angeles County Music Center for the Performing Arts and resident companies. Included are press clippings, programs, posters, and photographs.

47. UCLA Film and Television Archive
1015 N Cahuenga Blvd
Los Angeles, CA 90038

Contact: Edward Richmond, Curator; Dan Einstein, TV Archivist; Charles Hopkins, Motion Picture Archivist
(213) 462-4921
Hours: Mon-Fri, 9-6
Accessible to Public: Yes
Accessible to Scholars: Yes
Special Considerations: Appointments to view films and tapes must be made one week in advance; viewing time limited

This is the largest public collection of motion pictures, television programs, and radio programs in the U.S. outside the Library of Congress. The collection contains over 30,000 films, mostly American studio features, with many on original nitrate prints; 25,000 television films, tapes, and kinescopes dating from 1946-present; and over 30,000 radio broadcasts, most on original transcription disks covering the 1930s to the 1960s. The collection also includes over 300 items of antique and historic television equipment and receivers dating from the 1930s.

48. University of California at Los Angeles, Center for the Study of Comparative Folklore and Mythology
1037 Graduate School of Management, Library Wing
Los Angeles, CA 90024

Contact: Michael Owen Jones, Dir
(213) 825-4242
Hours: Mon-Fri, 8-5
Accessible to Public: Yes
Accessible to Scholars: Yes
Special Considerations: Call or write in advance

Visual Media Archive: Contains color microfiche of 15,000 images of the *Index of American Design* plus 40,000 slides and 100 videotapes about folklore and popular culture. Materials in the collection include slides of tarot cards, classic fairytale and science fiction illustrations, early 20th century postcards, early 20th century interiors, English broadsides from the 17th to 19th centuries, folklore in advertising and cartoons, and the

Travelog Magic Lantern Slides (1890-1940) of Burton Holmes.

D. K. Wilgus Archive of Folksong and Music: Contains 11,000 commercial recordings, 8,000 of which are LPs released since 1950. Emphasis is on folksongs, early race recordings, country and western music, and blues, with some other ethnic traditions as well as folksong revival material.

Archive of California and Western Folklore: Includes the Henry W. Splitter Collection of California and Western Folklore and History (1846-1900) with thousands of pages of material on pseudoscience, folk belief and medicine, eccentric characters, and occupational folklore. Also contains Andrew Jenkins's music materials and tens of thousands of examples of traditional speech and joke fads.

Folk Medicine Archive: Contains 750,000 index cards (one item per card) from field collections or publications including popular culture materials; a full range of remedies, diseases, and sources of information is represented.

Archive of American Popular Beliefs and Superstitions: Contains 900,000 index cards (one item per card) from field collections or published works including popular magazines and books. Concerns thousands of different beliefs and practices.

49. University of California at Los Angeles, Chicano Studies Research Library
405 Hilgard, 3121 Campbell Hall
Los Angeles, CA 90024

Contact: Richard Chabran
(213) 206-6052
Hours: Mon-Fri, 8-5
Accessible to Public: Yes
Accessible to Scholars: Yes

Consists of a large collection of print and audiovisual materials related to the Chicano experience.

50. University of California at Los Angeles, Department of Special Collections
A1713 University Research Library, UCLA
Los Angeles, CA 90024

Contact: James Davis, Rare Books Librarian
(213) 825-4879, 825-4988
Hours: Mon-Sat, 9-5
Accessible to Public: Yes
Accessible to Scholars: Yes
Special Considerations: Closed stack, noncirculating; material paged for readers

English Fiction, 1750-1900: Consists of 10,000 volumes, including works by Richard D. Blackmore, Rhoda Broughton, Theodore E. Hook, Joseph S. Le Fanu, Captain Frederick Marryat, Mrs. Frances Trollope, and Mary A. Ward; many of the important publishers' series of the period and an incomparable gathering of the cheaply-published "yellowbacks," the counterparts of modern paperback novels; works by Horace Walpole, Fanny Burney, and Ann Radcliffe; and extensive collections of manuscripts, correspondence, memorabilia, literary periodicals, original illustrations and prints, photographs, ephemera, and publishers' archives (includes the firms of Richard Bentley and Cadell & Davies).

California and Western Americana Collection: Includes printed books, pamphlets, ephemera, papers of John R. Haynes and Franklin Hichborn, and numerous other materials related to the state and region. Strong holdings related to printing and antiquarian book trade, the television and film industries, labor, civil liberties, theater, agriculture, landscape architecture, rare maps, photography, and national parks, with good representation of materials related to California, New Mexico, Arizona, and Nevada.

Children's Books Collection: Consists of 22,000 children's books (1750-1900) from England and America, and includes chapbooks, works related to folklore, songsters, and broadside ballads; 1,500 American textbooks (1790-1900); selected French, German, and other foreign materials are also available.

Popular Literature Collection: Principally from 1750-present, the collection includes English chapbooks (1775-1850); American songsters (1820-1900); American hymnals (1760-1870); English and American broadside ballads (1780-1890); American almanacs (1730-1880); strong collections of detective, western, mystery, romance, and science fiction pulp magazines (including long runs of *Argosy*, *Black Mask*, *Breezy Stories*, *Dime Detective Magazine*, *Munsey's Magazine*, *Street & Smith's Western Story Magazine*, *Weird Tales*, and *Wild West Magazine*); American paperbacks from 1880-present including collections of western novels with the authors' correspondence and manuscripts; a good collection of Haldeman-Julius publications (1929-1940); Tauchnitz editions; science fiction paperbacks; and a small but significant collection of English fiction directed to the working classes during the early 1800s.

Twentieth-Century Authors: Includes modern English and American authors represented by first and other important editions, notably Edward F. Benson, Bret Harte, Christopher Isherwood, Robinson Jeffers, James Joyce, Wyndham Lewis, William McFee, Robert Nathan, Gertrude Stein; extensive collection of Henry Miller's papers relating to his work and that of John C. Powys, William Fowlie, Claude Houghton Oldfield, Bernard H. Porter, Norman Douglas, Theodore Dreiser, Lawrence Durrell, H. Rider Haggard, Gerald Heard, Aldous Huxley, Anais Nin, George Bernard Shaw, and many others; local authors' personal papers, manuscripts, galley proofs, and oral history transcripts include works of Ray Bradbury, Edwin Corle, Raymond Chandler, Harold Lamb, Lawrence Lipton, Lawrence Clark Powell, Paul Jordan Smith, Irving Stone, Jim Tully, and Matt Weinstock; representative collection of English and American avant-garde literature, both poetry and prose; and 2,000 miscellaneous issues of little magazines.

Oral History Program: Consists of an extensive collection of oral history audiotapes related to the history and development of southern California.

UCLA University Archives: Extensive collection represents all noncurrent records of academic and administrative units as well as all manner of ephemera related to University history and life.

The Department of Special Collections also maintains significant holdings related to medieval and Renaissance manuscripts, Near Eastern studies, Hebraica and Judaica, Afro-American studies, Asian-American studies, Chicano and In-

dian studies, the history of women, family history, the history of science and technology, the history of photography, the history of television and film, the history of printing and the graphic arts, and the history of the book trade (including fictitious imprints and emblem books).

Oakland

51. Oakland Museum, History Department
1000 Oak St
Oakland, CA 94607

Contact: L Thomas Frye, Chief Curator of History
(415) 273-3842
Hours: Wed-Sat, 10-5; Sun, 12-7
Accessible to Public: No
Accessible to Scholars: Yes
Special Considerations: Researchers must write well in advance of proposed visit to outline specific research to be undertaken within the collections

The collection is a regional museum relating to California culture and includes rock music posters (1960s-1970s); war protest posters and arm bands (c. 1970); "hippie" clothing; surf boards (historic and contemporary); gay and lesbian literature and gay theatrical garments (1930s-1960s); sports equipment, programs, posters, and garments; fraternal order programs, garments, and related memorabilia; toys; Art Deco architectural fragments from the San Francisco Bay area; motorcycles; automobiles, license plates, posters, and motoring garments; games; hobbies and craft items (19th and 20th centuries); popular magazines from the 19th and 20th centuries; sheet music; a small collection of 45 rpm and 78 rpm recordings; California souvenir items from the 19th century and early 20th century; and large holdings of women's needlework from the 19th and 20th centuries, including samplers, quilts, mourning pictures, and similar items.

52. Oakland Public Library
125 14th St
Oakland, CA 94612

Contact: Kathy Page
(415) 273-3134

Hours: Mon-Thur, 10-8:30; Fri-Sat, 10-5:30
Accessible to Public: Yes
Accessible to Scholars: Yes

Collection includes 25 California elementary and high school textbooks (1874-1920); 4,000 programs (1868-present) in categories such as art, ballet, churches, circuses, clubs and societies, commemorative events, concerts, conventions, dances, dedications, fairs and expositions, fashion events, films, garden and flower shows, graduations, ice shows, lectures, musicals, operas, parades and pageants, recitals, sports events, and theaters; 4,000 stereoptican cards (1900-1940) in categories such as countries of the world, industries, World War I, and the Pacific Exposition of 1915; 2,000 postcards (1900-1960) of California counties; 1,000 business letterheads (1890-1940) from East Bay businesses; 200 trade cards (1880-1910) related to local businesses; 500 trade catalogs (1900-present) related to local businesses; and 7,000 items of sheet music for popular songs (1890-present).

Palo Alto

53. The Doll Studio
321-325 Hamilton Ave
Palo Alto, CA 94301

Contact: Evelyn Burkhalter
(415) 326-5841
Hours: Tues-Sat, 10-6
Accessible to Public: Yes
Accessible to Scholars: Yes

Collection houses "The Barbie Doll Hall of Fame," which includes more than 7,000 Barbie dolls, with representative dolls from each year of Barbie's existence and including most of the plethora of clothing manufactured for this doll.

Pasadena

54. Pasadena Tournament of Roses Association
391 S Orange Grove Blvd
Pasadena, CA 91184

Contact: William B Flinn
(818) 449-4100
Hours: Mon-Fri, 8:30-5:30
Accessible to Public: No
Accessible to Scholars: Yes

Special Considerations: As this is a regular business office, users must make an appointment; access generally not available from November through January

Collection includes souvenir programs from past Rose Parades and Rose Bowl Games, from the first parade in 1890 and from the first game in 1902. Film footage of past Rose Parades and Rose Bowl Games is available on a limited basis; the films are currently in the process of being archived and transferred to videotape. Rose Parade films from 1950 to the present are available for checkout, both to scholars and to the general public.

Riverside

55. University of California at Riverside, Tomas Rivera Library
PO Box 5900
Riverside, CA 92517

Contact: George Slusser, Curator
(714) 787-3233
Hours: Mon-Fri, 9-5
Accessible to Public: Yes
Accessible to Scholars: Yes
Special Considerations: Noncirculating

Collections consist of 50,000 science fiction books, including utopian and imaginary fiction, and 4,500 science fiction magazine issues; also includes 2,000 volumes of boys' books (1860-1920).

Sacramento

56. Sacramento Museum and History Division
1930 J St
Sacramento, CA 95814

Contact: James Henley, Dir
(916) 449-2072
Hours: Mon-Fri, 8-12, 1-5
Accessible to Public: Yes
Accessible to Scholars: Yes
Special Considerations: By appointment

Collections include documentary materials as well as artifacts that document life in the Sacramento Valley from about 1840 to the present. Holdings are numerous and extensive. Inquire as to specific interest areas prior to visit.

Saint Helena

57. Silverado Museum
PO Box 409
Saint Helena, CA 94574

Contact: Ellen Shaffer, Curator
(707) 963-3757
Hours: Tues-Sun, 12-4
Accessible to Public: Yes
Accessible to Scholars: Yes
Special Considerations: For qualified
  research workers

The museum is devoted to the life and works of Robert Louis Stevenson and his immediate circle. Contains some 7,900 items, including first and variant editions, letters, manuscripts, photographs, paintings, sculpture, and memorabilia.

San Diego

58. Cabrillo National Monument
PO Box 6670
San Diego, CA 92106

Contact: Contact the Superintendent
(619) 293-5450
Hours: Mon-Sun, 9-5:30
Accessible to Public: Yes
Accessible to Scholars: Yes
Special Considerations: Noncirculating

Contains 20 volumes related to Portuguese explorers, exhibits on Spanish exploration of the New World, and 15 volumes related to early lighthouses of the Pacific coast.

59. San Diego Aerospace Museum, N. Paul Whittier Library
2001 Pan American Plaza, Balboa Park
San Diego, CA 92101

Contact: Ray Wagner, Archivist
(619) 234-8291
Hours: Mon-Fri, 10-4:30; closed
  Thanksgiving, Christmas, and New
  Year's Day
Accessible to Public: No
Accessible to Scholars: Yes
Special Considerations: Advance
  appointment required

Juvenile Aviation Collection: Consists of the G. M. "Casey" Cameron collection (1887-1963), containing 461 titles, mostly fiction, emphasizing aviation heroes of futuristic adventure.

San Francisco

60. California Historical Society Library
2099 Pacific Ave
San Francisco, CA 94109-2235

Contact: Bruce L Johnson, Dir
(415) 567-1848
Hours: Wed-Sat, 1-5
Accessible to Public: Yes
Accessible to Scholars: Yes
Special Considerations: Please inquire as
  to specific holdings prior to visit

The Library has hundreds of thousands of items that relate to popular culture. Collections include sheet music, postcards, business cards, children's books, dime novels, stereographs, oral history tapes and transcriptions, manuscripts, photographs, etc.

Kemble Collections on Western Printing and Publishing: Hold well over 3,500 volumes and extensive ephemeral materials and include histories of printing, printing manuals, printer's dictionaries, printing-trade periodicals, type founders' specimen books, numerous manuscripts related to printing in the region, and the archives of the Taylor and Taylor Company (including broadsides 1906-1961, printers' copies of books and periodicals, pamphlets, work dockets, job tickets, and virtually all significant papers and printed items produced by this major San Francisco firm).

61. Cartoon Art Museum
1 Sutter St, Ste 205
San Francisco, CA 94104

Contact: M K White, Pres
(415) 397-3716
Hours: By appointment only
Accessible to Public: Yes
Accessible to Scholars: Yes
Special Considerations: Please phone
  ahead for appointment

Collections include 275 pieces of original cartoon art (drawings and paintings dating from 1914) and a library of cartoon art, anthologies, monographs, biographies of artists, comic books, and "how-to" books related to cartooning and cartoonists.

62. San Francisco Academy of Comic Art

2850 Ulloa St
San Francisco, CA 94116

Contact: Bill Blackbeard, Dir
(415) 681-1737
Hours: Make appointment
Accessible to Public: Yes
Accessible to Scholars: Yes
Special Considerations: Appointments
must be made at least one day in
advance; unavailable on holidays

Holdings are vast and include the following:

Comic Strip Collection: Includes 1,500,000 daily and Sunday strip episodes, 1896-present, individually clipped and organized by artist and title in published sequence (easy reference and access); covers virtually all nationally syndicated newspaper comics from first definitive strip (1896) to date; collection augmented by 47 new strip episodes daily.

Comic Book Collection: Consists of 11,000 comic books, 1897-present, filed by title and (if one artist is dominant) artist, and includes a full run of *Marvel* titles, *Barks Duck* titles and *WDC&S* episodes, *Pogo/Animal Comics,* Kurtzman *EC* titles, *Panic,* and many others.

Pulp Fiction Periodicals: Includes 6,500 pulps, 1893-1955, filed by title, excluding science fiction pulps. Notable strengths include a full run of *Argosy* (1900-1943), *Weird Tales* (1927-1945), *The Spider, Dime Detective, The Thrill Book,* and many others.

Science Fiction Collection: Consists of 8,500 science fiction and fantasy books, filed by author, plus full science fiction magazine runs of all titles (more than 3,500 issues).

Crime Fiction Collection: Includes 13,500 hard cover novels of crime and detection from 1764 to the present, with all *Queen's Quorum, Short Story Bibliography* titles plus over 1,000 additional titles. Also includes 2,500 paperback originals. Collections filed by author.

Dime Novel Collection: 6,500 dime novels, nickel thrillers, story papers, etc., filed by title. The British division of this collection includes 3,300 gothic novels, penny dreadful novels, shilling shockers, and boys' story papers and comics, many of which are in long bound runs; over 400 first issues of story papers and comics; set of *Reynolds' Miscellany.*

Children's Books Collection: Consists of 2,500 classic children's books (1840-present) with an emphasis on illustrations. Includes a full run of *Oz* books and L. Frank Baum titles, Leo Edwards, Captain Marryat, Judge Parry, Joel C. Harris, E. Nesbit, and many others, all filed by title.

British Periodical Collection: 10,000 issues, mostly bound in long or full runs, filed by title. Includes full sets of *Punch, The Idler, The Strand* (1891-1916), *The Tomahawk, Ainsworth's Magazine, Cruikshank's Comic Almanack,* and many others.

Motion Picture History Collections: 2,300 volumes and periodicals (1915-present) including all titles on many figures, from Ford and Hitchcock through W. C. Fields and Chaplin, filed by personality and function.

Bound Newspaper Collection: 3,500 bound volumes of historic, graphically relevant, or classically sensational newspapers, 1840-present, filed by title. Includes many Hearst titles from many cities from 1900 through the 1950s, including *New York World* (1878-1931), *Denver Post* (1000 1005), *New York Daily News* (1010 1038), *New York Post* (1941-1970), and many special single volumes that are related to such events as the San Francisco Earthquake of 1906, Lincoln's assassination, the Johnson-Jeffries prize fight, and the Jack the Ripper murders.

The Academy also holds numerous smaller collections of special interest, including: "True Crime Collection" of 900 titles, 1790-present, filed by author or by subject (Jack the Ripper, Lizzy Borden, etc.); "Western Fiction Collection" of 650 titles, 1893-present; "Adventure Fiction Collection" of 750 titles, 1830-present, with an emphasis on nautical adventure and piracy; a "General Literature Collection" of 3,300 titles of fiction, poetry, and *belles-lettres* by "establishment" authors, with an emphasis on relevance to genre fiction material in the other collections; 472 books, magazines, and pamphlets related to Sherlockiana; 221 books, magazines, and pamphlets related to Charles Dickens; 54 items related to *Alice in Wonderland;* 27 items related to *Wizard of Oz,* including an academically uncredited book by actor Richard Mansfield that preceded and paralleled the structure of Baum's book; 76 crime drama and film scripts; 6,300 science fiction fanzines, 1931-present; 2,400 detective fiction, pulp, and dime novel fanzines, 1921-present; 1,800 pulp and slick paper periodicals related to erotic fiction, 1894-present; 875 titles of erotic fiction, mostly paperback, 1875-present; literary periodicals, 1840-present, including full runs of the *Times Literary Supplement, Bookman* (United States), *Bookman* (Great Britain, 1910-1915), *New York Review of Books, Saturday Review of Literature* (1934-1945), *The Nation* (1925-1955), *The New Republic* (1929-1950), and many more; 202 Hollywood novels that cover the film world as central to the narrative, 1915-present; 52 comic strip artist novels; 115 newspaper novels, 1885-present; plays and scripts related to Hollywood, comic strip artists, and newspaper novels; 307 items related to Dashiell Hammett, including *Black Mask,* a scrapbook of his reviews, a script of first version of *The Thin Man,* newspaper and magazine reprints of his fiction, and first and variant editions of his books in hard cover and paperback; H. Rider Haggard collection of 72 items, all first and variant editions of his novels, including burlesques and periodical items; *Weird Tales* authors collection of 575 items, including all Arkham House firsts, other firsts, books and publications covering Lovecraft, Howard, and Smith, from 1935-present (includes authors helping to inspire Cthulhu Mythos, with first by Bierce, Chambers, Hodgson, and others); 1,200 items of original comic strip, cartoon, and magazine illustration art from George Herriman to Edd Cartier; 2,500 Walt Disney items, including books, magazines, a unique file of newspaper and magazine advertising and promotion art utilizing Disney characters, 1929-present (this collection includes many items not available in the Disney Archives); "Newspaper Magazine Collection" includes 3,500 items, including a full run of the *Hearst American Weekly,* and *This Week* (1937-1950), *New York Times Book Review* (1935-1960), *New York Herald-Tribune Magazine Section,* and *New York World Magazine Section;* and 5,500 American Slick Fiction Magazines, including runs of *Saturday Evening Post* (1934-1965), *Collier's* (1903-1955), *True* (1935-1955), *Liberty* (1943-1950), *Esquire* (1933-1970), *Hearst's Cosmopolitan* (1905-1950), and many others.

There are many other collections and materials of smaller volume, and researchers should inquire about individual interests and projects prior to visiting the Academy. A comprehensive brochure is currently in preparation. The Academy also holds 4,000 reference volumes relating to the above collections, including newspaper and genre subjects in general. This collection includes most rare works on gothic, detective, and boys' thriller fiction printed in the 19th and early 20th centuries, as well as virtually every specialized critical and reference text or periodical published with regard to these areas from 1950 to the present.

63. San Francisco Public Library, Special Collections Department
Civic Center
San Francisco, CA 94102

Contact: Johanna Goldschmid, Librarian (415) 558-3940
Hours: Tues, 10-6; Wed, 1-6; Thur-Sat, 10-6
Accessible to Public: Yes
Accessible to Scholars: Yes
Special Considerations: Closed stacks with paging of books through Rare Book Room

History of the Printed Book Collection: Contains over 2,500 reference works related to printing, binding, and papermaking; over 4,000 books exemplifying fine bookmaking from the world's most important presses; and representation of the entire scope of printing history in rare medieval books, ephemera by contemporary presses, early printer's manuals, pamphlets, and numerous other items.

Richard Harrison Collection of Calligraphy and Lettering: Includes over 400 pieces of original work from Great Britain, Europe, and the United States, along with 500 reference works and instruction manuals.

George M. Fox Collection of Early Children's Books: This collection of 18th and 19th century children's books with British and American imprints consists of over 2,000 items and is particularly strong in early books embellished with colored illustrations and wood carvings.

California Authors Collection: Numbers over 1,550 volumes and includes books, manuscripts, typescripts, portraits, and photographs of such California authors as George Sterling, Ambrose Bierce, Gertrude Atherton, Frank Norris, Ina Coolbrith, and Edwin Markham. Also includes a major Bret Harte collection, first editions of all Jack London books, and 23 notebooks and daybooks from the famous longshoreman Eric Hoffer.

Schmulowitz Collection of Wit and Humor: Includes over 17,000 volumes in 35 languages covering a span of over 400 years.

Holdings also include major collections related to Sherlock Holmes, the Panama Canal, and Robert Frost.

64. The Society of California Pioneers Library
456 McAllister St
San Francisco, CA 94102

Contact: Grace E. Baker, Librarian
(415) 861-5278
Hours: Mon-Fri, 1-4; closed month of
  Aug
Accessible to Public: Yes
Accessible to Scholars: Yes
Special Considerations: Visit in person
  and arrange research project in
  advance

Collection includes one carton of beverage labels and trade cards, one large envelope of Valentine cards, many postcards, over 1,000 stereo cards, scrapbooks, photograph albums, and sheet music.

65. Tattoo Art Museum
30 Seventh St
San Francisco, CA 94103

Contact: Judith Tuttle
(415) 775-4991
Hours: Mon-Fri, 12-6

Accessible to Public: Yes
Accessible to Scholars: Yes

Collection consists of 1,790 photographs of tattooed men, women, and tattoo artists and parlors (1892-present); 8,000 sheets of "flash" artists' tattoo designs; 500 tattoo machines; primitive tattoo instruments; 150 newspaper clippings; 98 tattoo supply catalogs; 2,851 business cards representing 1,905 tattoo artists; and 56 photographs, correspondence, tattoo signs, flash, and implements in the *Burchett Collection.*

San Rafael

66. Dominican College, American Music Research Center
Dominican College
San Rafael, CA 94901

Contact: Sister Mary Dominic Ray, Dir
(415) 457-4440
Hours: Mon-Fri, 11-4
Accessible to Public: Yes
Accessible to Scholars: Yes
Special Considerations: Rare books
  available only to qualified scholars

Comic Opera Collection (1728-1814): Consists of approximately 200 comic operas performed in America between 1735 and 1860. Most are photocopies, although several rare originals are available.

New England Singing Schools Collection: Consists of approximately 100 tunebooks (1726-1884), mostly original; numerous 16th, 17th, and 18th century New England Psalters with music; a collection of music representing the Singing School movement of the late 18th and early 19th centuries, including composers such as Charles Ives, C. T. Griffes, J. K. Paine, H. H. A. Beach, and many others.

California Mission Music (1769-1840): Contains about 200 excellent black-and-white photographs of the entire liturgical repertoire used in the mission period and three feet of shelf space for books on California mission music and life in the missions. Includes all important works on the subject by Maynard Geiger, O. F. M., and Owen Da Silva.

Other materials within the Dominican College Library include two rare journals by Marin County, California, ranchers; 450 long playing records, 50 78 rpm discs, and 1,500 slides that support the above collections; charts and maps of early and mid-18th century Boston, Philadelphia, New York, and St Louis; and a collection of fine materials on the Goldrush Days, minstrelsy, gospel music, and the Shakers.

67. Marin County Historical Society Museum
1125 B St
San Rafael, CA 94901

Contact: Dorothy C Morgan, Dir
(415) 454-8538
Hours: Wed-Sun, 1-4
Accessible to Public: Yes
Accessible to Scholars: Yes
Special Considerations: Donation requested

Collections consist of bound early newspapers (1861-1953), photographs of early Marin County (1850-present), brand registries from 1800s on Marin County (in bank vault), and voting registries from 1900 on (in Bank Vault).

Santa Barbara

68. University of California at Santa Barbara Library, Special Collections
University of California at Santa Barbara
Santa Barbara, CA 93106

Contact: Chris Brun, Dept Head
(805) 961-3062
Hours: Mon-Fri, 8-5; Mon-Thur, 7-10; Sat 11-5; Sun 12-3; closed Sun during school breaks and holidays
Accessible to Public: Yes
Accessible to Scholars: Yes
Special Considerations: Must present proper identification; use of some collections is restricted, and user may need to contact donor of materials prior to research

The Wyles Collection: The largest west coast collection of materials devoted to Abraham Lincoln, the Civil War and its origins, and the American westward expansion. The collection now contains over 35,000 items, including a large

Confederate collection, manuscripts, prints, photographs, Confederate imprints and money, periodicals, and major works of historical fiction dealing with the Civil War and westward expansion. The collection touches on all aspects of U.S. social and cultural history during the era of interest, including slavery, abolitionism, Mormon history, overland accounts, soldiers' letters, and many other related subjects. A five-volume catalog of the collection was published in 1970.

The Skofield Printers Collection: Contains a large and high quality collection of items on the history of printing and its allied crafts, many specimens of early and contemporary fine printing, and books on book making, calligraphy, inks, typography, and paper making. Collection includes over 800 William Edwin Rudge publications and a complete collection of Black Sparrow Press imprints; there are about 13,000 volumes in the collection.

Circus Collection: Includes materials on the circus, animal training, clowning, side shows, and magic in English and other languages. Consists of about 2,000 volumes listed by author.

Civil War Sheet Music and Song Books: Includes marches, military aires, funeral dirges, and mothers' laments from both Union and Confederate sides.

Morris L. Ernst Banned Book Collection: Consists of 700 volumes and includes books banned throughout the world for various reasons and at different times. These books were banned for political and theological reasons, and/or for reasons of obscenity.

Pamphlet Collection: Consists of two large file cabinet drawers with pamphlet literature collected on the UCSB campus and in the neighboring town of Isla Vista during the 1960s and 1970s; pamphlets are related to the civil rights movement, third world economy, the women's movement, the anti-war movement, ecology, and the environment.

University Archives: Consists of theses and dissertations, posters collected on the UCSB campus during the 1960s and 1970s, and materials related to student unrest, civil rights, women's movement, etc.

Special Collections Related to American and California Authors: Consists of 35,000 cataloged and 15,000 uncataloged volumes of books written by or about various American and California authors, along with magazines, both old and new, of science fiction and fantasy.

Romaine Trade Catalog Collection: Consists of 500 linear feet of trade catalogs from the 19th and 20th centuries, arranged in subjects such as artwork, celebration paraphernalia, entertainment, fairs, exhibitions, music, photography, sporting goods, and toys.

Manuscript Collections: Consists of manuscripts, personal papers, correspondence, photographs, and related materials on the following individuals and topics: Dame Judith Anderson (26 linear feet); Charles Bukowski (20 archive boxes); Community Development and Conservation Collection (covers development and beautification of Santa Barbara with numerous photographs and postcards); Tom Clark (18 linear feet); The Great War Collection (newspaper clippings, personal diaries, photographs, official British photographs, and posters of World War I in 11 archive boxes); Bernard Herrmann Archive (21 linear feet of original motion picture music scores); Madame Lotte Lehmann (20 linear feet); MacDonell Playbill Collection (7 archive boxes); Sinclair Collection of Television Scripts (10 archive boxes); 300 stereopticon slides with viewer; and the Wilke Collection (15 linear feet of printers' blocks and manuscripts related to the printer's art).

Santa Monica

69. Angels Attic—A Museum of Antique Dollhouses, Miniatures, Dolls, and Toys
516 Colorado Ave
Santa Monica, CA 90401

Contact: Jackie McMahan, Dir; Eleanor LaVove, Asst Dir
(213) 394-8331
Hours: Thur-Sun, 12:30-4:30; closed holidays and December 24
Accessible to Public: Yes
Accessible to Scholars: Yes

Consists of a large collection of dollhouses, toys, dolls, and miniatures, and related reference library.

Stanford

70. Stanford University Library, Department of Special Collections and University Archives
Green Library, Stanford University
Stanford, CA 94305

Contact: Michael Ryan
(415) 723-4054
Hours: Mon-Fri, 9-5; Sat, 9-12; closed Sat when school not in session
Accessible to Public: Yes
Accessible to Scholars: Yes
Special Considerations: Users must have a legitimate research project or interest

Collections fall into eight groups: *The Mary L. Schofield Collection* of 9,000 children's books, scores, and ephemera representing the late 19th and early 20th centuries; a theater collection of 1,540 volumes and nearly 240 linear feet of playbills, posters, scripts, scrapbooks, and photographs of the late 19th century American theater; movie posters and stills for selected "B" movies of the 1930s-1970s; 1,990 volumes of screenplays and teleplays, 1950-present; the *Carlton Morse Collection* of 47 linear feet of radio and television scripts, correspondence, news clippings, publicity material, photographs, television film, and sound recordings dating 1932-1982; the *Delmer Daves Collection* of 37 linear feet of correspondence, play and film scripts, drafts, adaptations, photographs, diagrams, and working papers dating 1930-1965; the *Panama-Pacific International Exposition Collection* of one linear foot of architectural plans, photographs, and a report (1913-1915); and the *Barker Collection* of 600 volumes of musicals and light operas.

Other materials in the general collections include literary manuscripts and collections of published materials relating to 1,000 American and English authors, with especially strong holdings in the late Victorian and Edwardian periods; a special collection documenting the publication of *Lady Chatterley's Lover*; a large collection of materials relating to all aspects of the history of science; a collection relating to California and Western history; and extensive materials on the history of the book and typography.

Stockton

71. Holt-Atherton Center for Western Studies
University of the Pacific
Stockton, CA 95211

Contact: Dr Ronald H Limbaugh, Dir
(209) 946-2404
Hours: Mon-Fri, 9-5
Accessible to Public: Yes
Accessible to Scholars: Yes
Special Considerations: Noncirculating, closed stack system; materials paged; researchers must fill out a request form prior to using manuscripts

Howard Pease Papers: Contains three linear feet of manuscripts, correspondence, and business records of children's author Howard Pease (1911-1964).

Amos Alonzo Stagg Papers: Contains one linear foot of records pertaining to early college football in the United States (1905-1936).

Hunt-Jacoby Prohibition Collections: Contains 60 items of campaign literature and printed matter relating to tobacco and liquor prohibition issues, 1914-1936.

Jack London Collection: Contains 100 items related to London's adventure fiction and social commentary, including first editions of London's books inscribed to his first wife, Bessie, and to their two daughters, Joan and Bess. Also includes some sample translations of his works into Dutch, French, Russian, German, and Pakistani.

Stockton, California, Photograph Collection: Consists of 30,000 images, many dealing with everyday life in Stockton and the northern San Joaquin Valley, 1850-1950.

Vallejo

72. Vallejo Naval and Historical Museum
734 Marin St
Vallejo, CA 94590

Contact: Captain J Nunneley
(707) 643-0077
Hours: Tues-Fri, 10-4:30; Sat, 1-4:30
Accessible to Public: Yes
Accessible to Scholars: Yes

The collections specialize in local and maritime history, with a special emphasis on Vallejo and on the Mare Island Naval Shipyard.

COLORADO

Bayfield

73. The Gem Village Museum
39671 Hwy 160
Bayfield, CO 81122

Contact: Elizabeth X Gilbert
(303) 884-2811
Hours: By appointment only
Accessible to Public: Yes
Accessible to Scholars: Yes
Special Considerations: Make appointment well in advance by phone or letter

Contains many local items of geology and archaeology, as well as miscellaneous books and items related to parapsychology.

Boulder

74. University of Colorado, Music Library
Campus Box 184, University of Colorado
Boulder, CO 80309

Contact: Nancy F Carter
(303) 492-3928
Hours: Sun-Thur, 8 am-11 pm; Fri-Sat, 8-5
Accessible to Public: Yes
Accessible to Scholars: Yes

Popular Music Collection: Includes 10,000 sheet music titles (1800-present), indexed by title, composer, lyricist, and first line; 100 titles of sheet music published by the Ingram publishing house of Denver (1900-1912); and the **Lumpkin Collection** of taped folk songs collected in Colorado.

Colorado Springs

75. Pro-Rodeo Hall of Champions and Museum of the American Cowboy
101 Pro Rodeo Drive
Colorado Springs, CO 80919

Contact: Patricia Florence, Asst Dir
(303) 593-8840, 593-8847
Hours: Mon-Fri, 9-5
Accessible to Public: No
Accessible to Scholars: Yes
Special Considerations: Research for public conducted by staff; special arrangements for scholarly access on weekend can be made; prior arrangements for research necessary

Collection contains 47 file envelopes, day sheets, rodeo programs, 1900-present (arranged by state); three file envelopes and four scrapbooks from California Frank Hafley's Wild West Show (contemporary to Buffalo Bill); four scrapbooks related to Everett Bowman, first president of the Professional Rodeo Association, 1936-1940; collection of early periodicals dealing with rodeo, 1934-1950s; complete collection of publications of Rodeo Cowboys' Association and Professional Rodeo Cowboys' Association; and Professional Cowboys' Association Archives.

Denver

76. Colorado History Museum and Library
1300 Broadway
Denver, CO 80203

Contact: Katherine Kane, Head, Public Service and Access
(303) 866-4601
Hours: Museum: Mon-Sat, 10-4:30; Sun, 12-4:30; Library: Tues-Sat, 10-4:30
Accessible to Public: Yes
Accessible to Scholars: Yes
Special Considerations: Call (303) 866-4697 for appointment to view

Decorative and Fine Arts Department materials

Stephen H. Hart Library: Contains Colorado items from the late 1800s and early 1900s, including Valentines, Christmas cards, theater programs, sheet music, menus, and 425,000 photographs of Colorado subjects.

Decorative and Fine Arts Department: Contains food containers, posters, Depression Glass, and toys, all related to Colorado and dating from the late 1800s.

77. Denver Art Museum, F. H. Douglas Memorial Library, Native Arts Department
100 W 14th Ave Pkwy
Denver, CO 80204

Contact: Richard Conn, Curator; Margaret Goodrich, Librarian (Vol)
(303) 575-2256
Hours: Tues; Also by appointment
Accessible to Public: Yes
Accessible to Scholars: Yes
Special Considerations: Access limited to scholars, Native Americans, researchers, and teachers

The F. H. Douglas Memorial Library of the Native Arts Department of the Denver Art Museum contains over 43,000 items, including 6,000 bound books; bound volumes and runs of journals and serials; pamphlets and clippings relating to native arts (worldwide), anthropology, ethnology, archaeology, dictionaries of Native American languages, and related subjects. Special collections include the dictionaries, linguistics, exhibition catalogs of artifacts, and materials on Gypsies, North and South American Indians, Eskimos, and peoples of Africa and Oceania.

78. Denver Public Library
1357 Broadway
Denver, CO 80203-2165

Contact: Eleanor M Gehres
(303) 571-2012
Hours: Inquire for hours of operation
Accessible to Public: Yes
Accessible to Scholars: Yes

Western History Collection: Extensive holdings in popular culture as related to the history of the West. Address specific inquiries to the staff prior to visit.

Several sections of the Denver Public Library have extensive holdings related to the field of popular culture; however, no detailed listing is available. Address specific inquiries to the staff prior to visit.

79. Denver Public Library, Folk Music Collection
1357 Broadway
Denver, CO 80203-2165

Contact: Henry O Vaag, Humanities
   Dept Mgr
(303) 571-2000
Hours: Mon-Wed, 10-9; Thur-Sat, 10-5:
   30; Sun, 1-5
Accessible to Public: Yes
Accessible to Scholars: Yes
Special Considerations: Interlibrary loans
   available but limited; photocopying
   available; collection open to public for
   reference use only

Collection contains folk music with emphasis on ballads and Anglo-American tradition; ethnomusicology; and contemporary folk music. Consists of 1,750 books and song collections, 47 bound periodical volumes, and 15 journals and other serials.

Fort Collins

80. Colorado State University Library
Colorado State University
Fort Collins, CO 80523

Contact: John Newman
(303) 491-1844
Hours: By arrangement
Accessible to Public: Yes
Accessible to Scholars: Yes
Special Considerations: Make prior
   arrangements by letter or telephone

Vietnam War Literature Collection: Consists of fiction, poetry, plays, and other imaginative works about Americans fighting in Vietnam, and includes 800 titles and 20 linear feet of manuscripts. Includes many vanity press items, rare discontinued journals, and a large collection of scholarly and critical works and reviews.

Western American Literature Collection: Collection is based on the works of 30 major western writers, including John Steinbeck, Willa Cather, Frank Waters, Owen Wister, Mari Sandoz, and Edward Abbey. Among these works is the **Charles F. Lummis Manuscript Collection,** which includes Lummis's manuscripts, signed copies of his books, his correspondence, and 1,000 of his photographs of Indian pueblos, archaeological sites, and similar subjects from California, Arizona, New Mexico, and Latin America.

The Germans from Russia Collection: Includes books, articles, issues of journals, theses, dissertations, oral history tapes and transcripts, manuscripts, documents, and photographs of early Colorado that are related to the migration of Germans to Russia's Volga River region and their ultimate settlement in the United States, especially in Colorado. Materials date from the 1760s.

Imaginary Wars Collection: Includes imaginary war fiction, including novels about future wars on Earth or the aftermath of such wars, and consists of 1,000 titles. Nuclear war and its avoidance is a special area of strength. The collection includes important titles by David Graham, Jerry Ahern, Marsden Manson, Marion White, and Ryder Stacy, among many others.

Leadville

81. Lake County Public Library
1115 Harrison Ave
Leadville, CO 80461

Contact: David R Parry, Dir
(303) 486-0569
Hours: Mon-Wed, 9:30-8; Thur, 9:30-5;
   Fri-Sat, 1-5
Accessible to Public: Yes
Accessible to Scholars: Yes
Special Considerations: Noncirculating
   collection; advance notice is
   appreciated but not required;
   photocopying and microfilm copying is
   permitted

Colorado Mountain History Collection: The collection contains materials related to Leadville and Lake County local history and genealogy, with an emphasis on the Leadville Mining District and surrounding Colorado mountain mining activities. Includes materials on the Tenth Mountain Division (ski troops) and their World War II encampment at nearby Camp Hale. Collection consists of 1,100 books, pamphlets, articles, and documents; 2,500 historic photographs (purchase of reproductions for one-time use is permitted); local newspapers on microfilm from 1878; census schedules with alphabetic index, 1860-1910; necrology index, 1878-1967; local cemetery directories (alphabetical); maps of the region; and Leadville city directories, 1878-present.

Pueblo

82. University of Southern Colorado Library
2200 Bonforte Blvd
Pueblo, CO 81001

Contact: Dan Sullivan, Acquisitions Librarian
Write for information
Hours: Wed, 1-5; Thur, 1-5; also by appointment
Accessible to Public: Yes
Accessible to Scholars: Yes
Special Considerations: Noncirculating

The Gornick Slavic Heritage Collection: Includes materials on Yugoslavia, and on Slovene and Serbo-Croatian immigrants to the United States, and particularly to Colorado. Approximately 800 cataloged books, plus files containing uncataloged manuscripts and personal documents and papers.

Vail

83. Colorado Ski Museum and Ski Hall of Fame
PO Box 1976
Vail, CO 81658

Contact: Michelle J Cahill, Exec Dir
(303) 476-1876
Hours: Tues-Sat, 12-5, June-Sept and Nov-Apr only
Accessible to Public: Yes
Accessible to Scholars: Yes
Special Considerations: Access for members only; individual membership $25, business/institutional membership $50

Includes a large selection of black-and-white photographs and negatives, old ski promotional films, and large library, all related to over 100 years of the history of skiing in Colorado, including the sports industry and skiing's original popularity as a form of transportation; material on equipment, military skiing, U.S. Forestry Service involvement, snowmaking, resorts, etc.

CONNECTICUT

Bristol

84. Edward Ingraham Library of the American Clock and Watch Museum
100 Maple St
Bristol, CT 06010

Contact: Chris H Bailey, Dir
(203) 583-6070
Hours: Museum: Mon-Fri, 11-5, Apr 1 through Oct 31; Library: open only by appointment
Accessible to Public: Yes
Accessible to Scholars: Yes
Special Considerations: Make advance appointment for library use

Collection consists of about 1,000 trade catalogs, pamphlets, and other trade materials on clocks and watches, 1852-present.

Farmington

85. Yale University, Lewis Walpole Library
154 Main St
Farmington, CT 06032

Contact: Catherine T Jestin, Librarian
(203) 677-2140; 677-9416
Hours: Mon-Fri, 8:30-1, 2-5
Accessible to Public: No
Accessible to Scholars: Yes
Special Considerations: By appointment only; write for permission in advance

The collections represent a research library for English 18th century studies, including 30,000 books and 37,000 prints. Areas of special interest include the most extensive collection of English 18th century political and social satires in the

United States, with prints catalogued by date, title, artist, engraver, publisher, and subject. Collection is ideal for researching satire, critical and political opinion, clothing styles, foods, furniture, and everyday life in Walpole's era.

Hartford

86. Connecticut Historical Society
1 Elizabeth St
Hartford, CT 06105

Contact: Everett C Wilkie, Head
   Librarian
(203) 236-5621
Hours: Library: Tues-Sat, 9-5 (closed Sat
   from Memorial Day-Labor Day);
   Museum: Tues, 12-7; Wed-Sun, 12-5
   (closed during summer)
Accessible to Public: Yes
Accessible to Scholars: Yes
Special Considerations: Library is free,
   but patrons must register and present
   proper identification; admission fee
   for use of museum

Collections relate to New England, with a focus on Connecticut, and cover the 17th through the early 20th centuries. Extensive holdings in children's books (3,600 volumes); 200 travel narratives; 70 cookbooks; 560 broadsides; 500 trade catalogs; 2,000 trade cards; 20 friendship albums; 15,000 photographs, including glass plate negatives, postcards, and stereopticon cards; and 1,100 prints. Holdings also include some sheet music, Valentines, and Christmas cards. Good materials relate to P. T. Barnum, Kellogg prints, printing and illustrating, and playbills.

87. The Stowe-Day Foundation and Library
77 Forest St
Hartford, CT 06105

Contact: Joseph S Van Why, Dir; Diana
   Royce, Librarian; Margherita Desy,
   Curator
(203) 522-9258
Hours: Mon-Fri, 9-4:30
Accessible to Public: Yes
Accessible to Scholars: Yes
Special Considerations: Closed stacks;
   noncirculating

Greeting and Trade Card Collection: Consists of 50 New Year's cards, 100 Valentines, 100 Easter cards, and 300 Christmas cards, 1870-1900; 300 trade cards, 1860-1900, for businesses and services in and around the Hartford area.

Theater Collection: Consists of 1,500 broadsides, tickets, programs, newspaper advertisements, illustrations, figurines, china, and research notes related to *Uncle Tom's Cabin* and "Tom" shows in general, 1852-1960, most collected by Harry Birdoff.

William H. Gillette Collection: Contains original and revised manuscripts of Gillette's plays, along with photographs, scrapbooks, and personal correspondence, 1860s-1937.

Nook Farm Residents Collection: Consists of a major research collection of diaries, letters, journals, and manuscripts from Nook Farm residents, including first editions of works by Harriet Beecher Stowe, Mark Twain, and Charles Dudley Warner; extensive collections of out-of-print works by such authors as Lydia H. Sigourney, Lyman Beecher, Catherine E. Beecher, Henry Ward Beecher, Isabella Beecher Hooker, Thomas K. Beecher, Calvin E. Stowe, Francis Gillette, William Gillette, and William Dean Howells, along with their correspondence with many leading figures of the era.

Mark Twain/Clemens Papers: Consists of 586 letters of Mark Twain and his family covering the Hartford years (1871-1891); 65 manuscript pages by Twain, including a 20-page outline of *The Gilded Age*; 59 volumes owned by Twain; numerous other notes and manuscripts related to his writings.

Harriet Beecher Stowe Manuscripts: Includes 227 letters, 28 manuscripts, travel journal and sketchbook, and numerous foreign editions of her works, along with sheet music, broadsides, and programs related to *Uncle Tom's Cabin.*

The Foundation also holds 100 trade catalogs (1860s-1900) related to American decorative arts manufacturers; 500 juvenile books and toy books, 1850-1890; numerous major manuscript collections relating to women's suffrage, law, letters, politics, the Saturday Morning Club, the Hartford Art Club (1901-1945), the history of American industry from 1770-

1900, social reform, decorative arts, landscape architecture, Black history, and related topics. Researchers should write for brochure prior to study.

88. Watkinson Library
Trinity College
Hartford, CT 06106

Contact: J Kaimowitz, Curator; M F
  Sax, Assoc Curator
(203) 527-3151 Ext 307
Hours: Mon-Fri, 8:30-4:30; Sat, 9:30-4:30
  (Sat only while school in session)
Accessible to Public: Yes
Accessible to Scholars: Yes
Special Considerations: Reference only

Collection is divided into categories by broad subject headings as follows: **Art:** 180 Currier and Ives prints; nearly 400 Valentines from England and America, 1830-1930, plus three scrapbooks with examples from 1875-1918; 120 English and American Christmas cards, 1870-1930s, plus eight scrapbooks containing examples from late 1800s; Easter cards, 1875-1910, in five scrapbooks; also postcards, fashion plates, and numerous miscellaneous catalogs and magazines.

Music: 26,000 pieces of American and English sheet music, 1790s-1960; 1,000 American song sheets, 1850-1890; 150 pictorial note paper songs, 1862-1869; several thousand New England and New York concert and theater programs, 1800s-1930s; numerous popular songsters, glee books, MS copybooks, and books on Jazz and popular music.

Theater: 400 English and American play bills, 1791-1840; numerous popular British and American plays from 18th and 19th centuries.

Literature: Broadside ballads (British); popular tracts (*Cheap Repository Tracts*, etc.); 10,000 items of children's literature, British and American, from the 19th and 20th centuries (includes the *Barnard Collection of Textbooks from the 18th and 19th centuries*); and numerous 19th century popular periodicals, novels, and dime novels.

History and Politics: U.S. Civil War scrapbooks containing envelopes, cards, political and satirical illustrations, etc.; political broadsides and songsters; 180 British caricatures, 1759-1848; 200 American World War I posters; and 257 Russian posters, 1914-1930s.

Miscellaneous: 1,000 English and American etiquette books for children and adults, 19th and early 20th centuries; 100 letter writing guides; 40 American and British women's magazines of the 18th and 19th centuries; several thousand American trade cards, 1875-1910; good collection of American and British books on popular medicine, phrenology, mental health, and early herbal guides.

New Haven

89. Yale University, Music Library
98 Wall St
New Haven, CT 06520

Contact: Harold E Samuel
(203) 432-0492
Hours: Mon-Fri, 8:30-5; Sat, 10-5; Sun, 2-10
Accessible to Public: Yes
Accessible to Scholars: Yes
Special Considerations: Noncirculating

Sheet Music Collection: 30,000 pieces of sheet music, both piano music and songs, published in the United States, 1800-1940.

The Alex Templeton Archives: 35 linear feet of materials (music manuscripts, correspondence, financial records, iconography, programs, and awards). Collection is not yet processed.

The Benny Goodman Archives: 100 linear feet of materials (1,500 arrangements; 800 tapes, scrapbooks, awards, and iconography). Processing is not yet complete.

The Ted Lewis Archives: 15 linear feet of materials (recordings, iconography, video programs, arrangements, and correspondence). Processing is not yet complete.

90. Yale University Library, Arts of the Book Collection
PO Box 1603A, Yale Station
New Haven, CT 06520

Contact: Gay Walker, Curator
(203) 432-1712, 432-1803
Hours: Mon-Fri, 2-5
Accessible to Public: Yes
Accessible to Scholars: Yes

Large collections of popular culture materials include 2,000 Victorian trade cards, mostly from the United States, including cut-outs and puzzle cards; 100 small Victorian advertising pamphlets; 100 early American greeting cards, many before 1900, including several of the earliest cards from Louis Prang's Boston company; 350 wine labels (in two notebooks), mostly from European wines; 100 chromolithographs of various subjects; 10,000 art prints, mostly historical engravings, portraits, and scenery, including several thousand from *Harper's Weekly*; 30 sets of photographic postcards from Oxford, England; 50 stereopticon cards of mixed subjects; 3,500 linecuts and wood engraved blocks from the first illustrated edition of *Webster's Dictionary*, 19th century; and 25 scrollwork patterns from turn-of-the-century popular ladies' magazines.

Western Americana Posters/Printed Ephemera Collection: Consists of 10 Buffalo Bill Circus posters; 50 lithographed lettersheets; 30 song sheets; and many other prints/pieces of ephemera.

91. Yale University Library, Benjamin Franklin Collection
1603A Yale Station
New Haven, CT 06520

Contact: Carter McKenzie, Admin Asst
(203) 432-1814
Hours: Mon-Fri, 9-5
Accessible to Public: Yes
Accessible to Scholars: Yes

Consists of a vast collection of manuscript and pictorial material relating to Benjamin Franklin and his contemporaries, and books and pamphlets relating to American history from the French and Indian War to 1800. The printed material numbers 15,000 volumes and consists of works written by Franklin, very important general American histories, and historical periodicals and publications of historical societies. Practically all important secondary works on colonial and Revolutionary U.S. history are included, along with extensive biographies of George Washington, Thomas Jefferson, Thomas Paine, John Paul Jones, and the Marquis de Lafayette, as well as of Franklin. The pictorial material consists of contemporary and later prints of the Franklin portraits and portraits of his contemporaries. Over 30,000 photocopies of Franklin-related manuscripts have been assembled from the U.S. and 13 other nations.

92. Yale University Medical Historical Library
333 Cedar St
New Haven, CT 06510

Contact: Ellen Zak Danforth, Curator
(203) 785-4259
Hours: Mon-Fri, 8:30-5
Accessible to Public: Yes
Accessible to Scholars: Yes
Special Considerations: Access to the collection is by appointment only; User's Manual is available at the Library

Collections consist of 3,000 artifacts (weights, scales, measures of length, volume, and time) and 50 linear feet of books, articles, journals, clippings, photographs, and ephemera relating to such topics as mensuration, metrology, and metrological history, particularly in the ancient world, Europe, and Asia. Materials date from 2900 B.C. through the early 20th century, and includes documentation on the history of the collections, on metrological associations, and on other metrological collections.

New London

93. Connecticut College
Charles E. Shain Library
New London, CT 06320

Contact: Mary Kent, Special Collections Librarian
(203) 447-7622
Hours: Mon-Fri, 8:30-12, 1-5
Accessible to Public: Yes
Accessible to Scholars: Yes

Almanac Collection: Consists of *The New England Almanac and Farmer's Friend*, 1773-1961, and numerous other miscellaneous 18th and 19th century almanacs.

Castle Postcard Collection: Contains 300 views of New London and environs, 1890-1930.

Gildersleeve Collection: Includes 2,600 children's books, primarily 19th and early 20th century.

Wyman Ballad Collection: Includes 375 titles of sheet music and folk songs.

Old Mystic

94. Indian and Colonial Research Center
PO Box 525
Old Mystic, CT 06372

Contact: Kathleen Greenhalgh, Librarian
(203) 536-9771
Hours: Tues, 10-4; Thur-Sat, 2-4; closed
   Dec to Mar
Accessible to Public: Yes
Accessible to Scholars: Yes
Special Considerations: Noncirculating

Consists of about 3,000 volumes dealing with early history until about 1865, and includes 50 cartons of pamphlets, over 1,000 early photographs of the area, 200 notebooks on genealogy, 150 notebooks on Indian culture, 100 notebooks on early colonial life, 500 rare American school texts (from early 1700s), oral history tapes made by senior citizens of the area, and hundreds of manuscripts, diaries, letters, bills of lading, and similar materials.

Storrs

95. The Molesworth Institute
148 Hanks Hill Rd
Storrs, CT 06268

Contact: Norman D Stevens
(203) 429-7051
Hours: By appointment only
Accessible to Public: Yes
Accessible to Scholars: Yes

Large collection of librariana, consisting of a variety of largely ephemeral material relating to librarians, librarianship, and libraries. It includes 20,000 picture postcards depicting American and foreign libraries; about 1,500 contemporary business cards of librarians; nearly 500 china and other commemoratives and souvenirs depicting libraries; and several hundred pieces of paper ephemera including posters, dedication programs, bookplates, etc.

96. University of Connecticut at Storrs, Homer Babbidge Library, Special Collections
U-5SC
Storrs, CT 06268

Contact: Ellen E Embardo
(203) 486-2524
Hours: Mon-Fri, 9-12, 1-5; between
   academic sessions Mon-Fri, 1-5
Accessible to Public: Yes
Accessible to Scholars: Yes
Special Considerations: Materials must
   be used in the Special Collections
   Reading Room

Children's Literature Collection: Includes 800 historical children's books, with an emphasis on American and British works between 1860 and 1930; 1,000 illustrated children's books, with an emphasis on significant illustrators of the 20th century (some 19th century illustrators included); original artwork of children's illustrators, including 1,200 pieces by Richard Scarry, manuscripts and artwork by Disney illustrator Hardie Gramatky, and manuscripts of 13 books and 400 additional pieces by James Marshall; and 5,000 fine illustrated children's books in the *Billie Levy Collection of Children's Books* (on loan until 1993) with an emphasis on American illustrators and those of other countries who had an influence on American children's book illustration.

Alternative Press Collection: Includes 3,500 journal titles (with 400 current subscriptions), 4,000 books and pamphlets, 75 linear feet of organizational files and ephemera, 2,700 U.S. Communist and Socialist books and pamphlets from 1900-1933, and the *Fat Liberation Archive* containing 500 pieces of correspondence and alternative publications. The Collection represents strong coverage from the mid-1960s to the present.

Terryville

97. Lock Museum of America
PO Box 104
Terryville, CT 06786

Contact: Thomas Hennessy, Curator
(203) 582-6897

Hours: Tues-Sun, Daily, May through
Oct; other times by appointment
Accessible to Public: Yes
Accessible to Scholars: Yes

Contains an enormous collection of
locks, including a large display of Yale
locks, 1870-1950, and is supported by the
largest collection of lock and hardware
company catalogs in the United States.

Willimantic

98. Eastern Connecticut State University, Connecticut Folklore Archive, Center for Connecticut Studies
83 Windham St
Willimantic, CT 06226

Contact: Barbara Tucker; David E
Philips
(203) 456-2231 Ext 443
Hours: Regular University Library hours
Accessible to Public: Yes
Accessible to Scholars: Yes
Special Considerations: Archive in
locked file cabinets; key must be
obtained at circulation desk

Connecticut Folklore Archive: Contains more than 200 folders of student
collecting projects done in undergraduate
folklore classes from 1966 to the present.
Individual collections include audiotapes
(some with typed transcripts), lists of
contents, slides and photographs, and
maps and artifacts related to folklore,
folklife, and oral history of the state.

**Popular Belief and Superstition Col-
lection:** Contains several thousand 4 X
6 file cards that list popular beliefs/su-
perstitions collected (mostly in Connecticut) by undergraduate folklore students.
Cards are filed and formatted according
to the Wayland Hand system.

DELAWARE

Winterthur

99. Winterthur Museum Library
Winterthur Museum
Winterthur, DE 19735

Contact: Dr Frank H Sommer, Head of
Library
(302) 656-8591
Hours: Mon-Fri, 8:30-4:30
Accessible to Public: Yes
Accessible to Scholars: Yes
Special Considerations: Identification
required

The general collection includes 70,880
bound volumes and secondary sources on
popular culture. Includes extensive collections in field of folk art (much related
to Pennsylvania German and Shaker
groups), large numbers of works listed in
Early American Imprints, U.S. colorplate
books, and children's books. Also contains 133,226 slides related to folk art,
decorative arts, and American crafts.

**Downs Collection of Manuscripts
and Microfilm:** 4,000 linear feet including large collections of popular prints.
The **Downs Collection** also includes
the *Thelma S. Mendsen Collection* of
printed ephemera (including trade cards,
greeting cards, calling cards, and picture
postcards), the *Maxine Waldron Collection* of paper antiques of childhood
(dolls, games, soldiers, etc.), and the *Edward Deming Andrews Memorial Shaker
Collection* of original manuscripts, architectural drawings, and advertising art.
The *Downs Collection* also includes
Pennsylvania German "fraktur" and related folk art manuscripts and account
books, day books, letter books, bills and
invoices, and materials such as weaving
patterns from American craftsmen.

**Decorative Arts Photographic Col-
lection (DAPC) and Photographic
Index of American Art and Design
(PIAAD):** Contains 138,000 photographs (8" X 10") of American-made art
(paintings, drawings, prints, furniture
and other woodwork, ceramics, base
metals, precious metals, and textiles) and
the original research notes of Phoebe
Prime on advertisements of craftsmen in

early American newspapers along with extensive files on American craftsmen.

DISTRICT OF COLUMBIA

Washington

100. American Film Institute, National Center for Film and Video Preservation
J. F. Kennedy Center
Washington, DC 20566

Contact: Amy Turim, Archivist
(202) 828-4070
Hours: Mon-Fri, 9-5:30
Accessible to Public: Yes
Accessible to Scholars: Yes
Special Considerations: Access by
   appointment; film collection is
   handled by the Library of Congress

The center seeks to discover and preserve American film heritage, with particular interest in films produced prior to 1951. There are more than 20,000 titles in the AFI Collection and the number is constantly growing. It would be impossible in a brief listing to catalog the wealth of materials available. Feature films, early television, documentary films, and newsreel footage are included. Researchers should contact AFI well in advance of a visit. *The National Moving Image Data Base* is one of the Center's most ambitious projects. When completed it will enable researchers to access the materials, both at AFI and elsewhere, more easily.

101. Broadcast Pioneers Library
1771 N Street, NW
Washington, DC 20036

Contact: Catharine Heinz
(202) 223-0088
Hours: Mon-Fri, 9-5
Accessible to Public: Yes
Accessible to Scholars: Yes
Special Considerations: General public
   access by appointment; faculty/
   researcher access by membership ($25
   fee)

Collection consists of oral histories, manuscripts, scrapbooks, photographs, sound recordings, and rare books and periodicals related to the history of broadcasting with special strengths in the early periods. A special service of the Library is in providing referrals to the best possible sources in broadcast history (both television and film). Important materials relate to RCA engineering pioneer Alfred N. Goldsmith, NBC correspondent Pauline Frederick, war correspondent Larry LeSueur, CBS news president William A. (Bill) Leonard, Elmo N. Pickerill, and John D. Fitzgerald. Holdings date from the mid-1800s to the present and include materials related to telegraphy.

102. The Library of Congress
(Address Inquiries to Specific Divisions
   as Listed Below)
Washington, DC 20540

Contact: (Address Inquiries to Specific
   Individuals as Listed Below)
(Specific Phone Numbers Listed Below)
Hours: Hours vary by divisions;
   generally open Mon-Fri, 8:30-5;
   inquire prior to visit
Accessible to Public: Yes
Accessible to Scholars: Yes
Special Considerations: Some special
   conditions, such as proper
   identification, apply to individual
   collections and reading rooms. Inquire
   prior to visit.

It would be the height of folly to attempt to categorize, classify, and list the enormous body of materials related to the study of popular culture held by The Library of Congress. Even broadly descriptive discussions of specific Divisions are unable to begin to delineate the resources available to the scholar. Hence, we list only the *major* Divisions that have the greatest volume of popular culture materials. We suggest that you contact the Library prior to your visit. Numerous guides and reference aids have been published to enable the researcher to gain access to the various collections. Reference librarians will be happy to help you plan your visit and will assist you in obtaining the best available reference aids related to your project. The Library of Congress contains, to use the words of one of the librarians, "the largest collection of materials pertaining to popuar culture in the world!"

Music Division: Contact Gillian B. Anderson, (202) 287-5504. Consists of the largest collection of materials related to music in the world, in a wide variety of forms and formats.

Recorded Sound Reference Center, Motion Picture, Broadcasting, and Recorded Sound Division: Contact Samuel Brylawski, Reference Librarian, or Edwin Matthias, Reference Librarian, (202) 287-7833. Excellent guides to this enormous collection are available.

Children's Literature Center: Contact Margaret N. Coughlan, Reference Specialist, no phone number available. Contains large numbers of Big Little Books, dime novels, Western Publishing's paperbacks, comic books, series books (including Oliver Optic, Horatio Alger, George Henty, Roger Garis, Thornton Burgess, Edward Stratemeyer, Laura Lee Hope, Carolyn Keene, F. W. Dixon, and Isabella Alden), and other forms and formats of children's literature. Please note that the Children's Literature Center is a *contact and reference point* for these materials—many of them are scattered throughout the collections and Divisions of The Library of Congress.

Motion Picture and Television Reading Room, Motion Picture, Broadcasting and Recorded Sound Division: Contact Reference Librarian, (202) 287-1000. A fairly complete listing of materials in this Division may be found in the publication *Special Collections in the Library of Congress.*

Archive of Folk Culture: Contact Joseph C. Hickerson, Head, (202) 287-5510. This collection consists of approximately 200 broadsides, 100,000 pieces of ephemera, 200 maps, 12,000 disc recordings, 20,000 tape recordings, 250 wire recordings, 8,000 wax cylinder recordings (all recordings are unpublished), 35,000 manuscript cards, 100,000 manuscript sheets, 5,000 photo prints, 60,000 photo negatives, and numerous other materials (including secondary resources) all related to the study of folklife, folk culture, and ethnomusicology. An excellent guide and several index systems are available.

103. Marine Corps Historical Center and Marine Corps Museum
Building 58, Navy Yard
Washington, DC 20374

Contact: Contact Head, Support System and Executive Officer
(202) 433-3840
Hours: Collections: Mon-Fri, 8-4:30; Museum: Mon-Sat, 10-4; Sun, 12-5
Accessible to Public: Yes
Accessible to Scholars: Yes
Special Considerations: Collections available by advance appointment only

The collections include 8,000 square feet of exhibits in the Museum that trace the history of the Marine Corps from 1775-present; 6,000 works of combat art (2/3 related to Vietnam War) from 1775-present; 2,000 individual collections of personal papers of prominent and other Marines (letters, diaries, photographs, documents, etc.); a library of 30,000 volumes related to the Marine Corps, naval history, military history, and diplomatic history; an oral history collection of 7,000 tapes of Vietnam era interviews, including 300 tapes by prominent Marines; *Official Archives* including Command Chronologies (war diaries) of all units to 1960; and the *Military Music Collection* including Marine Band and John Philip Sousa archival materials.

104. The Smithsonian Institution
(Address Inquiries to Specific Division as Listed Below)
Washington, DC 20560

Contact: (Address Inquiries to Specific Individuals as Listed Below)
(Specific Phone Numbers Listed Below)
Hours: Mon-Fri, 9-5; individual museums/collections vary slightly, inquire in advance
Accessible to Public: Yes
Accessible to Scholars: Yes
Special Considerations: Advance inquiries related to specific research projects and plans are a must

It would be impossible in a brief listing such as this to adequately characterize the richness of the holdings. Researchers are encouraged to contact the appropriate division as listed below well in advance of the proposed visit. All divisions have published guides and various research aids related to the holdings. Researchers are advised to obtain these materials prior to visiting Washington. The publication *Research Opportunities at the Smithsonian Institution* is available through the Office of Fellowships and Grants and is highly recommended.

National Museum of Natural History: Contact Paula Fleming, Museum Specialist, (202) 357-1976. Collections include the National Anthropological Archives with particularly strong holdings related to the study of American Indians, including over 250,000 photographs, extensive anthropological field notes, ethnographies, studies of Native American languages, and thousands of related materials.

Division of Political History, Museum of American History: Contact Edith Mayo, Larry Bird, or Keith Melder, Room 4109, Museum of American History, (202) 357-2008. Although numerous collections are available, important bodies of material include the *Political Campaign Collection* of 50,000 items, 1789-present (buttons, ribbons, badges, posters, bumper stickers, jewelry, and gimmicks); *White House/Inaugural Collection* of nearly 7,000 items related to White House social life and Inaugural events (invitations, souvenirs, prints, Christmas cards, favors, etc.); and the *Women's History, Reform, and Protest Collections* consisting of 5,000 items including buttons, ribbons, badges, posters, jewelry, handouts, leaflets, and similar materials relating to women's history, civil rights, voting rights, reform, antiwar protests, and the labor movement (mostly 20th century).

Department of Print, National Portrait Gallery: Contact Wendy Wick Reaves, Curator of Prints, 8th at F Streets, NW, (202) 357-1356. Collection consists of approximately 2,500 printed portraits of American subjects, and includes many popular art items ranging from 19th century lithographs to magazines, sheet music and almanac covers, book illustrations, posters, caricature drawings, illustrated broadsides, and cartoons.

National Museum of American History Branch Library: Contact Rhoda S. Ratner, Chief Librarian, (202) 357-2414. Collection includes monographs, serials, and trade catalogs in support of curatorial research in popular culture. Major holdings include the *Columbia Collection* of trade catalogues, 45,000 volumes of Patent Office trade journals, 15,000 cataloged and 250,000 uncataloged pieces of trade literature dating from the 19th and 20th centuries, city directories, and a major collection (over 1,500 items) related to international exhibitions and "world fairs." The Library collections include 165,000 volumes of books and bound journals related to engineering, transportation, military history, science, applied science, decorative arts, and domestic and community life.

Archives Center, National Museum of American History: Contact Robert S. Harding, (202) 357-1789, and for the *Faris and Yamna Naff Arab American Collection* contact John Fleckner, Director, or Alixa Naff, Associate Director, Room C340, National Museum of American History, (202) 357-3270. Among many others, collections of particular interest include *The Faris and Yamna Naff Arab American Collection,* a major resource for the study of all aspects of Americans of Arab origin, including oral histories, articles, statistical information, dissertations, photographs, personal papers and documents, and many other materials; *Warshaw Collection of Business Americana* consisting of over 1,000,000 items of trade cards, posters, pamphlets, labels, letterheads, advertisements, and business ephemera organized by type of product (1850-1950); *N. W. Ayer Advertising Agency Proofsheets* includes 400,000 items (1889-1970); *Modern Advertising History Projects* is developing a collection of oral histories and related advertisements and commercials for major post-World War II advertising campaigns (as of January 1987 the Pepsi-Cola, Marlboro Cigarettes, and Alka Seltzer campaigns have been completed); *Norcross Historical Greeting Card Collection* includes the official record copies of cards produced by the Norcross and Rust Craft companies and antique greeting cards collected by the two firms (over 1,000 cubic feet, 1800-1975); 25 account books (18th and 19th centuries) of small general stores and other small businesses; and numerous smaller manuscript collections related to the history of baseball, vaudeville, and other popular entertainment forms.

FLORIDA

Fort Lauderdale

105. International Swimming Hall of Fame Library

One Hall of Fame Dr
Fort Lauderdale, FL 33316

Contact: Marion Washburn, Librarian
(305) 462-6536
Hours: Mon-Fri, 9-4
Accessible to Public: Yes
Accessible to Scholars: Yes
Special Considerations: Noncirculating;
   call in advance if planning extensive
   research

The Rare Book Room contains hundreds of aquatic-related books (dating from 1696). Other materials include 5,000 aquatic books spanning pool construction, swimming, diving, synchronized swimming, water polo, histories of swimming, etc.; 35 national and international aquatic magazines (including back issues); tapes, histories, and photograph files on 300 aquatic superstars; and an extensive film and video library.

Gainesville

106. University of Florida, Baldwin Library

University of Florida Libraries
Gainesville, FL 32611

Contact: Ruth M Baldwin
(904) 392-0369
Hours: Mon-Fri, 1-4; by appointment,
   Mon-Fri, 8-12
Accessible to Public: Yes
Accessible to Scholars: Yes
Special Considerations: Noncirculating;
   some material may be xeroxed by
   special permission if the items are not
   too frail

Consists of over 40,000 children's books published before 1900 (strong collections of U.S. works prior to 1820, some English works prior to 1820, British and American editions of the same works, religious tracts, series books, and periodicals); 40,000 children's books published since 1900 (most published prior to 1950 (except for classics almost completely U.S., boys' and girls' series books, Little Golden Books, encyclopedias, and most titles of most popular children's authors); 4,600 comic books; 130 Big Little Books; about 90 figurines of children reading books, some figurines of characters from the books, and assorted memorabilia with characters (blocks, plates, etc.); and 4,000 almanacs from the late 1700s to the present along with a considerable collection of related material. A printed catalog guide to the collection is available.

107. University of Florida, Price Library of Judaica

18 Library East
Gainesville, FL 32611

Contact: Robert Singerman
(904) 392-0308
Hours: Mon-Fri, 9-5
Accessible to Public: Yes
Accessible to Scholars: Yes

Collection includes 350 calendars for the Jewish year (mostly 20th century), 30 postcards of Jewish interest, 10 bookmarks, and 400 posters and broadsides.

108. University of Florida Libraries, Belknap Collection for the Performing Arts

512 Library W, University of Florida
   Libraries
Gainesville, FL 32611

Contact: Marcia Brookbank; Mary Jane
   Daicoff
(904) 392-0322
Hours: Mon-Fri, 9-4
Accessible to Public: Yes
Accessible to Scholars: Yes

The collection is a depository for the ephemera of the performing arts (theater, dance, music, opera, radio, and cinema), including playbills, programs, posters, photographs, designs, clippings, scrapbooks, news releases, newsletters, and advertising circulars. Most materials relate to the United States and Canada, but Europe and Latin America are also well represented. The collection includes hundreds of thousands of individual examples. Specific collections include *The International Performing Arts Archives, College and University Arts Activities* (includes materials collected from representative colleges and universities in all

50 states), *Performance Programs, Production Information Files, Performing Arts Bibliographies, The Shakespearean Collection, Photographs and Prints Collection, Prompt Scripts Collection, Ringling Museum Theatre Collection,* and the *American Sheet Music Collection.* A special project currently underway is to collect and preserve information on the activities of all arts and cultural groups in Florida.

109. University of Florida Oral History Project
Florida State Museum
Gainesville, FL 32611

Contact: Samuel Proctor
(904) 392-1721
Hours: Mon-Fri, 9-5
Accessible to Public: Yes
Accessible to Scholars: Yes

Consists of oral history audio tapes and transcripts relating to the Indians of the southeastern United States, the University of Florida, Florida politics, and other subjects related to Florida.

Miami

110. Miami-Dade Public Library System
101 W Flagler St
Miami, FL 33130-1504

Contact: Alicia Godoy, Head Librarian; S J Boldrick, Florida Collection Librarian
(305) 375-2665
Hours: Mon-Wed, 9-6; Thur, 9-9; Fri-Sat, 9-6; Sun, 1-5
Accessible to Public: Yes
Accessible to Scholars: Yes

Spanish and Foreign Language Collection: The collection emphasizes services to the Spanish speaking community, and thus includes 20,000 Spanish language books (many popular works), a large collection of records and cassettes in Spanish, and a large 200-subject vertical file covering such areas as geography, travel, literature, folklore, music, art, history, and cinema. There is also a large "library within a library" consisting of works in French, German, Portuguese, and Italian, many of which are works of popular culture.

Florida Collection: Collection includes large group of Florida authors and/or Florida setting works, 75 dime novels set in the Everglades and South Florida, the Romer Photograph Collection of 17,500 negatives of South Florida life (1910-1950), sheet music collection of songs about Florida, and tourism promotional brochures from Florida, Cuba, the Bahamas, and the Caribbean area.

Orlando

111. Richard Crepeau Bicentennial Collection
History Department, University of Central Florida
Orlando, FL 32816

Contact: Dr Richard Crepeau
(305) 275-2224
Hours: By advance appointment
Accessible to Public: No
Accessible to Scholars: Yes
Special Considerations: This is a personal collection available to serious scholars by advance appointment only; noncirculating

The collection consists of several hundred items, including advertising materials, related to the popular culture surrounding the American Revolution Bicentennial. Included is a video tape of a Public Television program produced in Miami in which Jean Shephard utilizes material from the collection to comment on the popular celebration of the event.

Saint Petersburg

112. University of South Florida at Saint Petersburg, Nelson Poynter Memorial Library
140 Seventh Ave S
Saint Petersburg, FL 33701

Contact: Samuel Fustukjian, Library Dir
(813) 893-9125
Hours: Mon-Thur, 8 am-10 pm; Fri, 8-5; Sat, 9-5; Sun, 1-5
Accessible to Public: Yes
Accessible to Scholars: Yes

Contains over 1,200 negatives of photographs of old St. Petersburg, and visual and oral tapes related to the history of St. Petersburg, to Southern history in general, and to Nelson Poynter. Materials on Poynter include over 14,500 pieces of notes, letters, memos, memorabilia, and other materials related to the late publisher of The Times Publishing Company.

Tallahassee

113. Florida State University, Robert Manning Strozier Library
Special Collections Department
Tallahassee, FL 32306-2047

Contact: Contact Special Collections Librarian
(904) 644-3271
Hours: Mon-Thur, 9-6; Fri, 9-5
Accessible to Public: Yes
Accessible to Scholars: Yes
Special Considerations: Identification required

Collections include 304 dime novels, "Night Before Christmas" poem (256 versions, parodies, greeting cards, music, picture books, and miscellaneous items), 247 Christmas gift books, 108 linear feet of Victorian gift annuals and children's periodicals, 37 cassette tapes and 19 transcripts in the "Florida Civil Rights Oral History Project," and the *Robert M. Ervin, Jr., Comic Book Collection* of comics, comic books, monographs, posters, gum wrappers, prizes, cards, underground comics, science fiction and fantasy materials, and Big Little Books.

Tampa

114. Tampa-Hillsborough County Public Library
900 N Ashley St
Tampa, FL 33602

Contact: Jean Peters
(813) 223-8865
Hours: Mon-Thur, 9-9; Fri, 9-6; Sat, 9-5
Accessible to Public: Yes
Accessible to Scholars: Yes

Burgert Brothers Photography Studio Collection: Collection consists of over 14,000 negatives (including 100 glass plate negatives and 500 circuit negatives), and over 7,000 8 X 10 black-and-white archival prints, and represents a visual record of the development of the Tampa Bay area from the mid-1800s through the early 1960s.

115. University of South Florida Library, Special Collections Department
Library
Tampa, FL 33620

Contact: J B Dobkin, Special Collections Librarian
(813) 974-2731, 974-2732
Hours: Mon-Fri, 8-5
Accessible to Public: Yes
Accessible to Scholars: Yes

Collections include 6,000 American juvenile series books (1901-present); 8,000 dime novels and nickel libraries (1860-1920); 15,000 volumes of other juvenile literature in English (mostly American writers, 1790-1950); 3,000 issues of juvenile periodicals; 1,000 American toybooks (1790-1900); 1,200 volumes of American schoolbooks (1790-1900, mostly pre-1865); 40 linear feet of cigar labels, cigar bands, boxes, lithographic proof books, and related items; 5,000 trade cards and related items (1870-1900); 25,000 postcards, most of Florida views (1900-present); 5,000 pieces of sheet music by or about Afro-Americans (1818-present); 56 American songsters (1822-1900); 76 pieces of sheet music about Florida (1851-1950); 800 American almanacs (1707-1900); 96 American speakers and recitation books (1811-1900); 64 publishers' dummy books (1879-1920); and 1,000 Haldeman-Julius Little Blue Books.

White Springs

116. Florida Folklife Archives, Bureau of Florida Folklife Programs
PO Box 265
White Springs, FL 32096

Contact: Barbara Beauchamp, Archivist
(904) 397-2192
Hours: Mon-Fri, 8-5
Accessible to Public: Yes
Accessible to Scholars: Yes
Special Considerations: Some conditions apply to use of specific materials; charges apply to xeroxing and reproduction of photographs

Materials include those related to Florida folklore, folk arts, and folklife, and include the Florida Folk Festivals Collection.

Stetson Kennedy WPA Florida Folklore Collection: Consists of materials collected while Kennedy was director of the WPA Federal Writers' Project in Florida (1930s), and includes field notes, oral histories, folklore materials, indexes, visual documentation, and several articles on Florida folklife.

Thelma Ann ("Cousin") Boltin Papers and Folklore Collection: Extensive collection of notebooks assembled by Boltin while she was director of the Florida Folklife Festival (1954-1978), including folk tales, remedies, sayings, proverbs, riddles, and superstitions.

WPA Federal Writers' Project on Florida Folklore: Consists of nearly 3,000 pages from the WPA collections of the 1930s and 1940s. These materials document a broad range of folklife subjects from Florida's Cracker, Afro-American, Cuban, Seminole, Minorcan, and other ethnic cultures. Topics include beliefs, customs, folk tales and stories, dialects and jargon, agricultural lore, phrases and sayings, occupational lore, proverbs, songs, ballads, rhymes, cowboy and prison lore, and superstitions.

GEORGIA

Atlanta

117. Atlanta Historical Society
3101 Andrews Dr NW
Atlanta, GA 30305

Contact: Bill Richards, Dept Head; Anne Salter, Librarian; Rosa Dickens, Archivist; Elaine Kirkland, Visual Arts Archivist
(404) 261-1837
Hours: Mon-Sat, 9-5
Accessible to Public: Yes
Accessible to Scholars: Yes
Special Considerations: Users must register at research desk

Schillinglaw Cookbook Collection: Contains regional titles from the South-

east and rare books from the 18th century.

The collections also include 800 black-and-white and color postcards of Atlanta and Georgia, 50 trade cards representing Atlanta business firms (1880s-present), and one cubic foot of bills and letterheads from business and trade organizations in Atlanta (1880s-present).

118. Georgia State University Library, Special Collections Department
30 Courtland St SE
Atlanta, GA 30303-3083

Contact: Ms Christopher Ann Paton
(404) 658-2476
Hours: Mon-Fri, 8:30-5; research hours Mon-Fri, 9-5
Accessible to Public: Yes
Accessible to Scholars: Yes
Special Considerations: Some materials require special access

John H. Mercer Papers: Contains 28 linear feet of materials generated by and relating to the late lyricist Johnny Mercer, including correspondence, draft music and lyrics, biographical information, scores scripts, sound recordings, and 600 photographs (1927-1970s).

WSB Radio Collection: Consists of program logs, manuscripts, antique microphones, 44 linear feet of sheet music (mostly dance band arrangements, 1910-1950), 300 instantaneous transcription discs (mostly related to politics, 1940s-1950s), and nearly 55,000 sound recordings of popular and classical music, spoken word, and other types (World War II-1950s).

Sheet Music Collection: Contains 1,220 pieces of popular piano and vocal sheet music with an emphasis on Tin Pan Alley and film music (1891-1978).

Atlanta Country Music Project: Consists of photographs, manuscripts, and printed material relating to the history of country music and musicians in Atlanta (1930-1980s).

Carrollton

119. Irvine Sullivan Ingram Library, Annie Belle Weaver Special Collections

West Georgia College
Carrollton, GA 30118

Contact: Myron W House
(404) 834-1370
Hours: Mon-Thur, 8 am-10 pm; Fri, 8-5; Sat, 10-5; Sun, 3-10
Accessible to Public: Yes
Accessible to Scholars: Yes
Special Considerations: The Special Collections Library is open only during hours when Special Collections Librarian is present, but at other hours Special Collections materials are available through the reference desk on the main floor of the Library

Sacred Harp Music Collection: Consists of 78 volumes, 16 sound cassettes, four phonograph discs, and 333 other items related to Sacred Harp and other types of shaped note music.

Columbus

120. Columbus College, School of Business, Center for Business and Economic Research

School of Business, Columbus College
Columbus, GA 31907

Contact: Belle Zimmerly
(404) 568-2284
Hours: By appointment only
Accessible to Public: No
Accessible to Scholars: Yes

The collections contain a large body of newspaper, magazine, and outdoor advertising slides and a large collection of Coca-Cola advertising slides.

Fort Oglethorpe

121. Chickamauga and Chattanooga National Military Park

PO Box 2128
Fort Oglethorpe, GA 30742

Contact: John Cissell
(404) 866-9241

Hours: Mon-Sun, 8-4:45; closed Christmas Day
Accessible to Public: Yes
Accessible to Scholars: Yes

Fuller Gun Museum: Contains the largest single collection of American shoulder weapons in the United States (355 items on display).

Statesboro

122. Georgia Southern College, Zach S. Henderson Library

Landrum Box 8074
Statesboro, GA 30460-8074

Contact: Julius Ariail
(912) 681-5115
Hours: Mon-Fri, 8-5
Accessible to Public: Yes
Accessible to Scholars: Yes
Special Considerations: Check in at Special Collections Office

Early 20th Century American Sheet Music Collection: Contains three legal-size cabinets of 1,560 items of original American sheet music, mostly dating from 1900-1930. The collection catalog is organized by composer, lyricist, title and verse/chorus, and the collection is supported with an alphabetical composer shelflist.

HAWAII

Honolulu

123. Hawaii State Library

478 S King St
Honolulu, HI 96813

Contact: Shirley Naito (Edna Allyn Collection); Proserfina A Strona (Phillips and Thomas Collections); Fine Arts-Audiovisual Librarian (Music Collections)
(808) 548-2340, 548-2341, 548-2344
Hours: Mon-Sat, 9-5; Tues and Thurs, 5-8 pm
Accessible to Public: Yes
Accessible to Scholars: Yes
Special Considerations: Proper identification required; some material does not circulate

Edna Allyn Memorial Collection:
Special collection of reference books for
children consisting of 542 volumes, and
includes a variety of rare, out of print,
and Hawaiiana titles.

Hawaiian Music Collection: Consists
of a large collection of music about Hawaii and produced in Hawaii, including
sheet music and audio recordings (1920-
present).

Admiral Thomas Papers: This collection consists of a large volume of important manuscripts relating to Hawaii
(1841-1877), and also includes numerous
materials related to Tahiti and the Pacific in general.

James Tice Phillips Collection: This
is the most complete private collection
on Hawaii and its history, and consists
of 1,705 books, pamphlets, and manuscripts related to all aspects of Hawaiian
culture and life through the 1960s. A
detailed catalog to the collection is available to researchers.

IDAHO

Boise

124. Idaho State Historical Society, Old Idaho Penitentiary
2445 Old Penitentiary Rd
Boise, ID 83702

Contact: Kris Major, Education Spec
(208) 334-2844
Hours: Mon-Sun, 12-4; closed on state
holidays
Accessible to Public: Yes
Accessible to Scholars: Yes
Special Considerations: Call ahead for
research appointment

This prison museum contains collections
of contraband weapons made by inmates
and confiscated during shakedowns, and
prison paraphernalia such as balls-and-
chains and hanging ropes, as well as
prison records and reports. Collections
cover more than 100 years of western as
well as prison history.

Spalding

125. Nez Perce National Historical Park
PO Box 93
Spalding, ID 83551

Contact: Susan Kopczynski
(208) 843-2261
Hours: Mon-Sun, 8-4:30
Accessible to Public: No
Accessible to Scholars: Yes
Special Considerations: Available by
appointment to serious researchers

**Watson's and Salmon River General
Stores Collections:** Contain a wide variety of items (5,000 in total) from the
two stores. Artifacts date from 1904-
1963 and include postcards, stereopticon
slides, dime novels, medicines, clothing,
food and tobacco products, and household furnishings. Collections also include
the personal items of the stores' owners.

ILLINOIS

Chicago

126. Art Institute of Chicago Library
Columbus Dr at Jackson Blvd
Chicago, IL 60009

Contact: Nadene Byrne, Dir
(312) 443-3748
Hours: Mon-Fri, 9-5
Accessible to Public: Yes
Accessible to Scholars: Yes
Special Considerations: Advance
appointment required

Artists' Books Collection: Consists of
1,500 titles and exhibition catalogs and
supplemental information about collected
artists. Materials include books of formatted art created and produced by contemporary visual and literary artists.
There is a great variety within the collection which reflects the wide ranging
aesthetics and concerns found within the
field of artists' books. Included are large-
edition offset print books and periodicals; limited-edition letterpress, intaglio,
and lithographic books; one-of-a-kind
hand-drawn books; and similar materi-

als. The collection includes works created by notable Chicago artists.

127. Balzekan Museum of Lithuanian Culture

6500 Pulaski Rd
Chicago, IL 60629

Contact: Stanley Balzekas, Jr, Pres
(312) 582-6500
Hours: Mon-Sun, 1-4
Accessible to Public: Yes
Accessible to Scholars: Yes

Includes exhibits on rare amber, textiles, rare maps, rare books, Lithuanian folk art, Lithuanian wooden folk art, philately, numismatics, and a children's museum.

128. Center for Research Libraries

6050 S Kenwood Ave
Chicago, IL 60637

Contact: Circulation Dept
(312) 955-4545
Hours: Mon-Fri, 9-4
Accessible to Public: No
Accessible to Scholars: Yes
Special Considerations: Persons wishing to use the collection should call in advance

Children's Book Collection: Consists of 56,000 children's books, fiction and nonfiction, mostly published after 1951. Most titles retain their original dust covers. Books are arranged alphabetically by author. Most titles are American imprints, although British editions and many English translations of books from foreign countries are included.

Civilian Conservation Corps Camp Newspapers Collection: Consists of several thousand titles of newspapers (mostly on mimeograph) written and produced by CCC enrollees in the Corps' camps during the 1930s. This is probably the largest and most complete such collection in existence.

129. Chicago Historical Society

Clark St at N Ave
Chicago, IL 60614

Contact: Archivist
(312) 642-4600
Hours: Tues-Sat, 9:30-4:30

Accessible to Public: Yes
Accessible to Scholars: Yes
Special Considerations: Advance appointment required for use of prints and photographs (appointments available Tues-Sat, 1-4:30)

The general collections include 6,000 19th and early 20th century trade cards representing Chicago companies, arranged by type of business.

Print and Photograph Collection: The department holds nearly 1,000,000 pictorial items, including the following: 10,000 picture postcards (mostly of Chicago), 15,000 posters and broadsides (mostly advertising and political), 10,000 reels of newsfilm from WGN-TV (1948-1973), 700 television kinescopes of *Kukla, Fran, and Ollie,* 50,000 prints (500 by Currier and Ives), 25,000 documentary photographs of Chicago neighborhoods made after 1948 by members of the Chicago Area Camera Clubs Association, 250,000 *Chicago Daily News* negatives (1902-1960s), 10,000 *cartes de viste,* 20,000 cabinet cards, and 10,000 stereographs.

130. Chicago Public Library, Music Information Center

78 E Washington
Chicago, IL 60602

Contact: Richard Schwegel
(312) 269-2886
Hours: Mon-Thur, 9-7; Fri, 9-6; Sat, 9-5
Accessible to Public: Yes
Accessible to Scholars: Yes
Special Considerations: Valid identification required

The general collections include over 300 titles of popular music periodicals covering rock, jazz, new wave, punk, reggae, etc.; a comprehensive collection of 7,000 titles of popular music literature related to jazz, rock, the music business, the recording industry, gospel music, and discography (includes dissertations); a reference collection of 10,000 popular LP recordings; and 10,000 titles of popular sheet music in original covers dating from 1830.

Balaban and Katz Popular Orchestra Collection: Contains over 15,000 dance band arrangements, light classical pieces, sheet music, musical comedy selections, film music scores, original arrangements, and documentary materials gathered from local movie palaces in use 1920-1950.

Chicago Blues Archives: Consists of an archival collection of videotapes, recordings, photographs, and miscellaneous items covering the history of the blues (1,000 items).

131. Chicago Public Library Cultural Center, Thomas Hughes Children's Library
78 E Washington St
Chicago, IL 60602

Contact: Laura Culberg, Head
(312) 269-2835
Hours: Mon-Fri, 9-5:30; Sat, 9-5
Accessible to Public: Yes
Accessible to Scholars: Yes

Collection contains a retrospective *Children's Literature Collection* of 6,000 volumes (fiction and nonfiction, 1900-1950), including a complete run of *St. Nicholas Magazine;* 2,900 titles of folk and fairy tales; 40 Walt Disney stories and film books; and a sampling of children's books representing 21 foreign languages.

132. Newberry Library
60 W Walton
Chicago, IL 60610

Contact: Cynthia Peters, Head of Reader's Services
(312) 943-9090
Hours: Tues-Sat, 9-5
Accessible to Public: Yes
Accessible to Scholars: Yes
Special Considerations: Admission on a "need to use" basis

Collections include 100,000 pieces of sheet music (mostly American imprints through 1920), the *J. Francis Drisoll Sheet Music Collection,* and 4,000 road maps (mainly American).

133. The Peace Museum
430 W Erie
Chicago, IL 60610

Contact: Marianne Philbin
(312) 440-1860
Hours: Tues-Sun, 12-5; Thur, 12-8
Accessible to Public: Yes
Accessible to Scholars: Yes
Special Considerations: General public not admitted to research collection; request a research appointment in

advance and outline the specific nature of the project in the request

Collections are vast and relate to all aspects of war and peace studies. Materials include 2,000 posters, 1,000 buttons, 1,000 miscellaneous items, manuscripts, artwork, and 400 fabric panels from "The Ribbon Project," which formed an 18-mile long peace ribbon with which to wrap the Pentagon in 1985.

134. Sears, Roebuck and Company Archives
Department 703, Sears Tower 40-10
Chicago, IL 60684

Contact: Lenore Swoiskin, Archivist
(312) 875-8321
Hours: Mon-Fri, 8-4
Accessible to Public: No
Accessible to Scholars: Yes
Special Considerations: Available by prior appointment; forward letter or phone with details of research project.

Collections include original Sears catalogs (general, Christmas and special books) from the late 1890s to date. Microfilm collections of general catalogs are also located at libraries throughout the United States. Contact the archives for the collection nearest you. Collections also include retail store and Catalog Distribution Center photographs, and a set of stereoscope views on Sears' operations dating from about 1906.

135. University of Chicago, Chicago Jazz Archive
1100 E 57th St
Chicago, IL 60637

Contact: Hans Lenneberg, Music Librarian
(312) 702-8449
Hours: Mon-Fri, 9-5
Accessible to Public: No
Accessible to Scholars: Yes
Special Considerations: Requires valid identification from an academic or scholarly institution

Collection consists primarily of Chicago Jazz (400 hours of recordings) on 78 rpm and LP discs. Collection is only partially cataloged.

136. University of Chicago Library, Department of Special Collections
1100 E 57th St
Chicago, IL 60637

Contact: Robert Rosenthal, Curator
(312) 702-8705
Hours: Mon-Fri, 8:30-5; Sat, 9-1
Accessible to Public: Yes
Accessible to Scholars: Yes
Special Considerations: Collection is reserved for scholarly research needs only

Comic Book Collection: Consists of 2,300 comic books published between 1949 and 1959, with the bulk from 1952-1959. An index is available.

Edwardsville

137. Southern Illinois University at Edwardsville, Lovejoy Library
Lovejoy Library, SIU
Edwardsville, IL 62026

Contact: Gary Denue, Library Dir;
   Therese Zoski, for Music Materials;
   Milton C Moore, Rare Book Librarian
(618) 692-2711, 692-2670 (Music),
692-2665
Hours: Mon-Fri, 8:30-4:30
Accessible to Public: Yes
Accessible to Scholars: Yes

Music and Related Materials: Includes 4,500 arrangements for silent movie orchestras, instruments, and voices; 800 19th century hymnals and American songbooks; over 30,000 standard orchestral scores, popular, jazz, and band (to about 1950); 500 player piano rolls; over 10,000 phonograph records (mostly 78 rpm with a very strong collection of jazz); 1,000 radio show tapes (1920s-1950s); and over 40,000 items of American sheet music (early 1800s-1960s).

The Romain and Ellen Proctor Puppetry Collection: This major collection relates to all aspects of puppetry around the world, and includes 746 books, 57 serial titles, and numerous manuscripts, posters, and related materials (imprints date from 1806).

The collections also include several thousand comic books, 1,000 dime novels, and several hundred postcards (mostly related to Illinois and Missouri).

Elmhurst

138. Lizzadro Museum of Lapidary Art
220 Cottage Hill Ave
Elmhurst, IL 60126

Contact: Elaine Poepp
(312) 833-1616
Hours: Tues-Sat, 10-5; Sun, 1-5
Accessible to Public: Yes
Accessible to Scholars: Yes
Special Considerations: Noncirculating

Collections contain a large number of books and periodicals, many very old and rare, related to geology, archaeology, jewelry, lapidary arts, minerals, and stones.

Evanston

139. National Foundation of Funeral Service, Beryl L. Boyer Library
1614 Central St
Evanston, IL 60201

Contact: Contact Librarian
(312) 328-6545
Hours: Mon-Fri, 9:30-4:30
Accessible to Public: No
Accessible to Scholars: Yes
Special Considerations: Collection generally available only to funeral directors; inquire in advance for appointment and access possibilities

Consists of a large collection of books (3,000), prints, and pamphlets related to death, grief, and the funeral.

140. National Woman's Christian Temperance Union, Frances E. Willard Memorial Library
1730 Chicago Ave
Evanston, IL 60201

Contact: Marilyn F Staples
(312) 864-1396
Hours: Mon-Fri, 9-12, 1-4; closed holidays and one week each summer
Accessible to Public: Yes
Accessible to Scholars: Yes

Contains an extensive collection of materials related to temperance and total abstinence from alcohol throughout history.

141. Northwestern University Library, Special Collections Department
Northwestern University
Evanston, IL 60201

Contact: R Russell Maylone
(312) 491-3635
Hours: Mon-Fri, 8:30-5; Sat, 8:30-12
Accessible to Public: Yes
Accessible to Scholars: Yes

Collections include 700 titles of comic books, 275 titles of underground comic books, 120 *Big Little Books*, 1,500 travel books (including gazetteers, railroad guides, etc.), 2,200 science fiction monographs and serials, 5,000 posters (women's movement, political, revolution, etc.), four linear feet of archival materials relating to the 1968 Democratic National Convention, and 4,000 files of ephemeral materials related to women (topical files documenting contemporary women's movement).

Naperville

142. North Central College, Oesterle Library
320 E School Ave
Naperville, IL 60566

Contact: Edward Meachen
(312) 420-3425
Hours: Mon-Thur, 8 am-11 pm; Fri, 8-6:30; Sat, 9-5:30; Sun, 12-1
Accessible to Public: Yes
Accessible to Scholars: Yes
Special Considerations: Access through Librarian or Deputy Librarian for Special Collections

Collection includes eight linear feet of uncataloged materials on American conscientious objectors (1920s-1950s), including pamphlets, articles, and unpublished papers of conscientious objectors.

Oak Park

143. Institute for Advanced Perception
719 S Clarence Ave
Oak Park, IL 60304

Contact: Harold S Schroeppel
(312) 386-1742
Hours: By appointment
Accessible to Public: No
Accessible to Scholars: Yes
Special Considerations: Contact Insitute in advance of visit

Contains 1,000 books relating to the occult, ESP, and related topics. Includes some journals.

Rock Island

144. Augustana College Library, Special Collections
Augustana College
Rock Island, IL 61201

Contact: Judy Belan
(309) 794-7317
Hours: Inquire
Accessible to Public: Yes
Accessible to Scholars: Yes

Collection includes local trade cards, but they are not cataloged.

Springfield

145. Illinois Bell Oliver P. Parks Telephone Museum
529 S 7th St
Springfield, IL 62721

Contact: Geri Braun
(217) 753-8436
Hours: May-Sept, Mon-Sun, 9-4:30; Apr and Oct, Mon-Sat, 9-4:30; Nov-Mar, Mon-Fri, 9-4:30
Accessible to Public: Yes
Accessible to Scholars: Yes
Special Considerations: Wheelchair access and hands-on displays for the blind

Collection includes 79 antique phones, including wooden wall phones, candlesticks, cradle designs, glass insulators, coin phones, and two switchboards in the *Oliver P. Parks Collection*, and materials related to the history of Illinois

Bell's operations, including picturephone, touchtone, and fiber optic displays.

146. Sangamon State University, Oral History Office

Brookens 377
Springfield, IL 62708

Contact: Cullom Davis
(217) 786-6521
Hours: Mon-Fri, 9-4
Accessible to Public: Yes
Accessible to Scholars: Yes
Special Considerations: Some memoirs are restricted; write in advance for information on holdings.

Oral History Collection: Includes nearly 1,000 interviews, most of them transcribed, of regional scope and diverse subject matter. Major topics include Illinois statecraft (government and politics), coal mining and union activities, farming and farm life, ethnic and racial minorities, women's history, the Lincoln legend, political activism, and local history.

Urbana

147. University of Illinois at Urbana-Champaign, Education and Social Science Library

1408 W Gregory Dr
Urbana, IL 61801

Contact: Nancy O'Brien
(217) 333-2305
Hours: Mon-Thur, 8 am-Midnight; Fri, 8 am-10 pm; Sat, 9 am-10 pm; Sun, 1-Midnight
Accessible to Public: Yes
Accessible to Scholars: Yes
Special Considerations: Test collection does not circulate

Odell Test Collection: Consists of 7,000 educational and psychological tests to measure intellectual skills, aptitude, and intelligence.

Merton J. Mandeville Collection: Contains 6,000 titles in the occult sciences.

School Collection of Children's and Young Adult Literature: Consists of more than 30,000 volumes of literature

and nonfiction works written for children and young adults (1800-present), including numerous rare volumes.

The library also contains 3,000 volumes related to arms control, disarmament, and international security, and 12,000 volumes of elementary and secondary textbooks, teachers' manuals, curriculum guides, filmstrips, and audiocassettes.

148. University of Illinois at Urbana-Champaign, Music Library

2136 Music Building, 1114 W Nevada
Urbana, IL 61801

Contact: William M McClellan
(217) 333-1173
Hours: Mon-Thur, 8 am-10 pm; Fri, 8-5; Sat, 9-5; Sun, 1-10; between academic terms, Mon-Fri, 9-5
Accessible to Public: Yes
Accessible to Scholars: Yes
Special Considerations: Sound recordings and special collections are noncirculating

Morris N. Young Collection: Consists of 20,000 items of early American popular music (1790-1910), including 48,000 music titles and comprising 10,500 sheet music items, of which the Black American collection of 3,500 items is particularly important. Also contains 90 bound volumes of sheet music and other sheet music collections, including 165 patriotic items, 120 advertising items, 900 theater-music items, 1,000 items in small format, 175 college and organizational songs, 825 songsters, 50 broadsides, 125 manuscripts, vocal and instrumental anthologies, 50 dance folios, 100 programs and other items of memorabilia, 2,000 photographs, 500 books about music, and 1,000 sound recordings.

The general collections of the Music Library include numerous items related to popular music, including jazz, rock, theater music, folk music, country, gospel, and other popular forms. These include 370 periodical titles, 1,600 books, 200 discographies, 1,000 folios of popular songs, 1,000 collections of folk songs, 200 titles of Broadway musicals (scores and editions), over 13,000 LP discs (traditional and vernacular music, North American and British popular music, jazz, film sound tracks, musicals, and a wide range of music from Russia, the

Middle East, Africa, Oceania, South America, etc.), over 25,000 sheets of vocal music (mainly United States, 1800-1970), 1,200 piano rolls, and piano and ensemble sheet music (dance band, silent film music, radio station WGN sheet music, etc.).

149. University of Illinois Library at Urbana-Champaign, Rare Books and Special Collections
1408 W Gregory Dr
Urbana, IL 61801

Contact: Nancy L Romero, Admin; Gene K Rinkel, Curator
(217) 333-3777
Hours: Mon-Sat, 9-5; hours vary during school breaks
Accessible to Public: Yes
Accessible to Scholars: Yes
Special Considerations: Access limited to residents of Illinois and research scholars

Popular culture materials are scattered through several areas of the Special Collections Department, and include 200 dime novels; 10,000 items related to censorship and intellectual freedom, American political and social movements, court cases, books, pamphlets, posters, and cartoons; 200 science fiction novels, stories, and anthologies; 100 editions of *Little Black Sambo;* 8,500 items related to American wit, humor, and folklore (Mark Twain editions, photographs, etc.); 350 motion picture screenplays, books, periodicals, and stills; 5,000 items in the *Motley Collection* of theater and costume designs by Motley (Shakespeare and other productions, 1932-1976); the *Carl Sandburg Collection* of 2,000 books and 1,500 linear feet of papers and correspondence; and 3,600 historic children's books dating from about 1900 through 1925.

Wauconda

150. Lake County Museum
Lakewood Forest Preserve
Wauconda, IL 60084

Contact: Katherine Hamilton-Smith, Special Collections Curator
(312) 526-8638
Hours: Mon-Fri, 8:30-4:30

Accessible to Public: Yes
Accessible to Scholars: Yes
Special Considerations: Access to the postcard collection is by appointment only, although a permanent general interest exhibit is open to the public

The Curt Teich Postcard Collection: The Collection consists of the industrial archive of the Curt Teich Company of Chicago. The company was once the largest volume producer of advertising and view postcards in the world and was in operation from 1898 through 1974. The company retained examples of all images produced as well as the production or job files for the cards. Production files include photographs, negatives, copy negatives, pasteups, drawings, and client instructions. There are 2,970 linear feet in the collection, and this includes postcards, panorama view cards, advertising blotters, brochures, trade cards, souvenir booklets, and maps. There are nearly 1,000,000 postcards in the archive. Access is by computer catalog and can be searched by date, geographic location, or subject.

Wheaton

151. Wheaton College, Marion E. Wade Collection
Wheaton College
Wheaton, IL 60187

Contact: Lyle W Dorsett, Curator
(312) 260-5908
Hours: Mon-Fri, 9-12, 1-4; Sat, 9-12; closed during academic breaks
Accessible to Public: Yes
Accessible to Scholars: Yes

Marion E. Wade Collection: Contains materials related to Owen Barfield (94 volumes, letters, manuscripts), G. K. Chesterton (over 2,400 volumes, letters, manuscripts), C. S. Lewis (over 4,000 volumes, letters, manuscripts, and his personal library), George MacDonald (nearly 900 volumes, letters), Dorothy L. Sayers (1,100 volumes, letters, manuscripts), J. R. R. Tolkien (700 volumes, letters, manuscripts), and Charles Williams (566 volumes, letters, manuscripts). Holdings also include 30 oral history interviews, 250 theses and dissertations, audiotapes, videotapes, 40 detective fiction reference volumes, 90 volumes of Arthuriana, 140 fantasy reference volumes, photographs, and artwork.

Winnetka

152. Rosemary Wells "Tooth Fairy" Collection
1219 Scott
Winnetka, IL 60093

Contact: Rosemary Wells
(312) 492-1400 Ext 374; evenings and weekends (312) 446-3842
Hours: By appointment
Accessible to Public: Yes
Accessible to Scholars: Yes
Special Considerations: Advance appointment and permission to use materials is required

This is the only known "Tooth Fairy Collection." This ever-growing collection of art and artifacts related to the "Tooth Fairy" includes children's books, articles, short stories, art, cartoons, reproductions of artists' concepts of the "Tooth Fairy," slides, and over 300 drawings of the "Tooth Fairy" by children. Also contains nearly 100 "Tooth Fairy" pillows, shirts, dolls, tooth containers, craft kits, jewelry, etc.

INDIANA

Auburn

153. Auburn-Cord-Duesenberg Museum
PO Box 271
Auburn, IN 46706

Contact: Julia W Page
(219) 925-1444
Hours: Oct-Apr, Mon-Sun, 10-5; May-Sept, Mon-Sun, 9-9
Accessible to Public: Yes
Accessible to Scholars: Yes
Special Considerations: Access to research collection is by advance appointment

Tri Kappa Collection of Automotive Literature: Consists primarily of sales and service brochures and manuals dealing with the automobiles built in Auburn. Includes over 10,000 items, including periodicals, correspondence, and pho-

tographs from the Auburn Automobile Company.

Raymond Wolff Collection: Includes 900 original 8 X 10 negatives from the advertising department of the Auburn Automobile Company, 1925-1937.

Bloomington

154. Indiana University, Archives of Traditional Music
Morrison Hall
Bloomington, IN 47405

Contact: Anthony Seeger, Dir; Mary E Russell, Librarian
(812) 335-8632
Hours: Mon-Fri, 9-5
Accessible to Public: Yes
Accessible to Scholars: Yes
Special Considerations: Many items are for in-house use only. Some items may not have listening copy (dub) available for immediate use, so advance inquiries are suggested. Field collection dubbing requires written permission of collector.

Collections include 33,500 commercial sound recordings of folk, ethnic, jazz, blues, and popular music; 40,000 discs, 30,000 tapes, and extensive collections on wax cylinders and wire recordings; Hoagy Carmichael memorabilia (manuscripts, videos, recordings); field recordings dating to late 19th century of music and spoken word from many culture groups, with especially strong holdings of American Indian and African materials (1,500 field collections); and collections of conversations, recitations, and pedagogical sessions in 300 languages of the world.

155. Indiana University, Black Culture Center Library
Afro-American Studies Department, 109 N Jordan
Bloomington, IN 47405

Contact: Wilmer H Baatz, Librarian
(812) 335-9271
Hours: Mon-Fri, 9-6; some evening hours available
Accessible to Public: Yes
Accessible to Scholars: Yes

Contains nearly 2,100 books, current Black periodicals and newspapers, a large pamphlet file, and the *Arno Press/ New York Times* series of reprints on Afro-American history and literature. This collection is augmented by a fine research collection housed in the University Library (Room W521).

156. Indiana University, Elizabeth Sage Historic Costume Collection
203 Wylie Hall
Bloomington, IN 47405

Contact: Kathleen Rowold, Curator;
  Pamela Schlick, Asst Curator
(812) 335-5223
Hours: Mon-Fri, 9-5
Accessible to Public: Yes
Accessible to Scholars: Yes
Special Considerations: Special appointment must be made for access to storage area; public exhibits open as listed above

Contains over 6,000 items of 19th and 20th century apparel (women's, men's, and children's) and accessories. Collections are primarily North American and European, and include, but are not limited to, designer fashions.

157. Indiana University, Kinsey Institute for Research in Sex, Gender and Reproduction
Room 313, Morrison Hall
Bloomington, IN 47405

Contact: David Frasier; Gwen Pershing
(812) 335-7686
Hours: Mon-Fri, 9-4:45
Accessible to Public: No
Accessible to Scholars: Yes
Special Considerations: Scholars must send a letter outlining their research project and their academic or institutional credentials. A brochure is available on request.

The general holdings include 71,000 journals and reprints documenting all aspects of sex behavior, gender, and reproduction. The art collection houses some 25,000 pieces of flat art plus a collection of 3,500 three-dimensional objects. These collections are augmented by a collection of 70,000 still photographs dating from 1855 to the present, and a 6,500-reel film collection dating from the earliest days of the medium to the present, including commercial erotic films, medical films, and documentaries dealing with sex and reproduction.

Men's Magazine Collection ("J" Collection): Contains nearly 15,000 magazines ranging from adult humor magazines of the 1920s through the current adult newstand fare. Collection is particularly strong in titles of the 1950s and also contains complete runs of *Playboy* and *Screw*.

Vertical File Collection: Contains newspaper clippings, newsletters, photocopies, and ephemera (52 file drawers arranged by topic), including a significant body of sexually related folklore, graffiti, jokes, poems, and songs.

Eight-Pager Collection: Includes 3,000 examples of this early form of underground comic, the sexually explicit parody and satire form that emerged in the 1920s.

Russ Meyer Collection: Consists of over 300 interviews, film reviews, and newspaper articles that document the life and career of pioneer soft-core sexploitation filmmaker Russ Meyer. Also included are videotapes of all commercially available Meyer feature films.

"W" Film Collection: This recent addition includes 1,500 feels of film, including a large body of homosexual films (1968-present), heterosexual "peep-show" films, promotional and publicity films, and similar materials.

158. Indiana University, Lilly Library
Lilly Library, Rare Book and
  Manuscript Collection
Bloomington, IN 47405

Contact: L C Rudolph
(812) 335-2452
Hours: Mon-Fri, 9-5
Accessible to Public: Yes
Accessible to Scholars: Yes
Special Considerations: Some individual collections have restrictions on use

The collections of the Rare Book and Manuscript Division are extensive, with numerous materials relating to popular culture. Some of the most important materials include *The Michael Sadleir London Low Life Collection*, and the *Vir-*

ginia Warren Collection of Street Cries; a large body of guide books, travellers' accounts, city plans, and local histories related to Paris, France (1650-1900); hundreds of collections of literature, manuscripts, letters, and papers related to writers from the United States, Germany, Great Britain, France, and Czechoslovakia (many popular writers such as Daniel Defoe, Charles Dickens, and Jules Verne are included; consult the library for specific author inquiries; materials date from the 1600s); 16,000 British plays from the 19th century, including playbills and related theatrical literature; 10,000 volumes of children's literature, including 2,100 chapbooks (British, American, French, and German); extensive collections of detective and science fiction, including pulp magazines; manuscripts and papers of Orson Welles (19,875 items); letters, scripts, production materials, and manuscripts of John Ford (7,000 items); 4,000 items in the manuscripts and papers of film producer and distributor Richard Edward Norman; 227 items of materials related to the production of the film *The Wizard of Oz*; 2,000 film scripts ranging from the silent era to the present, including Darryl Zanuck's scripts; the papers of freelance writer Shirley Thomas; a large collection of television scripts, including 102 annotated scripts for *Rowan and Martin's Laugh-In* and a complete run of *Star Trek* scripts (most scripts from 1960s and 1970s); the papers of radio and television writer John McGreevey; extensive collections of the papers and field notes of folklorists Stith Thompson and Richard Dorson; a major collection of materials related to 19th century international trade expositions held in London, Paris, Lyon, Vienna, Moscow, New York, Philadelphia, Chicago, and other cites 1851-1900; includes programs, official reports, guides, periodicals, etc.); extensive materials related to the art of the book (illuminated manuscripts, incunabula, fine printing, etc.); Gilbert and Sullivan librettos and other related materials; 100,000 pieces of American sheet music, dating from the late 1700s; a comic art collection of original illustrations for comic books, newspaper comic sections, pulp magazines, film animations, and newspaper political cartoons (1906-1967, including work by Fontaine Fox, Dale Messick, Charles Addams, Ernie Bushmiller, Milton Caniff, Al Capp,

Rudolph Dirks, Hal Foster, George McManus, Charles Schulz, Chic Young, and others); and a large collection of materials by and about children's book illustrators (artists include Edward Ardizzone, Paul Bransom, Judith Gwyn Brown, Gordon Frederick Browne, Randolph Caldecott, Juliana Horatia Ewing, Chris Conover, Walter Crane, Walt Disney Studios, E. H. Shepard, and many others).

159. Indiana University, Oral History Research Center
512 N Fess
Bloomington, IN 47405

Contact: John Bodnar
(812) 335-2856
Hours: Mon-Fri, 8-5
Accessible to Public: Yes
Accessible to Scholars: Yes

Consists of tapes of ordinary people throughout Indiana in the 20th century, especially autoworkers, miners, women, and Blacks. Collections are strongest for Indianapolis, South Bend, and Anderson.

160. Indiana University Libraries
Folklore, Anthropology, Sociology, and
  Women's Studies Librarian
Bloomington, IN 47401

Contact: Polly Grimshaw
(812) 335-1550
Hours: Open whenever University
  Library is open
Accessible to Public: Yes
Accessible to Scholars: Yes

Contains a rich folklore collection, including more than 30,000 monographs and 686 serial titles. Reference and other printed materials (books and serials) often relate to popular culture. Field collections are mainly from Indiana, Ohio, Michigan, and Kentucky. Collection also includes 5,000 limericks, a legend file of 7,500 items, a material culture and folklife file in excess of 1,200 manuscripts, 90 files of Micronesian folktales, slide collections of material culture, and cassette tapes of thousands of field interviews.

161. Stone's Scout Museum of Girl and Boy Scout Memorabilia
2290 W Bloomfield Rd
Bloomington, IN 47401

Contact: Thornton Stone; Constance
Stone
(812) 336-5031
Hours: By advance appointment
Accessible to Public: Yes
Accessible to Scholars: Yes
Special Considerations: No set hours, so
appointment is required

Collections and exhibits relate to all aspects of Boy and Girl Scouting, with an emphasis on Indiana. Researchers should inquire for holdings related to specific projects in advance of visit.

Crawfordsville

162. Wabash College, Lilly Library Archives
PO Box 352
Crawfordsville, IN 47933

Contact: Johanna Herring, Archivist
(317) 362-1400
Hours: Mon-Fri, 10-12, 1-3
Accessible to Public: Yes
Accessible to Scholars: Yes

Horsethief Detective Association Collection: This vigilante and quasi-legal organization was founded in Montgomery County in the 1840s and later expanded to nearby states. Collection includes minute books, roll books, and constitution and by-law booklets for a number of local companies, as well as for the national association. The records date from 1845, when the Council Grove Minute Men organized near Crawfordsville, and continue through the 1930s when laws were enacted to take away the Association's powers as peace enforcers. There are about 100 separate titles in the collection from organizations in Indiana, Illinois, and Ohio. There are also a few artifacts, including badges, seals, and stamps.

Evansville

163. University of Southern Indiana Library, Special Collections and University Archives
8600 University Blvd
Evansville, IN 47712

Contact: Gina R Walker, Archivist
(812) 464-1896
Hours: Mon-Fri, 9-4
Accessible to Public: Yes
Accessible to Scholars: Yes
Special Considerations: Researchers
should call prior to visit

Center for Communal Studies: 210 current and 50 historic communal societies are represented by cataloged books, cassettes, photographs, clippings, brochures, and newsletters, 1800-present.

Jeanne Suhrheinrich Collection: Consists of over 400 movie promotion press kits from all types of motion pictures, 1950-present.

Evansville-Vanderburgh School Cooperation: Consists of 3,800 glass lantern slides, including instructional slides for fine arts, language arts, health, mathematics, science, and social science, 1910-1930.

Oral History Collection: Includes tapes and transcripts of prominent Evansville citizens. Subjects covered include early Evansville and the German influence in Evansville.

Indiana Labor History Collection: Consists of oral interviews, books, and memorabilia concerning labor unions in Indiana in the early 1920s and 1930s through the 1960s.

The library also holds two boxes of postcards (divided by subjects, 1890-present), and 30 sheets of music (religious, secular, and patriotic, 1900-1950).

Fort Wayne

164. Friends of the Third World, Inc.
611 W Wayne St
Fort Wayne, IN 46802

Contact: Jim Goetsch
(219) 422-1650

Hours: Tues-Sat, 10-6
Accessible to Public: Yes
Accessible to Scholars: Yes
Special Considerations: Noncirculating;
photocopying available

Collections consist of newsletters and publications relating to social change in economics, poverty, and international development, and include approximately 4,000 pamphlet files.

Indianapolis

165. Butler University, Hugh Thomas Miller Rare Book Room
4600 Sunset Ave
Indianapolis, IN 46208

Contact: Gisela Terrell
(317) 283-9265
Hours: Mon-Fri, 9-5; evening and weekend hours by appointment
Accessible to Public: Yes
Accessible to Scholars: Yes
Special Considerations: Patrons must register

Dellinger Collection: Consists of educational materials printed in the United States prior to 1945, including readers, grammars, primers, math and science books, etiquette books, etc. There are 200 items in this growing collection, which is cataloged and indexed.

American Popular Music Collection: Consists of pre-1900 American sheet music, including 300 titles which are cataloged and indexed. Collection also includes 6,000 items of popular 20th century American sheet music (held in the Music and Fine Arts Library).

Kin Hubbard/Gaar Williams Collection: This partially cataloged collection consists of original cartoons, drawings, sketchbooks, books, correspondence, clippings, and memorabilia by these Hoosier cartoonists and humorists.

166. Butler University, Music and Fine Arts Library
4600 Sunset Ave
Indianapolis, IN 46208

Contact: Phyllis J Schoonover
(317) 283-9270

Hours: Mon-Thur, 8 am-11 pm; Fri, 8-5;
Sat, 9-5; Sun, 12-11; Summer Hours:
Mon-Fri, 8-4:30
Accessible to Public: Yes
Accessible to Scholars: Yes
Special Considerations: Noncirculating

Harper and Stit Collections: Contain 6,000 titles of popular sheet music, 1900-present.

167. Indianapolis Motor Speedway Hall of Fame Museum
4790 W 16th St
Indianapolis, IN 46222

Contact: Jack L Martin, Dir
(317) 248-6747
Hours: Mon-Sun, 9-5; closed Christmas Day
Accessible to Public: Yes
Accessible to Scholars: Yes

Collections include materials related to the history of the Speedway and to auto racing in general.

168. Indianapolis-Marion County Public Library
PO Box 211
Indianapolis, IN 46206

Contact: Daniel H Gann, Head of Arts Division
(317) 269-1705
Hours: Mon-Fri, 9-9; Sat, 9-5; Sun, 1-5
Accessible to Public: Yes
Accessible to Scholars: Yes
Special Considerations: Collections are "reference" and may be used only in library

Old Song Collection: Consists of 7,000 sheet music titles of American popular songs (1850-1980, most 1900-1950), with access by title (composer/lyricist index being developed).

Julia Connor Thompson Memorial Collection: Collection relates to "the finer arts of homemaking" and contains a reference collection of books on domestic architecture, interior decoration, furniture, gardening, landscape architecture, and the arts and crafts of the home. This rapidly growing collection consists of more than 5,000 titles.

Indianapolis 500 Auto Race Collection: Contains official programs of the Indianapolis Motor Speedway for the years 1909, 1911, 1919-1941, and 1946-1970, and official yearbooks for 1949-1950, 1952-1954, and 1956-present.

169. National Track and Field Hall of Fame Historical Research Library
4600 Sunset Ave, Butler University,
Irwin Library
Indianapolis, IN 46208

Contact: Gisela Terrell
(317) 283-9265
Hours: Mon-Fri, 9-5
Accessible to Public: Yes
Accessible to Scholars: Yes
Special Considerations: Available by appointment

Collection consists of books, periodicals, competition programs, biographies, descriptions, technical works, rules, directories, and related materials covering the history of track and field in the United States. The collection is the research division of the National Track and Field Hall of Fame which is located at 1 Hoosier Dome, Indianapolis, (317) 261-0483.

Muncie

170. Ball State University Library, Special Collections
Alexander M Bracken Library
Muncie, IN 47306

Contact: David C Tambo, Head of
Special Collections
(317) 285-5078
Hours: Mon-Fri, 8-5; Wed, 7:30-9:30 pm
Accessible to Public: Yes
Accessible to Scholars: Yes

Rare Books and Manuscripts: Includes 150 trade catalogs, many relating to Indiana companies and others related to glass and auto industries.

Elisabeth Ball Poster Collection: Contains 2,000 items, primarily World War II, from a wide range of countries including the United States, Great Britain, France, Germany, and numerous colonial territories.

Ball State University Archives: Contains 70 volumes of school yearbooks (1913-present), 65 volumes of school newspapers (1922-present), and 100 films and aural tapes of school events such as homecoming parades and basketball games.

Stoeckel Archives: Contains 2,000 linear feet of manuscripts and county records, 10,000 photographic prints and negatives, 900 maps, 300 hours of interviews, and miscellaneous items related to local history of Delaware County and east central Indiana. Materials relate to such topics as business, labor, family history, religion, Black history, Jewish history, local government, education, recreation, cultural activities, and social and fraternal organizations.

Middletown Studies Collections: Consists of approximately 500,000 feet of film and videotape, 500 hours of aural tape, and 200 linear feet of other records and printed material pertaining to the study of Muncie as "Middletown." Includes Middletown III and Black Middletown studies materials, and unused footage of Middletown Film Project materials, by filmmaker Peter Davis, a series that aired first on PBS.

John Steinbeck Collection: Consists of 1,000 volumes in several languages and 25 linear feet of manuscripts, photographs, films, videotapes, and phonodiscs related to Steinbeck and his work.

Nazi Collection: Contains 650 volumes and related items such as postcards, currency, and stamps.

Ku Klux Klan Collection: Materials include 80 titles, .4 linear feet of manuscripts, and 90 photographs on the Klan in the early 20th century, with an emphasis on Indiana.

Conservative Collection: Contains five linear feet of pamphlets, newsletters, and other ephemera, mostly from the 1960s.

Radical Pamphlets Collection: Contains 850 titles, including pamphlets, newsletters, and ephemera (1900-1970).

Modern American Poetry Collection: Contains several thousand titles in a variety of formats, mostly limited edition, signed by authors. Primary access is by author and title.

171. Center for Middletown Studies
Ball State University
Muncie, IN 47306

Contact: Dwight W Hoover, Dir; David Tambo, Archivist
(317) 285-8037
Hours: Mon-Fri, 8-5
Accessible to Public: Yes
Accessible to Scholars: Yes
Special Considerations: Users must secure permission of the Director to view films

Collections contain 1,600 negatives of Muncie in the 1920s and 1930s; 1,500 negatives of Muncie from 1900-1920; 500 negatives of the Marsh family from 1880-1900; various other family photographs, papers, and miscellaneous items; various oral history collections (100 oral histories of Black Munsonians, 20 oral histories of Jewish Munsonians, and several other citizens of the town); and over 500 hours of film outtakes from the Middletown Film Project taken of the town during the years 1979-1981.

Nashville

172. The John Dillinger Historical Museum
PO Box 869
Nashville, IN 47448

Contact: Joe M Pinkston
(812) 988-7172, 988-7381
Hours: Mon-Sat, 10-6
Accessible to Public: Yes
Accessible to Scholars: Yes
Special Considerations: Admission fee ($2.50); photographs by permission only

Contains the nation's largest collection of materials related to Dillinger and his 1930s crime spree, including newspaper clippings, memorabilia, and ephemera.

Peru

173. Circus City Festival, Inc., Museum
154 N Broadway
Peru, IN 46970

Contact: Betty Black, Exec Sec
(317) 472-3918
Hours: Mon-Fri, 9-12, 1-4; special hours during second and third weeks in July
Accessible to Public: Yes
Accessible to Scholars: Yes

Contains a large collection of circus lithographs, photographs, costumes of famous performers, trapeze, rigging, harness, mouthpieces, furniture from the Wallace Circus Home and the Mugivan Home, wild animal cages, miniature circus wagons, miniature circuses made to scale, paintings by circus artists, and many other items of circusiana.

Valparaiso

174. Valparaiso Technical Institute of Electronics, Wilbur H. Cummings Museum of Electronics
1 Center St
Valparaiso, IN 46383

Contact: Arthur L Hershman, Curator
(219) 462-2191
Hours: Mon-Fri, 8-5; Sat, 8-12; other times by appointment
Accessible to Public: Yes
Accessible to Scholars: Yes

Collections include 5,000 magazines covering the early days of radio and wireless telegraphy, from the 1930s and 1940s, with some materials dealing with the 1920s and 1950s.

175. Valparaiso University, Moellering Library
Moellering Library
Valparaiso, IN 46383

Contact: Margaret Perry
(219) 464-5364
Hours: Mon-Thur, 8 am-11 pm; Fri, 8 am-9 pm; Sat, 9-5; Sun, 12-11; summer hours vary
Accessible to Public: Yes
Accessible to Scholars: Yes

Collections contain 120 cartoon books (Charles Addams, Walt Kelly, Norman Thelwell, and dozens of other artists are represented; good selection of cartoon "Best of . . ." collections) and the *Hesse Collection of Humor Books* (29 items).

IOWA

Ames

176. Iowa State University Library, The Parks Library, Department of Special Collections

The Parks Library, Iowa State
University
Ames, IA 50011-2140

Contact: Dr Stanley Yates
(515) 294-6672
Hours: Mon-Fri, 8-11:50, 1-5
Accessible to Public: Yes
Accessible to Scholars: Yes
Special Considerations: Materials for use within Department of Special Collections only

Collections include 1,883 underground comic books, 83 issues of *E.C. Comics,* a large grouping of science fiction novels and major science fiction magazines, a large collection of materials related to creationists and evolutionists (61 books, 13 journals, and six linear feet of letters and manuscripts), 2,210 Little Blue Books, and 120 centennial and sesqui-centennial histories of Iowa towns.

Cedar Falls

177. Cedar Falls Historical Society

303 Franklin St
Cedar Falls, IA 50613

Contact: Rosemary Beach
(319) 277-8817
Hours: Wed-Sun, 2-4
Accessible to Public: Yes
Accessible to Scholars: Yes

The collections include an oral history collection of 200 tapes of interviews with local residents.

Decorah

178. The Norwegian-American Museum

502 W Water St
Decorah, IA 52101

Contact: Marion J Nelson, Dir
(319) 382-9681

Hours: Mon-Fri, 8-5
Accessible to Public: Yes
Accessible to Scholars: Yes
Special Considerations: Make appointment one week in advance of visit

Consists of 1,000 objects covering the full range of popular culture materials that were part of the lives of Norwegians in America. There is also a major collection related to folklore.

Des Moines

179. Grandview College Library, Danish Immigrant Archives

1351 Grandview Ave
Des Moines, IA 50316

Contact: Dr Rudolph Jensen
(515) 263-2879
Hours: Mon-Fri, 8-5; hours vary when school not in session
Accessible to Public: Yes
Accessible to Scholars: Yes
Special Considerations: Advance appointment is encouraged, though not required

Danish Immigrant Archives: Consists of a wide variety of books, periodicals, documents, photographs, family histories, and related materials pertaining to Danish immigrants to the United States. The Danish Lutheran Church and Danish Bishop N. F. S. Grundtvig are emphasized. Most items are in Danish. The collection covers 600 linear feet of shelving.

Iowa City

180. University of Iowa, Women's Resource and Action Center

130 N Madesian, Sojourner of Truth Library
Iowa City, IA 52242

Contact: Cherry Muhanji
(319) 335-1486
Hours: Mon-Thur, 9-7; Fri, 9-5
Accessible to Public: Yes
Accessible to Scholars: Yes

Collection represents one of the oldest women's libraries in existence, and contains 1,500 entries, including old and new books, women's magazines (many now out of print), and related materials.

181. University of Iowa Libraries, Special Collections
University of Iowa Libraries
Iowa City, IA 52242

Contact: Robert A McCown, Head of Special Collections
(319) 353-4854
Hours: Mon-Fri, 9-12, 1-5; closed holidays
Accessible to Public: Yes
Accessible to Scholars: Yes

Library contains large manuscript and archival collections of scrapbooks, advertising cards, playbills, broadsides, theater clippings, ballads, folklife materials (games, folk sayings, riddles, supersitions, remedies, etc.), Chautauqua collections, editorial commentaries from Iowa television stations (KCAU, KCRG, KWWL, WHO, and WMT), Jay Norwood Darling's papers, theater programs (from Chicago, New York, St. Louis, and Oshkosh), Dessa Manion's music collection (transcripts of lyrics and sheet music), playscripts from the Federal Theatre Project (1936-1938), Vaudeville and moving picture business records of B. F. Keith and E. F. Albee, TV and movie scripts by Charles E. O'Neal, and concert programs.

Motion Picture and Television Related Collections: Consists of an extensive body of materials (scripts, scenarios, stills, papers, and manuscripts) related to such producers of film and television as Robert Blees Productions, David Swift Productions, Albert J. Cohen Productions, Arthur A. Ross Productions, Victor Animatograph Company (1878-1961), Albert Zubsmith, Ralph M. Junkin, Norman Felton, Twentieth Century-Fox, Luis Bunuel, Nicholas Meyer, and Stewart Stern. Collections also include screenplays for numerous major motion pictures. Inquire as to exact holdings prior to visit.

Le Mars

182. Westmar College Library
Westmar College
Le Mars, IA 51031

Contact: Dr Mary Pope; Janet Wiener
(712) 546-7081
Hours: Mon-Fri, 8-5
Accessible to Public: Yes
Accessible to Scholars: Yes
Special Considerations: Prior notice of visit required

Collections include the *Nicholson Collection* of more than 2,000 crosses, rosaries, and religious artifacts of various styles and media, and approximately 100 hymnals (late 19th and early 20th centuries). Emphasis is on the Evangelical United Brethren denomination.

Mason City

183. Van Horn Antique Truck Museum
Hwy 65 N, Rte 4
Mason City, IA 50401

Contact: Lloyd Van Horn; Margaret Van Horn
(515) 423-0655, 423-0550
Hours: May 25-Sept 22, Mon-Sat, 10:30-4; Sun, 11-6; closed remainder of year
Accessible to Public: Yes
Accessible to Scholars: Yes
Special Considerations: Admission charge ($3)

Consists of antique trucks dating 1909-1930, including trucks manufactured by 55 different companies; old garage and gas station tools and equipment; old lights and lanterns; and a large collection of truck literature.

Mount Pleasant

184. Museum of Repertoire Americana
Threshers Rd
Mount Pleasant, IA 52641

Contact: James V Davis, Pres
(319) 385-8937
Hours: By advance appointment
Accessible to Public: Yes
Accessible to Scholars: Yes

Special Considerations: Make appointment in advance

This is the largest collection of early Tent Repertoire Theatre, Opera House, and Chautauqua memorabilia in the nation, including the Toby Hall of Fame. Includes pictures, show heralds, advertising sheets, scrap books, and newspaper clippings (all materials date from the early 1850s). Also contains books, scripts, tape recordings, and films related to early history of tent theaters in the United States.

West Branch

185. Herbert Hoover Presidential Library Valentines
Hoover Presidential Library
West Branch, IA 52358

Contact: Dale C Mayer
(319) 643-5301
Hours: Mon-Fri, 8:45-4:45
Accessible to Public: Yes
Accessible to Scholars: Yes

Collection consists of presidential papers, including Hoover's personal files. Of particular interest are 10.5 archival containers of birthday greetings (cards, letters, and telegrams, 1929-1932), and an archival container of Valentine greetings (cards, letters, and telegrams, 1930-1933).

KANSAS

Abilene

186. Greyhound Hall of Fame
407 S Buckeye
Abilene, KS 67410

Contact: Ed Scheele
(913) 263-3000
Hours: Apr through Oct, Mon-Sun, 9-5; Nov through Mar, Fri-Sun, 9-5
Accessible to Public: Yes
Accessible to Scholars: Yes
Special Considerations: Library use requires advance appointment; no restrictions on museum use

Library collections include general material on greyhounds, including books, magazines, photographs, clipping files, videotapes, and racing programs.

187. Museum of Independent Telephony
412 S Campbell
Abilene, KS 67410

Contact: Peg Chronister
(913) 263-2681
Hours: Apr through Oct, Mon-Sat, 10-4:30; Sun, 1-5; Nov through Mar, open weekends only, except by advance appointment
Accessible to Public: Yes
Accessible to Scholars: Yes
Special Considerations: Curator must be present to access files; make advance appointment, especially Nov-Mar

Collections include a library of 1,000 manuscripts, histories, magazines, books, and booklets related to all phases of telephone related subjects. An oral history collection of 100 cassettes covers the early pioneers in the field, and 4,000 artifacts are accessioned.

Independence

188. Independence Community College Library
College Ave and Brookside Dr
Independence, KS 67301

Contact: Del Singleton, Library Dir
(316) 331-4100 Ext 280
Hours: Mon-Thur, 7:45 am-9 pm; Fri, 7:45-4:30
Accessible to Public: Yes
Accessible to Scholars: Yes
Special Considerations: Inge Collection available by advance appointment only

The William Inge Collection: Contains a vast collection of materials related to playwright and screenwriter William Inge, including 400 manuscripts, plays, screenplays, one-act plays, novels, and short stories. Additionally, the collection includes foreign editions of Inge's work, many biographical materials, and theater programs and playbills from his plays.

La Crosse

189. Rush County Historical Society, Inc.

202 W 1st St
La Crosse, KS 67548

Contact: Tillie Miller, Sec Treas; Ruth Johnson, Tour Guide
(913) 222-3560
Hours: Apr through Oct, Mon-Sat, 10-4: 30; Sun, 1-4:30; closed Nov through Mar
Accessible to Public: Yes
Accessible to Scholars: Yes

Collections include the *Post Rock Museum*, which demonstrates how rock was used for fence posts, and a number of exhibits and materials related to the history of central Kansas.

Lawrence

190. Kenneth Spencer Research Library, Department of Special Collections

University of Kansas
Lawrence, KS 66045-2800

Contact: Alexandra Mason, Spencer Librarian
(913) 864-4334
Hours: Mon-Fri, 8-6; during academic year also Sat, 9-1
Accessible to Public: Yes
Accessible to Scholars: Yes
Special Considerations: Material for use in rare book reading room only; no ink, no food, no drink, etc.

Science Fiction Collection: Contains 4,000 volumes of printed science fiction, including over 100 periodical titles (mainly 20th century, and mainly paperback), and includes foreign works and editions; archives of the Science Fiction Oral History Association (300 tapes); official North American repository of World SF; archives of Science Fiction Research Association; the papers of James E. Gunn, Lloyd Biggle, and Lee Killough; large holdings of papers of Cordwainer Smith and small collections of other authors' papers; and 6 linear feet of fan literature (uncataloged).

The Library also holds 7,000 volumes of children's literature, mainly American and British (late 18th to mid-20th century), and 150 volumes of 19th century railway stall novels (known as "Yellowbacks").

191. University of Kansas Libraries, Kansas Collection

Kenneth Spencer Research Library, University of Kansas
Lawrence, KS 66045

Contact: Sheryl K Williams, Curator
(913) 864-4274
Hours: Mon-Fri, 8-5; Sat, 9-1; hours vary when school not in session
Accessible to Public: Yes
Accessible to Scholars: Yes

Wilcox Collection: Consists of extremist political literature from the Right and Left since 1960, and includes 4,000 serials, 5,000 books and pamphlets, 400 audiotapes, and 50,000 pieces of ephemera representing 7,000 organizations.

Haldeman-Julius Press Collection: Includes 5,000 titles of *Little Blue Books* and other series dating from the early 20th century.

Albert Reid (1873-1955) Collection: Contains 406 political cartoons, primarily pen and ink drawings, dating 1919-1931.

Pittsburg

192. Pittsburg State University, Leonard H. Axe Library

Pittsburg State University
Pittsburg, KS 66762

Contact: Gene DeGruson, Special Collections Librarian
(316) 231-7000 Ext 4883
Hours: Mon-Fri, 8-4:30; additional hours by appointment
Accessible to Public: Yes
Accessible to Scholars: Yes

E. Haldeman-Julius Collection: Includes 20,000 *Little Blue Books* and 2,000 *Big Blue Books*, as well as the personal library and business correspondence of the E. Haldeman-Julius Publishing Co., Girard, Kansas. Collection includes six linear feet of manuscripts; six linear feet of archival materials; 300 photographic prints; and paintings, furniture, and other realia from the Haldeman-Julius home and office.

J. A. Wayland Collection: Contains variant editions of the *Appeal to Reason*, the most influential American Socialist newspaper, with diaries and correspondence of founding editor J. A. Wayland (1854-1912) and office correspondence of managing editor Fred D. Warren. Consists of seven linear feet of manuscripts, one linear foot of archives, 120 photographic prints, and taped interviews with family members.

Ted Watts Sports Art Collection: Contains books and programs illustrated by Watts (b. 1942), with 850 posters, lithographs, and original art, supplemented by records of the Ted Watts Studio, Inc. (three linear feet of manuscripts, one linear foot of archives, and 300 photographic prints).

L. V. Roper Collection: Includes books, galleys, manuscripts, and clippings of Lester Virgil (Sam) Roper (b. 1931) who also writes romance under the pseudonym of Samantha Lester (one linear foot of manuscripts, one linear foot of archives).

Irene P. Ertman Science Fiction Collection: Consists of 1,248 science fiction titles published 1932-1985.

Bill Martino Collection: Includes writings from men's and travel magazines by free-lance writer James William Martino (b. 1933).

William R. Hunter Collection: Consists of manuscripts (two linear feet), scrapbooks, and publications of William R. (Bill) Hunter (1940-1984), free-lance writer and photographer and editor of *Ford News* and *Flagship News* (one linear foot of archives, 800 photographic tapes, three video tapes, and 10 computer discs).

Marietta Holley Collection: Includes 40 books by Holley (1836-1926), first American female humorist.

Zula Bennington Greene Collection: Includes photographs by Lynn Martin and books of Kansas authors inscribed to Greene, dean of Kansas journalists, supplemented with correspondence (one linear foot of manuscripts, one linear foot of archives, 300 photographs, and 100 books).

Charles M. Sheldon Collection: Consists of 46 books and pamphlets by Sheldon (1857-1946), including numerous editions of *In His Steps*.

Albert Bigelow Paine Collection: Consists of 26 book titles, one linear foot of manuscripts, and three photographic prints of Paine (1861-1937), children's author, novelist, and literary executor of Mark Twain's estate.

Vance Randolph Collection: Contains 83 book titles, one linear foot of manuscripts, and five photographic prints of Randolph (1892-1980), folklorist of the Ozarks.

Harold Bell Wright Collection: Includes 34 books and one linear foot of archival material related to Wright (1872-1944), Christian minister and novelist. Collection is supplemented by an exhaustive clipping file documenting Pittsburg, Kansas, and Wright's career.

Bertie Cole Bays Collection: Consists of nine books and one linear foot of manuscripts of Bays (1899-1972), the last appointed poet laureate of Kansas.

Topeka

193. Kansas State Historical Society Library
120 W 10th
Topeka, KS 66612

Contact: Portia Allbert
(913) 296-1770
Hours: Mon-Fri, 9-5; Sat, 8-12; closed holidays and holiday weekends
Accessible to Public: Yes
Accessible to Scholars: Yes
Special Considerations: Access to folklore collections is by advance appointment

Collections include 1,480 *Little Blue Books* printed by Haldeman-Julius of Girard, Kansas (1919-1951); 281 items, mostly books and printed materials, concerning cats and collected by Nelson Antrim Crawford; three pamphlet boxes of political and business cards (mostly pre-1950); four large pamphlet boxes of musical and theatrical programs, mostly from Topeka, Kansas; and 50 linear feet of pamphlet boxes of Women's Club yearbooks, mostly 1900-1940 (from the clubs that belong to the Kansas Federation of Women's Clubs).

Kansas Folklife Collection: Consists of a large body of materials collected in 1980 by the University for Man, Manhattan, Kansas. This statewide collection of folklore and folk art contains 600 cassette and reel-to-reel tapes (oral interviews and performances), 2,000 black-and-white images, and 2,500 color slides.

William Koch Collection: Contains 12 linear feet of folklore materials collected by Koch and his Kansas State University students.

Wichita

194. The Suzanne Frentz Collection of Television Soap Opera Scripts

Department of Speech Communication, Wichita State University
Wichita, KS 67208

Contact: Contact Librarian
(316) 682-9121
Hours: By advance appointment only
Accessible to Public: No
Accessible to Scholars: Yes
Special Considerations: This is a private collection and is available only to scholars and only by appointment

Collection contains 1,500 television scripts from "The Young and the Restless," April 1976-April 1983.

195. Wichita State University, Department of American Studies

Box 63, Wichita State University
Wichita, KS 67208

Contact: Gregory S Sojka
(316) 689-3148
Hours: Mon-Fri, 8:30-4:30
Accessible to Public: No
Accessible to Scholars: Yes

Sojka Sheet Music Collection: Contains 530 pieces of original sheet music dating from 1910-1970s, with most from 1940s and 1950s. Subjects range from George M. Cohan to the Beatles.

Ross McLaury Taylor Collection: Materials (882 books) relate to Southwest and military history, Great Plains culture and folklore, and include some rare volumes and editions. Additional research papers and maps dealing with re-

gional and local culture are located at the Ablah Library on the WSU campus.

KENTUCKY

Ashland

196. The Jean Thomas Museum and Cultural Center

1105 Bob McCullough Dr
Ashland, KY 41101

Contact: Mary Lou Putnam
(606) 329-1919
Hours: Mon-Fri, 8:30-4:30
Accessible to Public: Yes
Accessible to Scholars: Yes

The Museum displays artifacts, photographs, books, records, paintings, and Victorian furniture, and generally relates to Appalachian folk arts. An extensive archives for research is available.

Bardstown

197. The Oscar Getz Museum of Whiskey History and Bardstown Historical Museum

114 N 5th St
Bardstown, KY 40004

Contact: Flaget M Nally, Curator; Mary Hite, Curator
(502) 348-2999
Hours: Nov through Apr, Tues-Sat, 10-4, Sun, 1-4; May through Oct, Mon-Sat, 9-5; Sun, 1-5
Accessible to Public: Yes
Accessible to Scholars: Yes
Special Considerations: No special access for handicapped users

Collections include over 200 bottles (1825-1925), jugs and other containers, advertising art for bourbon manufacturers, old documents, the *Bardstown Historical Museum*, Civil War memorabilia, documents written by John Fitch (builder of the first steamboat), clothing of the 1850s, and numerous items related to the history of whiskey and to local history of Nelson County.

Berea

198. Berea College Library, Special Collections
Berea College
Berea, KY 40404

Contact: Gerald F Roberts
(606) 986-9341 Ext 289
Hours: Mon-Fri, 9-12, 1-5
Accessible to Public: Yes
Accessible to Scholars: Yes

Weatherford-Hammond Appalachian Collection: Contains 12,000 volumes on history, literature, folklore, and culture of southern Appalachia.

Bowling Green

199. Western Kentucky University, Folklife Archives
Kentucky Library
Bowling Green, KY 42101

Contact: Patricia M Hodges
(502) 745-6086
Hours: Mon-Fri, 8-4:30; closed
  University holidays
Accessible to Public: Yes
Accessible to Scholars: Yes
Special Considerations: Noncirculating;
  patrons must fill out circulation forms

Folklore Archives: This vast collection includes 2,000 cataloged field research collections (urban folklore, social folk customs, material culture, ethnographies, and folk arts); 3,800 tapes, a large folksong collection, belief collections, the *Gordon Wilson Collection of Folk Speech* (18,500 cards and 48 tapes); a large collection of political folklore; material culture studies; collections of games, rhymes, tales; and the *Courtney M. Ellis Collection* of photographs (3,305); and a large body of other materials relating to steamboats of the Ohio and Mississippi River Valleys.

200. Western Kentucky University, Kentucky Museum and Library
Reading Room, Kentucky Museum and
  Library
Bowling Green, KY 42101

Contact: Nancy Baird; Connie Mills
(502) 745-6263

Hours: Mon-Fri, 8-4:30; Sat, 9-4:30
Accessible to Public: Yes
Accessible to Scholars: Yes
Special Considerations: Noncirculating
  and closed stacks; photocopying
  available if materials are in good
  physical condition

Greeting Card Collection: Consists of three boxes of birthday, Christmas, Valentine, and Easter cards, 1870s-present, with most dated 1890-1920.

Gerard Photo Collection: Contains 400 photos of Bowling Green, Kentucky, places and people, 1890-1960.

Devasier Record Collection: Contains approximately 5,000 phonograph records (78 rpm) by popular artists, with an emphasis on the Big Band sound (1935-1960).

Southard Collection: Contains the schedules, posters, tickets, lobby cards, photo stills, and related materials of James Short Southard who operated a tent theater and a drive-in movie theater in Butler, Muhlenburg, and Ohio Counties, Kentucky, 1930s-1950s.

Rather Political Americana Collection: Contains about 500 items of political memorabilia for 350 candidates who campaigned in Kentucky, including buttons, broadsides, bumper stickers, brochures, canes, glassware, manuscripts, and correspondence (1840s-present, but most from 20th century).

Elizabethtown

201. Elizabethtown Community College, Media Center
College St Rd
Elizabethtown, KY 42701

Contact: Ann Thompson
(502) 862-4702
Hours: Mon-Thur, 8-8; Fri, 8-5
Accessible to Public: Yes
Accessible to Scholars: Yes
Special Considerations: Some materials
  in Archives Collection are confidential

Kentucky Collection: Consists of materials by Kentucky authors or about the state, and includes 400 books and 36 linear feet of other materials.

Archives for Elizabethtown Community College History: Contains 36 linear feet of materials and manuscripts related to the institution's history.

202. The Schmidt Coca-Cola Museum

PO Box 647
Elizabethtown, KY 42701

Contact: Janet B Schmidt
(502) 737-4000
Hours: Mon-Fri, 9-4
Accessible to Public: Yes
Accessible to Scholars: Yes
Special Considerations: Admission fee
($1 per adult); special rates for
children, senior citizens, and bus tours

This is the largest private collection of the memorabilia of Coca-Cola, including trays, calendars, posters, clocks, thermometers, dispensers, school aids, magazine ads, ashtrays, gum wrappers, playing cards, cigar bands, candy wrappers, games, and dozens of other types of Coca-Cola ephemera.

Frankfort

203. Kentucky Historical Society

PO Box H, 300 Broadway (Old Capitol
Annex)
Frankfort, KY 40602-2108

Contact: Mary E Winter, Potographic
Archivist; Mary Margaret Bell,
Manuscripts; Cathy Zwyer, Museum
(502) 564-3016
Hours: Mon-Sun, 8-4:30
Accessible to Public: Yes
Accessible to Scholars: Yes
Special Considerations: Advance
appointment is advised for use of
archival materials; all materials used
under the direct supervision of the
staff

Collections include .3 cubic feet of postcards and greeting cards (early 20th century); 31 stereopticon cards and viewer (1930 world travelogue scenes); 38 volumes of photo albums (1859-1978) cover such topics as Civil War portraits, family albums, and special events; 121 lantern slides, including black-and-white views of Mammoth Cave and hand-colored views of prominent Kentucky personalities and places; a large collection of broadsides, handbills, newspaper extras, announcements, and documents (commercial, mili-

tary, political, and noncommercial); and a large scrapbook collection (scrapbooks contain greeting cards, calling cards, pressed flowers, clippings, documents, commercial items such as gum wrappers, and photographs).

Lexington

204. John W. Landon Collection of Popular and Theatre Pipe Organ Music

809 Celia Ln
Lexington, KY 40504

Contact: Dr John W Landon
(606) 278-6245
Accessible to Public: No
Accessible to Scholars: Yes
Special Considerations: This is a *private*
collection and is accessible only by
advance appointment; there are no
regularly scheduled hours

Collection includes 10,000 records on 78 rpm discs dating from the earliest days of recording until the 1960s, with most from the period 1920-1935 (classical and popular and indexed by artist, song title, and manufacturer's serial number); 2,000 LP discs, many of which are reissues of the 78 rpm recordings listed above; numerous recordings of theater pipe organ music and silent movie music; and a large number of books, pieces of sheet music, photographs, and other archival materials.

205. University of Kentucky Art Library

4 King Library N
Lexington, KY 40506

Contact: Meg Shaw, Art Librarian
(606) 257-3938
Hours: Mon-Thur, 8 am-10 pm; Fri, 8-4:
30; Sat, 1-5; Sun, 2-10; when school
not in session, Mon-Fri, 8-4:30
Accessible to Public: Yes
Accessible to Scholars: Yes

Consists of approximately 30,000 volumes covering the literature of art history, art criticism, art studio, theater history, and play production, including a collection of over 2,000 acting editions of plays.

Louisville

206. Kentucky Derby Museum

PO Box 3513
Louisville, KY 40201

Contact: Leslie A Bush
(502) 637-1111
Hours: Mon-Sun, 9-5
Accessible to Public: Yes
Accessible to Scholars: Yes
Special Considerations: Admission fee
  ($3 for adults; $2.50 for senior
  citizens; $1.50 for children)

Contains a large assembly of materials related to the Kentucky Derby. Inquire in advance of research visit for details.

207. University of Louisville, Photographic Archives

Ekstrom Library
Louisville, KY 40292

Contact: David Horvath
(502) 588-6752
Hours: Mon-Fri, 8-4:30
Accessible to Public: Yes
Accessible to Scholars: Yes

The general collections include about 750,000 items of documentary and fine art photographs. Collections also include antique media and equipment. Although popular culture materials are scattered throughout the Archives, several collections of special interest exist.

Lou Block Collection: Contains photographs dating from 1934-1969. Block, an associate of Walker Evans, focused most of his attention on New York City in the 1930s, Rikers Island, mural painting, and the Artists Strike of 1935.

Caulfield and Shook Studio: Consists of 400,000 negatives produced by Louisville's largest photography studio (1904-1978); images cover all aspects of life and culture in Louisville.

Lin Caufield Collection: This commercial photographic collection provides documentation of the post-World War II era in Louisville and also includes advertising, social events, construction progress, sports, and other commercial subjects (85,000 negatives).

Erotic Photography Collection: Consists of several hundred photographic prints from various sources dating from the 1880s to the 1950s. The images vary in subject matter and include both commercially produced photographs and those intended for personal viewing.

The Royal Photo Company Collection: Contains 25,000 black-and-white negatives (1937-1973) and is a valuable source of information about commerce, industry, and major construction in Louisville. The collection is particularly rich in photographs of social and cultural interest.

The Standard Oil of New Jersey Picture Library: This collection is the result of a vast photo-documentation project directed by Roy Stryker and his successors (1943-1951). The project was concerned with depicting the oil industry in general as well as its effect on life in the 20th century. The 85,000-item collection is significant because of its intense coverage of small town life in America in the 1940s.

The Roy Stryker Papers: Contains Stryker's personal collections of photographs, correspondence, and other primary and secondary materials relating to his career in documentary photography. The projects Stryker worked on included The Farm Security Administration (1935-1942); the Office of War Information (1943); The Standard Oil of New Jersey Picture Library (1943-1950); The Pittsburgh Photographic Library (1950); and the Jones and Laughlin Steel Corporation Picture Library (1952-1960).

Flexner Slide Collection: Consists of 8,000 color transparencies (1951-1968) of excellent travel images from around the world.

Arthur Y. Ford Albums: Consists of albums of photographs documenting Kentucky life and culture from 1890-1900 and the 1904 Louisiana Purchase Exposition in St. Louis.

The Macauley Theatre Collection: Includes photographs, many autographed, of actors and actresses who appeared in Macauley's theater in Louisville, 1873-1925. The collection includes photographs of virtually every important American performer of the era.

Manvell Collection of Film Stills:
Contains 12,000 motion picture stills representing all countries and all periods. Special areas of interest are Stalin-era Russian film stills, hundreds of documentary stills, and many stills from film productions of the plays of Shakespeare.

Also of note are the *R. G. Potter Collection* of photographs of Louisville and the *Jean Thomas "The Traipsin' Woman" Collection* of several hundred images of life in the mountains of eastern Kentucky (1920s-1950s). The Archives also contains a small collection of reference works and pamphlets in support of scholarly research, including an excellent collection of photographically illustrated books dating from 1850.

208. University of Louisville Library, Rare Book Department

Rare Book Department, University of
    Louisville Library
Louisville, KY 40292

Contact: Delinda Stephens Buie; George
    T McWhorter, Curator for Burroughs
    Collection
(502) 588-6762
Hours: Mon-Fri, 9-5
Accessible to Public: Yes
Accessible to Scholars: Yes
Special Considerations: Identification
    required; closed stack system

The Nell Dismukes McWhorter Memorial Collection of Edgar Rice Burroughs Materials: Consists of 20,000 items, including all serial editions, first and reprint editions, foreign editions, comics, Sunday and daily syndicated newspaper strips, original paintings and drawings, correspondence, author's memorabilia, fanzines, periodical collection of Burroughsiana, biography and bibliography, posters, films and tapes, scrapbooks and photographs, games and toys, the author's personal school texts, and related items.

Pulp Magazine Collection: Consists of 10,000 volumes including *Black Mask, Doc Savage, Adventure, All-Story, Argosy, Blue Book*, and many others.

Dime Novel Collection: Consists of over 1,100 volumes, including *Beadle's, Deadwood Dick, Nick Carter, Happy Days, Wild West Weekly*, and many others.

Science Fiction Collection: Includes more than 500 paperbacks and a special collection of Ursula LeGuin materials.

L. Frank Baum Collection: Contains about 200 volumes, including the Van Dyne titles, along with Baum's pseudonymous works, posters, toys, and Oz books written by other authors.

Yenawine American Humor Collection: Contains 2,500 volumes of 19th and 20th century humor, poetry, and graphics.

World Wars I and II Poster Collection: Consists of approximately 1,500 posters with a videotaped index, and includes posters from Austria-Hungary, Canada, France, Germany, Great Britain, Italy, Russia, South Africa, the Netherlands, and the United States.

Middlesboro

209. Cumberland Gap National Historical Park

PO Box 1848
Middlesboro, KY 40965

Contact: Daniel A Brown
(606) 248-2817
Hours: Mon-Sun, 8-5
Accessible to Public: Yes
Accessible to Scholars: Yes
Special Considerations: Prior
    arrangements for use of library should
    be made with park historian.

Hensley Settlement Oral History Tapes: Consists of 82 taped interviews with residents of the mountain community, 1906-1951. Transcripts are available.

Pippa Passes

210. Appalachian Oral History Project

Alice Lloyd College
Pippa Passes, KY 41844

Contact: Katherine R Martin
(606) 368-2101
Hours: Mon-Fri, 8-4; closed mid-May
    through mid-Aug
Accessible to Public: Yes
Accessible to Scholars: Yes

Appalachian Oral History Project: A consortium of four institutions devoted to collecting the oral history of the Appalachian regions of Kentucky, North Carolina, and Virginia. The collections include information on folklore, history, sociology, music, language, crafts, and all other aspects of the region, and currently include 5,000 hours of interviews. The addresses and phone numbers of the other institutions are as follows: Lee's Junior College, Breathitt County, Jackson, KY, (606) 666-7521; Emory and Henry College, Emory, VA 24327, (703) 944-3121; Appalachian State University, 202 Appalachian St., Boone, NC 28607, (704) 262-2095.

LOUISIANA

New Orleans

211. Earl K. Long Library, Archives and Manuscripts/ Special Collections Department

University of New Orleans
New Orleans, LA 70148

Contact: D C Hardy, Archivist; Beatrice Owsley; Marie Windell; Raymond Nussbaum
(504) 286-6543, 286-7273
Hours: Mon-Fri, 8-4:30; Sat, 10-2; closed on all school holidays
Accessible to Public: Yes
Accessible to Scholars: Yes

Newlin Rock and Roll Collection: Consists of 534 original phonograph records of rock and roll music, 1952-1970.

Saucier Phonodiscs, Louisiana Folklore Society Collection: Consists of Louisiana French folk songs and stories recorded on phonodiscs by folkorist Corinne L. Saucier (around 1948), along with explanatory notes and an inventory.

Claude R. J. Wolsch Collection: Contains original campaign pins of U.S. Presidents Franklin D. Roosevelt, Dwight D. Eisenhower, and John F. Kennedy.

Jean LaFitte National Historical Park Collection: Includes source materials collected by the National Park Service to document historical and cultural aspects of Jean LaFitte National Historical Park. The materials include numerous audiotapes and videotapes of interviews with area residents (southeast Louisiana) about their social, economic, and cultural life (1970s and 1980s).

212. New Orleans Public Library, Louisiana Division

219 Loyola Ave
New Orleans, LA 70140

Contact: Collin B Hamer, Jr, Head
(504) 596-2610
Hours: Mon-Thur, 9-6; Sat, 9-6
Accessible to Public: Yes
Accessible to Scholars: Yes
Special Considerations: Register to use rare material and present valid photo identification

Carnival Collection: Contains 11,000 items, including programs, costume designs, and memorabilia relative to the annual New Orleans Mardi Gras festivities, 1852-present.

Jambalaya Program: Consists of the collected audiotapes of the National Endowment for the Humanities *Jambalaya Program* (1977-1980), a series of lectures, discussions, exhibits, and related activities examining the history and culture of New Orleans.

Louisiana News Index: Contains 528,000 cards and references to persons, places, and activities from throughout Louisiana, 1804-1963.

Louisiana and New Orleans Picture File: Contains 46,700 items from the 1880s to modern times.

Other important materials within the collections include two cubic feet of menus from New Orleans and Louisiana; a vertical file of rare ephemeral material related to Louisiana and dated pre-1930; 1800 postcards of New Orleans and Louisiana; a large collection of scrapbooks dating from the Civil War (includes those of Huey Pierce Long, Yves R. Lemonier, and de Lesseps Story Morrison); 100 cubic feet of post-1930 Louisiana ephemeral material; 30 dolls made by the WPA Toy Renovation Project (dolls depict New Orleans street characters, historical figures, and international costumes); and 6,300 newsreels from New Orleans television station WVUE (1968-1980).

213. Tulane University, Howard-Tilton Memorial Library

Tulane University Libraries
New Orleans, LA 70118

Contact: Wilbur E Meneray, Head of
 Rare Books and University Archives
(504) 865-5685, 865-5686
Hours: Mon-Fri, 8:30-5; Sat, 9-1
Accessible to Public: Yes
Accessible to Scholars: Yes
Special Considerations: Closed stack
 system; valid identification required

The materials in Rare Books, Manuscripts, and University Archives include over 3,500 manuscript collections that in one way or another relate to popular culture (12,000 linear feet of materials). Included are manuscripts related to Mardi Gras, the *Friends of the Cabildo Oral History Collection,* and many others. A collection of political ephemera includes 177 reels of microfilm, 74 file drawers, 135 linear feet of books, and 31 cubic feet of storage boxes representing 5,000 organizations and individuals. There is an outstanding collection of science fiction, including long runs of such titles as *Amazing Stories, Astounding, Analog, Fantastic, Fantasy and Science Fiction, Galaxy, If,* and others.

Louisiana Collection: Includes Louisiana sheet music, vertical files, photographs, pamphlets, and a Louisiana art vertical file. Materials date from 1717. (Contact Gary Craft, 504-865-5643.)

William Ransom Hogan Jazz Archive: This is a major repository for information and source materials associated with the birthplace of this musical genre, and includes 25,000 discs, 1,000 audiotapes, 7,000 photographs, 30,000 pieces of sheet music, 24 cylinders, 1,500 reel-to-reel tapes of interviews with musicians and other individuals involved with jazz (many have been transcribed). (Contact Curt Jerde, Curator for Jazz Archive, 504-865-5688.)

Southeastern Architectural Archive: Holds over 150,000 original architectural drawings, correspondence, specifications, photographs, maps, books, research papers, and artifacts. The emphasis of the collection is on Louisiana from 1835 to the present. (Phone 504-865-5699, 504-865-5697.)

Latin American Library: Holds 150,000 volumes relating to all aspects of Latin American history and culture, with many items related to popular culture. Collections include manuscripts, books, photographs, periodicals, rare books, and ephemera.

214. Tulane University, William Ransom Hogan Jazz Archives

Howard-Tilton Memorial Library,
 Tulane University
New Orleans, LA 70118

Contact: Curtis D Jerde, Curator
(504) 865-5688
Hours: Mon-Fri, 8:30-5; Sat, 10-12
Accessible to Public: Yes
Accessible to Scholars: Yes

Oral History Collection: Contains approximately 1,500 reels of taped interviews with musicians and other people involved with jazz, and transcripts or summaries with editorial explanations on 1,200 of the reels.

Recorded Sound Collection: Consists of 23,000 discs in all formats, 800 tapes, 24 cylinders, and more than 50 piano rolls. The primary emphasis is on New Orleans style jazz as played by local musicians, but there are also examples of a variety of related musical styles, including blues, gospel, and Cajun, as well as African and West Indian forms.

Print and Manuscript Collection: Includes over 40,000 pieces of popular sheet music and orchestrations dating well back into the 19th century, with rags, cakewalks, coon songs, minstrel airs, sentimental parlor pieces, and religious compositions among the assortment.

Graphics Collection: Contains more than 7,000 prints and negatives and 250 art and advertising posters dating from the late 19th century.

Vertical Files: These materials consist of several files that bring together data on bands, musical persons, discology, jazz-related subjects, the musicians' union, and the developmental history of the archive itself, along with research notes of scholars, books, serials, and museum artifacts.

Dominic LaRocca Collection: Materials consist of 28,444 items, including posters, photographs, correspondence, scrapbooks, interview material, advertisements, films, phonograph recordings, contracts, and affidavits related to the experience of the Original Dixieland Jazz Band.

Souchon Collection: This collection of the Souchon Brothers, Dr. Edmond and Harry V., Sr., contains phonorecords of blues, rags, Caribbean folk music, jazz items, and rare V Discs and press testings; includes 559 tapes, many jazz books, journals, photos, and assorted correspondence and memorabilia.

Al Rose Collection: Contains over 15,000 pieces of print and manuscript music, nearly 2,000 phonodiscs consisting of original jazz recordings, and over 1,000 photographs.

William Russell Collection: Includes published and unpublished writing notes, films, oral history interviews, music tapes, phonodiscs, photographs, and sheet music.

Roger C. Gulbrandsen Collection: Contains approximately 4,500 phonodiscs, 86 books, serials, pamphlets, and correspondence.

Robichaux Collection: Includes 7,236 pieces of print music from the collection of John Robichaux, violinist, who led society dance bands between the 1890s and the 1930s.

Ralston Crawford Collection: Contains photographs of more than 600 images of New Orleans urban folk culture.

Musicians' Union File, 174-496: Contains affidavits, board minutes, contracts, correspondence, ledgers, logs, publications, and receipts of the New Orleans local of the American Federation of Musicians.

MAINE

Boothbay

215. Boothbay Theatre Museum
Corey Ln
Boothbay, ME 04537

Contact: Franklyn Lenthall, Curator
(207) 633-4536

Hours: Mon-Sat, by appointment only June 15-Sept 15
Accessible to Public: Yes
Accessible to Scholars: Yes
Special Considerations: Mail inquiries are handled all year

The collections consist of theatrical memorabilia from the 18th century to the present and include stage jewelry, costumes, portraits, photographs, sculpture, playbills, figurines, holograph material, set models, and toy theaters; all materials relate to the history of theater in the United States.

Deer Isle

216. Haystack Mountain School of Crafts
Haystack Mountain School of Crafts
Deer Isle, ME 04627-0087

Contact: Nancy Ross, Asst Dir
(207) 348-2306
Hours: Mon-Fri, 9-4:30; weekend and additional hours during summer
Accessible to Public: Yes
Accessible to Scholars: Yes
Special Considerations: Although not required, an advance telephone call is suggested

Collection consists of 5,000 books on craft objects and materials, including exhibition catalogs and books on related art and technical areas, and 2,000 copies of craft periodicals.

Kennebunkport

217. Seashore Trolley Museum/New England Electric Railway Historical Society
Drawer A
Kennebunkport, ME 04046

Contact: Dorothy Warner, Office Mgr
(207) 967-2712
Hours: June-Labor Day: Mon-Fri, 10-5: 30; Labor Day-June: Mon-Fri, 12-5
Accessible to Public: Yes
Accessible to Scholars: Yes
Special Considerations: Other hours possible with advance appointment

Collections include 175 units of mass transit vehicles (streetcars, buses, trolley coaches, rapid transit cars, and related work cars and vehicles), industry artifacts, slide presentations related to the history of mass transit, and a library of technical documents, books, publications, and supporting materials.

Orono

218. Raymond H. Fogler Library, Special Collections Department
University of Maine
Orono, ME 04469

Contact: Eric S Flower
(207) 581-1686
Hours: Mon-Fri, 8-4:30; during fall and spring semesters: Sun, 1-5
Accessible to Public: Yes
Accessible to Scholars: Yes
Special Considerations: Standard archival rules apply to use of materials

The collection is a center for the study of Maine, and collects in virtually all available areas of printed bibliographical, historical, and descriptive works on the state, as well as literary titles by Maine authors. The collections of published items include books, pamphlets, manuscripts, state documents, and other forms of materials that provide extensive coverage of Maine's cities, towns, counties, people, and institutions. Collections also include extensive materials for the study of family history, travel and tourism (including several collections of travel films and large numbers of postcards), the American Revolution Bicentennial, children's literature (including manuscripts of children's authors from Maine), photographs of Maine, motion pictures by Maine artists, the papers of Floyd Phillips Gibbons (cartoonist, writer, radio personality, and journalist), papers and letters of the Great Northern Paper Company, the *Hoffman Postcard Collection*, 2,000 black-and-white photographs from throughout the state in the *Maine Historical Photographs Collection*, records and oral history interviews of the Maine Music Educators Association, the *Charley Miller Collection* (photographs, notebooks, and motion picture films related to the camps of the famous Maine guide and sportsman), scrapbooks related to Maine theatrical productions, the *Erskine Clifton York*

Collection of circus memorabilia, information on restaurants, and hundreds of similar materials and Maine manuscripts.

219. University of Maine at Orono, Northeast Archives of Folklore and Oral History
Department of Anthropology, S Stevens Hall
Orono, ME 04469

Contact: Pat Phillips; Sandy Ives
(207) 581-1891
Hours: Mon-Fri, 8-4
Accessible to Public: Yes
Accessible to Scholars: Yes
Special Considerations: Other hours available by special appointment; some portions of the collection have special conditions for access and researchers should inquire in advance of visit

The repository includes tape recordings, transcripts of tapes, related photographs, and manuscript material relevant to the folklore and folklife of Maine and the Atlantic Provinces of Canada, and now holds over 1,600 collections, about 2,500 hours of tapes, and over 5,000 photographs. One of the largest bodies of material relates to the lumberman's life, including beliefs, values, customs, stories, daily routines, songs, and similar materials. Other occupational groups represented include lobstermen, farmers, hunters, guides, and even poachers. The scope of the collection is considerable and the materials are varied. A brief published guide is available to researchers, and advance inquiries will enable the researcher to determine just what materials are available to assist in the anticipated research project.

Waterville

220. Miller Library, Special Collections
Colby College
Waterville, ME 04901

Contact: Fraser Cocks, Curator
(207) 872-3284
Hours: Mon-Fri, 8:30-12, 1-4:30
Accessible to Public: Yes
Accessible to Scholars: Yes

Collections include 2,000 volumes of children's literature, with 500 Jacob Abbot titles and works by Mary Ellen Chase, Elizabeth Coatsworth, Lawrence Housman, John Masefield, Laura E. Richards, Kate Douglas Wiggin; a complete run of *Tip Top Magazine* (1896-1912); 100 scrapbooks of Colby students (late 19th and early 20th century); and 200 glass plate negatives of scenic and historic spots in eastern and southeastern U.S. (late 19th century).

MARYLAND

Baltimore

221. Alternative Press Center

PO Box 33109, 1443 Gorsuch Ave
Baltimore, MD 21218

Contact: Peggy D'Adamo
(301) 243-2471
Hours: Tues-Sat, 10-4
Accessible to Public: Yes
Accessible to Scholars: Yes
Special Considerations: Apply in person
  for library card; xeroxing on request

Includes publications of alternative, progressive, and radical nature dating from 1969. Collections contain newspapers, magazines, and journals that cover socialist movements, feminism, gay and lesbian rights, Black liberation, animal rights, environmental and ecological movements, and many similar topics. There are nearly 1,000 different titles. There is also a smaller collection (about 500 titles) of books, and a complete run of the *Alternative Press Index* covering 200 periodicals published since 1969.

222. Baltimore Public Works Museum

701 Eastern Ave
Baltimore, MD 21202

Contact: Nancy A Fenton, Curator
(301) 396-5565
Hours: Mon-Fri, 8:30-4:30
Accessible to Public: Yes
Accessible to Scholars: Yes
Special Considerations: Advance notice
  is required

Collections include approximately 4,000 items, most of which are photographs and glass plate negatives depicting the construction of various public works facilities in Baltimore from 1905-1930.

223. Enoch Pratt Free Library, Fine Arts and Recreation Department

400 Cathedral St
Baltimore, MD 21201

Contact: Joan Stahl, Dept Head
(301) 396-5490
Hours: Mon-Thur, 9-9; Fri-Sat, 9-5; Sun
  (Oct-May only), 1-5
Accessible to Public: Yes
Accessible to Scholars: Yes
Special Considerations: Use of the *Hilda
  Holme Collection* requires advance
  appointment

Hilda Holme Collection: Consists of a chronological record of 413 illustrated books, a reference collection, and specimen pages (291).

The library also holds a small collection of early hymnals dating from the late 1800s (about 75) and a large popular music collection (sheet music and song books). Excellent indexes are available.

224. Flickinger Foundation for American Studies, Inc.

300 St Dunstan's Rd
Baltimore, MD 21212

Contact: B Floyd Flickinger
(301) 323-6284
Hours: By appointment
Accessible to Public: No
Accessible to Scholars: Yes
Special Considerations: Write in advance
  describing proposed research project

Collections consist of 10,000 volumes related to American Studies, including materials on the Civil War, Colonial America, the Revolution, Virginia, West Virginia, and Maryland. Collections also include manuscripts, pictures, and various forms of unbound materials (charts, brochures, TV programs, etc.).

225. Johns Hopkins University

Milton S. Eisenhower Library, Special
  Collections
Baltimore, MD 21218

Contact: Cynthia H Requardt,
Manuscripts Librarian
(301) 338-5493
Hours: Mon-Fri, 8:30-5
Accessible to Public: Yes
Accessible to Scholars: Yes

Lester S. Levy Collection of Sheet Music: This collection of popular American sheet music consists of nearly 30,000 items dating from the late 18th century to the mid-20th century. The music is divided into 38 subject categories, and has a card catalog that indexes the music by song title, composer, author, publisher, lithographer, and the first line of the song. A detailed guide has been published and is available to researchers.

226. Johns Hopkins University, John Work Garrett Collections, Milton S. Eisenhower Library
4545 N Charles St
Baltimore, MD 21210

Contact: Judith Gardner-Flint, Garrett
Librarian
(301) 338-7641
Hours: Mon-Fri, 9-5
Accessible to Public: No
Accessible to Scholars: Yes
Special Considerations: Patrons should
telephone in advance for an
appointment; anyone with a valid
scholarly reason for using the
collections is able to gain access.

Greeting Cards: Consists of 800 greeting cards, the majority 19th century, comprising cards for Christmas, New Year, Thanksgiving, Valentine's Day, and Easter, plus calendar cards and miscellaneous, in various shapes and sizes, some with silk edges and some cut-outs and shaped, appliquie1s and stand-up, including cards by Louis Prang.

Trade Cards: Includes approximately 1,500 trade cards, circulars, and stickers, for various trades and products, including tobacco, soaps and creams, sewing machines, thread, seeds and farmers' needs, scales, railroads, travel, hotels, pianos and organs, photographers, printers, ink, paint, jewelers, florists, insurance companies, furniture, carpets, foods, books, boots and shoes, hats, coffee and tea, department stores, and

drugs, in various shapes and sizes and most from the 19th century.

Campaign Collection: Contains 700 campaign medals, pins, tokens, ribbons, buttons, and other political memorabilia, from George Washington through Ronald Reagan, with most dating from mid-1900s.

The collections also include 1,500 volumes of children's books dating from the mid-1800s to the mid-1900s.

227. Lacrosse Foundation Hall of Fame
Newton H. White, Jr., Athletic Center
Baltimore, MD 21218

Contact: Steven B Stenersen, Exec Dir
(301) 235-6882
Hours: Mon-Fri, 9-5
Accessible to Public: Yes
Accessible to Scholars: Yes

Collections relate to the history of Lacrosse and are international in scope.

228. Maryland Historical Society Library
201 W Monument St
Baltimore, MD 21201

Contact: Marcy Silver, Prints and
Photographs Librarian
(301) 685-3750
Hours: Tues-Fri, 11-4:30; Sat, 9-4:30
Accessible to Public: Yes
Accessible to Scholars: Yes
Special Considerations: Nonmembers
must pay admission fee; appointment
needed for access to Prints and
Photographs Division

The Reference Division contains 100 boxes of sheet music and over 100 broadsides from the late 18th to the mid-20th centuries. The Prints and Photographs Division contains a collection of printed ephemera related to Maryland (200 boxes), including business and trade cards, letterheads, announcements, programs, cards, tickets, playbills, postcards, and obsolete bank notes. Another collection includes prints and photographs that document everyday life in the state from the late 1700s to the present.

229. Towson State University, The Gerhardt Collections
Fine Arts Building, Rm 457
Baltimore, MD 21204

Contact: Edwin L Gerhardt
(301) 242-0328
Hours: By appointment
Accessible to Public: Yes
Accessible to Scholars: Yes
Special Considerations: Alternate
  address: 4926 Leeds Ave, Baltimore,
  MD 21227; make prior appointment

Gerhardt Marimba Xylophone Collection: This is a unique and comprehensive accumulation of marimba and xylophone lore, including literature, phonograph and tape recordings, catalogs, music, methods, pictures, correspondence, personal reminiscences, and miscellaneous information. It is *not* a collection of instruments. A detailed outline of the holdings is available on request.

Gerhardt Library of Musical Information: Consists of a representative collection of music literature, phonograph and tape recordings, pictures, and artifacts. It includes special sections on Thomas Alva Edison and the phonograph, John Philip Sousa and bands, old popular songs, and percussion. Most of the material is out of print and hard to find. The collection is *not* a grouping of scores and manuscripts. A detailed outline of the holdings is available on request.

230. University of Baltimore, Langsdale Library
1420 Maryland Ave
Baltimore, MD 21201

Contact: Gerry Yeager
(301) 625-3135
Hours: Mon-Fri, 8:30-4
Accessible to Public: Yes
Accessible to Scholars: Yes
Special Considerations: Appointment is
  suggested but not required

The collections include WMAR-TV newsfilm from 1947-1981 (7,000,000 feet), and the *Steamship Historical Society of America Collection* of approximately 100,000 ship photographs and related ship materials. There are also 70 other collections in the library with at least some popular culture materials (inquire prior to visit).

231. University of Baltimore, Langsdale Library, Special Collections Division
1420 N Charles St
Baltimore, MD 21201

Contact: Geraldine Watkins
(301) 625-3135
Hours: Mon-Fri, 8:30-4:30
Accessible to Public: Yes
Accessible to Scholars: Yes
Special Considerations: Prior notice of at
  least one working day is required

Maritime History of the Chesapeake Bay: This collection includes 50 tapes (15 minutes each) of interviews dealing with all aspects of Bay history and culture (military, fisheries, ports, ship design, immigration, etc.).

Catonsville

232. University of Maryland Baltimore County, Department of Modern Languages and Linguistics
5401 Wilkens Ave
Catonsville, MD 21228

Contact: Edward Larkey
(301) 455-2104, evenings at 366-7463
Hours: By advance appointment
Accessible to Public: No
Accessible to Scholars: Yes
Special Considerations: This is a private
  collection, and an advance
  appointment is required

Collection consists of various East German rock music recordings (1971-present). Includes 60 LP recordings.

233. University of Maryland Baltimore County, Special Collections
Albin O. Kuhn Library and Gallery
Catonsville, MD 21228

Contact: Janet Murray, Special
  Collections Library
(301) 455-2356
Hours: Mon-Fri, 9-5
Accessible to Public: Yes
Accessible to Scholars: Yes

Special Considerations: Inquire about additional hours

Azriel Rosenfeld Science Fiction Research Collection: Contains over 6,000 first editions of hardcover and paperback volumes and 5,000 issues of major science fiction magazines.

Walter Coslet Collection: Consists of approximately 15,000 fanzines; manuscripts, including some by Isaac Asimov and Roger Zelazny; and cover art and posters by Frank Kelly Freas.

Popular Culture Collection: Includes 1,200 E. Haldeman Julius "Little Blue Books"; over 1,200 comic books, including underground comics and especially strong holdings in 1930s and 1940s comic books; 3,500 adventure and detective pulps covering the years 1860-1950s; and approximately 500 television scripts, including *The Beverly Hillbillies* and *Mission Impossible* scripts.

Poster Collection: Consists of 30 war posters and five Ringling Brothers and Barnum and Bailey Circus posters.

Henry Burke Postcard and Stereoview Collection: Includes 9,000 postcards from European galleries, photographic postcards from around the world, and 1,000 stereopticon slides of such subjects as the Spanish American War and World War I.

World's Fair and Expositions Collection: Contains 250 items, including catalogs, reports, and other publications relating to world's fairs and expositions. Fairs from 1851 to 1900 are covered, including the first international exposition (London, 1851), the Centennial Exposition (Philadelphia, 1876), the World's Columbian Exposition (Chicago, 1893), and many smaller exhibitions.

B&O Railroad Glee Club Collection of Sheet Music: Consists of approximately 45,000 octavo scores used by the Baltimore and Ohio Railroad Glee Club. Pieces in this collection of sheet music range from popular to religious in style. The Glee Club was in existence from 1914 to 1968.

College Park

234. University of Maryland, Department of Textiles and Consumer Economics
2100 Marie Mount Hall
College Park, MD 20742

Contact: Jo B Paoletti
(301) 454-6494, 454-2141
Hours: Mon-Fri, 9-5; Summer hours by appointment only
Accessible to Public: Yes
Accessible to Scholars: Yes
Special Considerations: Call or write prior to visit; copies of completed research papers prepared using the collection's materials and any photographs of collection materials taken by researchers must be donated after use of collection

Collections consist of 3,500 examples of women's, children's, and men's clothing, including some textiles and related materials (paper patterns, photographs, etc.), and 125 coverlets from the 19th century.

Columbia

235. Keesing Musical Archives
8862 Blue Sea Dr
Columbia, MD 21046

Contact: Hugo A Keesing
(301) 381-8494
Hours: By appointment; evenings and weekends are most convenient
Accessible to Public: No
Accessible to Scholars: Yes
Special Considerations: This is a private collection; advance appointment necessary

The collection is divided into eight categories: *Pop/Rock Books,* consisting of more than 2,000 titles in eight languages, covering reference books, artists' biographies, "how to" books, rock criticism, record price guides, and related topics (most post-1964); *Records and Tapes,* including 15,000 discs (78 rpm, 45 rpm, and LP), with over 50,000 song titles, 1930s-present (special sections include materials related to World War II, Vietnam, American presidents, and topical issues); *Sheet Music*, including over 1,000 pieces from late 1920s to early 1970s, with a virtually complete run of all number one songs from 1930-1957; *Newspaper and Magazine Clipping Files*, 1957-present, and all related to popular music (six cubic feet); *"Top Hit Lists"* from radio stations and record stores, mid-1950s to the present, and including nearly 2,000 lists (U.S. and Holland); *Record Auction Lists* (three cubic feet); *Pop and Rock Artifacts*, consisting of gum cards, comics, puzzles, pins, jewelry, lunch boxes, souvenir programs, movie posters, etc.; and more than 4,000 slides (35mm) of popular culture personalities, artifacts, events, sheet music, album covers, picture sleeves, etc.

Hunt Valley

236. Unitarian and Universalist Genealogical Society

10605 Lakespring Way
Hunt Valley, MD 21030

Contact: Willis Clayton Tull, Jr, Exec
  Dir
(301) 628-2490
Hours: By advance appointment only
Accessible to Public: No
Accessible to Scholars: Yes
Special Considerations: By appointment
  for members and scholars only

Maintains 1,300-volume library of biographies, church histories, and polemic works by or about Universalists and other religious liberals, including extensive bio-bibliographical files.

Towson

237. Goucher College, Julia Rogers Library

Dulaney Valley Rd
Towson, MD 21204

Contact: Betty R Kondayan, Librarian
(301) 337-6000
Hours: Mon-Fri, 9-5
Accessible to Public: No
Accessible to Scholars: Yes
Special Considerations: Call in advance
  for appointment to use special
  collections

The Brownlee Sands Corrin Collection: The collection consists of five major divisions: *Humor*—including 280 books and anthologies of written comedy and satire and 500 LP recordings of professional stand-up comics and comedy teams; *Show Business*—containing 110 books on various aspects of the entertainment business, 50 LP recordings of old-time radio shows, 130 musical stage and revue records, 35 movie soundtracks, and 200 LP recordings of 20th century American music (folk, blues, rock, barbershop, gospel, and protest); *Science Fiction and Fantasy*—with 1,800 books (1918-1985); *Politics and Public Affairs*—consisting of 220 audioand videotapes (newscasts, interviews, and public affairs documentaries, 1930-1980), 300 audioand videotapes of politicians before the media (1950-1980), 110 film and tape copies of political spot advertising, and seven boxes of artifacts related to American political campaigns (flags, buttons, handbooks, signs, bumper stickers, posters, direct mail appeals, and similar materials, 1956-1980); and *Commercial Advertising*—with 55 films, audio-, and videotapes of representative commercial spots from a variety of media.

MASSACHUSETTS

Amherst

238. Amherst College Library

Special Collections
Amherst, MA 01002

Contact: John Lancaster
(413) 542-2299
Hours: Mon-Fri, 8:30-4:30; Summer:
  Mon-Fri, 8-4
Accessible to Public: Yes
Accessible to Scholars: Yes
Special Considerations: Identification
  required

The Library contains an extensive collection documenting amateur dramatic productions from the early 19th century to the present.

S. G. Goodrich/Peter Parley Collection: Contains about 600 volumes of works by Goodrich, including publications under the Parley pseudonym in imitation or piracy of Goodrich's work.

Van Nostrand Theatre Collection: Consists of 35,000 acting editions of plays for home and amateur performance, many from the 19th century.

Marshall Bloom Collection of Underground Newspapers: Includes 500 boxes (1966-present). This is an uncataloged collection and requires prior interview and appointment for access.

239. National Yiddish Book Center
PO Box 969, Old East St School
Amherst, MA 01004

Contact: Devorah S Sperling; Paula Parsky
(413) 256-1241
Hours: Mon-Thur, 9-5; Fri, 9-3:30
Accessible to Public: Yes
Accessible to Scholars: Yes
Special Considerations: Call ahead for appointment and specific information related to use of the collection

This is not a library, but a supplier of used and out-of-print Yiddish books. Current holdings include about 500,000 volumes, with catalogs of readily accessible materials available. Materials are for sale to institutions and individuals.

Boston

240. Berklee College of Music Library
150 Massachusetts Ave
Boston, MA 02115

Contact: John Voigt, Librarian
(617) 266-1400 Ext 407
Hours: By advance appointment
Accessible to Public: No
Accessible to Scholars: Yes
Special Considerations: For serious scholars only; noncirculating

Extensive holdings of jazz and rock sheet music are available, as are holdings of materials dealing with technological implications of popular music (synthesizers, MIDI, etc.). Collections also include videotapes of jazz performances and historic rock performances. Reference collection includes basic history texts in popular music.

241. Boston University, Mugar Memorial Library, Department of Special Collections
771 Commonwealth Ave
Boston, MA 02215

Contact: Howard B Gotlieb, Dir of Special Collections
(617) 353-3696
Hours: Mon-Fri, 9-5
Accessible to Public: Yes
Accessible to Scholars: Yes
Special Considerations: Researchers with no academic affiliation should call or write ahead for appointment

Twentieth Century Archives: This special collection consists of over 1,200 individual collections of papers, photographs, and memorabilia relating to some 75 film personages, over 125 mystery and suspense writers, and journalists, science fiction writers, stage actors, scriptwriters, and cartoonists (including Henri Arnold, E. Simms Campbell, Al Capp, Harold Gray, Art Gates, Ferd Johnson, Hank Ketcham, Robert Leffingwell, Jack Rosen, Otto Soglow, Joseph Stern, Raeburn Van Buren, and Mort Walker). The comics and cartoon collections are particularly extensive and include thousands of strips, color proofs, papers, and original artworks. Other categories include literature, public affairs, and television. The book collection contains more than 20,000 volumes of works by persons whose papers are collected. Detailed guides to the collection have been published and researchers are invited to inquire prior to their visit as to specific holdings.

Historical Manuscript Collection: This collection consists of letters, historical documents, and manuscripts from the Revolutionary era to the 20th century. A major strength of the collection is in British literary manuscripts, including materials related to such figures as Samuel Taylor Coleridge and Sir Walter Scott. Inquire as to specific holdings.

Zion Research Collection: Consists of a large collection of Bibles, theological manuscripts, and related materials pertaining to the history of Christianity.

Bortman Collection of Americana: Holdings include some 2,000 printed and manuscript sources that document the first two centuries of American life, with emphasis on the early history of New England, church history, military affairs, and the history of Canada and the West Indies.

Other collections of note within the Library are related to Abraham Lincoln, military history, Walt Whitman, private press books, the history of nursing in America, Theodore Roosevelt, modern poetry, Robert Frost, the Mystery Writers of America, and many similar and supporting topics.

242. French Library in Boston, Inc.
53 Marlborough St
Boston, MA 02116

Contact: Librarian
(617) 266-4351
Hours: Mon-Fri, 10-5; Wed, 10-7; Sat, 10-4
Accessible to Public: Yes
Accessible to Scholars: Yes
Special Considerations: Membership necessary to check materials out of Library

Collections include eight catalog drawers of French postcards depicting cities, provinces, costumes, customs, and monuments.

243. John Fitzgerald Kennedy Library
Columbia Point
Boston, MA 02125

Contact: Barbara L Anderson, Archivist
(617) 929-4534
Hours: Mon-Fri, 9-5
Accessible to Public: Yes
Accessible to Scholars: Yes
Special Considerations: Inquire in advance as to specific holdings

The Kennedy Library holds voluminous materials covering every aspect of Kennedy's career and times, including extensive oral history interviews and audiovisual records of the Kennedy era, vast collections of photographs, and information by and about many dozens of public figures related to Kennedy and his administration. Many holdings relate to various aspects of popular culture. There is no way a brief entry could reflect the richness of the collection. Researchers

should write in advance and request a copy of the Library's printed guide.

244. New England Conservatory of Music, Firestone Library
290 Huntington Ave
Boston, MA 02115

Contact: Kenneth Pristash, Audio Librarian
(617) 262-1120 Ext 301
Hours: Mon-Thur, 8:30 am-10:30 pm; Fri, 9-6; Sat, 9-5; Sun, 1-9
Accessible to Public: Yes
Accessible to Scholars: Yes

Contains New England Conservatory concert tapes (1969-present), with performances by the Jazz Department and the Third Stream Department (several performances annually).

Cambridge

245. Massachusetts Institute of Technology, Archives and Special Collections
14N-118 MIT
Cambridge, MA 02139

Contact: Kathy Marquis, Reference Archivist
(617) 253-5136
Hours: Mon-Fri, 9-5
Accessible to Public: Yes
Accessible to Scholars: Yes
Special Considerations: Some archival materials and manuscripts have restrictions on use; consult archivist for further information

Archives of Useless Research: Contains books and pamphlets collected by Albert G. Ingalls, associate editor of *Scientific American.* Much of the material rejects contemporary theories of the physical sciences, particularly theoretical and planetary physics; a smaller portion builds upon contemporary science and explores hypotheses not yet accepted. Many items are concerned with the conflicts between science and religion, often in very personal terms.

David Oakes Woodbury Papers: Consists of Woodbury's papers, notes, interview notes, letters, etc., dealing with his *Collier's* column, "Your Life Tomorrow," on the household applications of World

War II technology. Also includes his notes and research material for his autobiography of Elihu Thomson, and correspondence concerning his public lectures on the peaceful uses of atomic energy and other topics related to science.

246. Massachusetts Institute of Technology Science Fiction Society
MIT Rm W20-473
Cambridge, MA 02139

Contact: Curator
(716) 225-9144
Hours: most evenings by appointment
Accessible to Public: Yes
Accessible to Scholars: Yes
Special Considerations: Hours are irregular and an advance appointment is required; no smoking is permitted

Collections consist about 15,000 book titles out of a total of 45,000 items. Materials also include foreign books, almost all English-language science fiction magazines, 5,000 fanzines, and numerous related print items and artifacts.

247. Radcliffe College, Arthur and Elizabeth Schlesinger Library on the History of Women in America
10 Garden St
Cambridge, MA 02138

Contact: Eva S. Moseley, Curator of Manuscripts
(617) 495-8647
Hours: Mon-Fri, 9-5; limited evening hours during academic year
Accessible to Public: Yes
Accessible to Scholars: Yes

The collection is a major resource for the study of all aspects of American women's history, and includes manuscripts, photographs, monographs, tapes, and other materials. Coverage includes such topics as women's rights and suffrage, social welfare, reform, pioneers in the professions, family history, health, child-bearing and child-rearing, women in politics, the labor movement and women, and information on such important figures as Susan B. Anthony, the Beecher-Stowe and Blackwell families, Julia Child, Betty Friedan, Charlotte Perkins Gilman, Emma Goldman, Ame-

lia Earhart, Elizabeth Holtzman, Lydia Pinkham and her medicine company, and many others. The library is the official repository for the records of the National Organization of Women, the Women's Equity Action League, and several other organizations, including the YWCAs of Boston and Cambridge. The books alone number 30,000, including 4,000 on cooking and home management and etiquette books dating from 1811-1982. The library subscribes to 400 periodical titles related to women's issues and also has extensive vertical and clipping files. This is one of the largest and most complete collections related to women and women's history available anywhere.

Deerfield

248. Pocumtuck Valley Memorial Association Library and Henry N. Flynt Library of Historic Deerfield, Inc. (The Memorial Libraries)
PO Box 53
Deerfield, MA 01342

Contact: David R Proper, Librarian
(413) 774-5581 Ext 125
Hours: Mon-Fri, 9-5
Accessible to Public: Yes
Accessible to Scholars: Yes
Special Considerations: Many materials are stored in closed stacks

The Library contains printed books, manuscripts, photographs, and related material gathered largely from local sources. The bulk of the collection was formed between 1870 and 1916, and represents to an extraordinary degree the life and thought of one small town from the close of the 17th century to the opening of the 20th. For example, the printed book collection represents the reading matter of several generations of the people of Deerfield, and is an index to the intellectual climate and popular culture of the town through two centuries. Strong collections also relate to history of the area, education (including most schoolbooks from the community), religion (including nearly a full run of 19th century Massachusetts election sermons, hymnals, printed sermons, etc.), agriculture in the area, travel accounts (many locally produced), a large number of encyclopedias and dictionaries, account books from numerous local businesses ranging from the 17th century (taverns, small businesses, stores, etc.), local diaries (18th through 20th centuries), town records, church records, voluntary society records, family papers, photographs, and many supporting reference materials. In short, the holdings represent a complete portrait of the history and popular culture of a small town, a portrait that is unique and unusually varied.

Fall River

249. Edward T. LeBlanc Collection (Private Collection)
87 School St
Fall River, MA 02720

Contact: Edward T LeBlanc
(617) 672-2082
Hours: By advance appointment only
Accessible to Public: No
Accessible to Scholars: Yes
Special Considerations: Available to
  serious scholars only; this is a private
  collection

Collection consists of 25,000 dime novels, story papers, and periodicals (1860-1933); 30,000 English equivalents of dime novels, including 100 "Penny Dreadfuls" (1840-1860); 20,000 boys' and girls' journals; and 10,000 story papers and libraries.

Greenfield

250. Handwriting Analysis Research Library
91 Washington St
Greenfield, MA 01301

Contact: Robert E Backman, Curator
(413) 774-4667
Hours: Mon-Fri, 9-5
Accessible to Public: Yes
Accessible to Scholars: Yes
Special Considerations: Visitors who
  must travel more than 75 miles may
  arrange special evening and weekend
  hours with an advance appointment of
  at least three days

The Library collects published and unpublished materials on graphology, handwriting, handwriting analysis, the history of writing, penmanship (theory, practice, and teaching), and questioned documents. The collections include materials in Chinese, Danish, Dutch, English, French, German, Italian, Japanese, Magyar, Norwegian, Polish, Portuguese, Spanish, and Swedish. Holdings include more than 105,000 items in hundreds of formats, and represents the finest collection in the nation for the study of handwriting and related topics.

New Bedford

251. Whaling Museum Library, Old Dartmouth Historical Society
18 Johnny Cake Hill
New Bedford, MA 02740

Contact: Virginia M Adams, Librarian
(617) 997-0046
Hours: Library: Mon-Fri, 9-5; Museum:
  Mon-Sat, 9-5, Sun, 12-5
Accessible to Public: Yes
Accessible to Scholars: Yes
Special Considerations: Advance notice
  of visit is useful, although not
  required

The collections emphasize the history of the American whaling industry and southeastern Massachusetts. Includes popular texts on whales and whaling from the 17th century to the present. Local history collection contains broadside play bills, theater programs, trade cards, etc. (about 1,000 items).

Northampton

252. Northampton Historical Society
46 Bridge St
Northampton, MA 01060

Contact: Ruth E Wilbur, Dir
(413) 584-6011
Hours: Tues-Fri, 9-5; Tours: Wed, Sat,
  Sun, 2-4:30
Accessible to Public: Yes
Accessible to Scholars: Yes
Special Considerations: Researchers
  should make advance appointment

Collections relate to Northampton history and culture and include 1,800 stereoptican cards, 200 trade cards, 600 greeting cards, 80 oral histories, 36 shelf feet of ephemera, 24 shelf feet of photographs, 500 Daguerreotypes, 12 shelf feet of sheet music and bound music volumes, and nine file drawers of clippings and related materials.

253. The Sophia Smith Collection and Women's History Archive
Smith College
Northampton, MA 01063

Contact: Susan Boone, Curator
(413) 584-2700 Ext 2972
Hours: Sept-May, Mon-Fri, 9-5; June-Aug, Mon-Fri, 8-4
Accessible to Public: Yes
Accessible to Scholars: Yes

The collection is a manuscript repository related to women's history, and includes family and personal papers, organization records, diaries, letters, and similar materials, all of which have at least some interest to popular culture scholarship. Collections of special interest include those related to Frances Gillette Bemis (a department store public relations specialist) whose files include materials and photographs concerning Louis Bromfield, Lillian Gish, Fiorello LaGuardia, Mary Pickford, Robert Merril, Jackie Robinson, and many others (along with information on fashion and design); the papers of Helen Gurley Brown and her personal collection of clippings, recordings, etc.; the papers of Mary Alletta Crump; and materials related to author Phyllis Duganne. Additional materials in subject files include suffrage memorabilia such as buttons and various articles sold to raise money for suffrage activities (playing cards, sewing kits, Valentines, etc.), etiquette books, and memorabilia related to the 1960s women's movement.

Pittsfield

254. Berkshire Athenaeum, Music and Arts Department
1 Wendell Ave
Pittsfield, MA 01201

Contact: Mary Ann Knight, Dept Head
(413) 499-9487

Hours: Mon, Wed, Fri, Sat, 10-5; Tues, Thur, 10-9
Accessible to Public: Yes
Accessible to Scholars: Yes

Collections include more than 1,000 pieces of sheet music, 1856-1960s, with most dating 1900-1950.

255. Hancock Shaker Village Library
PO Box 898
Pittsfield, MA 01202-0898

Contact: Robert F W Meader, Librarian-Archivist
(413) 443-0188
Hours: Mon-Fri, 10-5
Accessible to Public: No
Accessible to Scholars: Yes
Special Considerations: Prior arrangements must be made (no "drop-ins"); no interlibrary loans

Collections are dedicated to the interpretation and preservation of the culture of the Shaker religious group.

Plymouth

256. Pilgrim Hall Museum
75 Court St
Plymouth, MA 02360

Contact: Caroline D Chapin, Curator of Manuscripts and Books
(617) 746-1620
Hours: Mon-Fri, 9:30-4:30
Accessible to Public: Yes
Accessible to Scholars: Yes
Special Considerations: Appointments are requested, though not absolutely necessary; telephone and mail reference assistance is available

Collections consist of manuscript and printed materials relating to the history of Plymouth, Massachusetts, and to the history and image of the Pilgrim settlement in New England. The general research collection, which focuses on the history of Plymouth and its first colonists, contains a variety of popular histories that treat the Pilgrim story in a topical manner. Some of the materials include 2,000 stereo and postal card views of Pilgrim subjects and 10 linear feet of ephemera (greeting cards, commemorative materials, promotional items, pamphlets, guide books, and related items depicting the Pilgrims and their story). Collections also include several runs of Plymouth newspapers (1786-1921), a map collection, a large collection of photographs of Plymouth (including early glass plate negatives), and many early church and civic records.

257. Plimoth Plantation
PO Box 1620, Warren Ave
Plymouth, MA 02360

Contact: Jeremy Bangs, Chief Curator
(617) 746-1622
Hours: Mon-Fri, 9-5
Accessible to Public: No
Accessible to Scholars: Yes
Special Considerations: Make prior
  appointment via phone or mail

Pilgrims in Popular Culture: Collection includes postcards, paintings, prints, chinaware, and other items portraying Pilgrims, and is supported by a library containing books, primarily novels, concerning Pilgrims.

Salem

258. Essex Institute, James Duncan Phillips Library
132 Essex St
Salem, MA 01970

Contact: Eugenia Fountain, Reference
  Librarian
(617) 744-3390
Hours: Library Hours: Mon-Fri, 9-4:30;
  Museum Hours: Mon-Sat, 9-5, Sun, 1-5, holidays, 1-5
Accessible to Public: Yes
Accessible to Scholars: Yes
Special Considerations: Nonmembers
  must pay $2 admission fee per day

Collections center on the history and culture of New England and early America, with an emphasis on Essex County and Salem, and are extensive, including 300,000 books, pamphlets, broadsides, maps, newspapers, and periodicals. There is also an extensive manuscript collection. Topics of special strength include Nathaniel Hawthorne, witchcraft in Salem, commercial activity in Essex County (especially in the late 19th century), U.S. Customs Service files from Salem and surrounding ports, abolitionism, women's rights, music, medicine, literature, agriculture, domestic life, family histories, and the *Frederick Townsend*

Ward Collection on the history of Imperial China (with 10,000 items, this is one of the best collections on this topic in the U.S.). The museum offers numerous exhibits and restored buildings related to the history and culture of Essex County. Brochures and guides are available, and researchers are advised to call ahead for more detailed information.

Sharon

259. Kendall Whaling Museum
27 Everett St, PO Box 297
Sharon, MA 02067

Contact: Curator
(617) 784-5642
Hours: Tues-Fri, 1-5; Sat, 10-5; other
  times by appointment
Accessible to Public: Yes
Accessible to Scholars: Yes
Special Considerations: Serious scholars
  may gain access to the collections
  during hours when the museum is not
  open by making advanced
  appointment

The museum includes artifacts and resources for the study of whaling and its cultural history, and is international in scope.

South Carver

260. Edaville Railroad Museum of New England Heritage
PO Box 7
South Carver, MA 02366

Contact: Kenton T Harrison
(617) 866-4526
Hours: June-Aug, Mon-Sun, 10-5:30;
  Nov-Dec, Mon-Fri, 4-9; Nov-Dec, Sat-Sun, 2-9
Accessible to Public: No
Accessible to Scholars: Yes
Special Considerations: Advance
  appointment required

Contains numerous sources and resources related to railroad history, with an emphasis on New England. Selected materials include the *Fall River Line Journal* (a publication distributed free to passengers of the steamship line) and employee magazines published by New

York Central Railroad, New York, New
Haven & Hartford Railroad, and the
Boston & Miami Railroad.

Waltham

261. Brandeis University Library
415 South St
Waltham, MA 02254

Contact: Victor Berch, Special
   Collections Librarian
(617) 736-4682
Hours: Mon-Fri, 9-4
Accessible to Public: Yes
Accessible to Scholars: Yes
Special Considerations: Access requires
   identification and statement of
   purpose

Collections include more than 1,000 dime
novels, Frank Meriwell novels, story papers, Horatio Alger novels, complete
runs of *Tip Top Weekly* and *New Tip
Top Weekly*, Oliver Optic novels, Harry
Castlemon novels, and more than 5,000
items of popular American sheet music.

262. WCRB-FM (Charles River Broadcasting, Inc.)
750 South St
Waltham, MA 02154

Contact: George C Brown, Music Dir
(617) 893-7080
Hours: Mon-Sun, 24 hours a day
Accessible to Public: Yes
Accessible to Scholars: Yes
Special Considerations: Access to general
   public is limited to Mon-Fri, 9-5

Collection consists of recordings of Boston Symphony Orchestra and Boston
Pops Orchestra dating back several dec-
ades, and also includes a growing collection of interviews with composers, musicians, and artists.

Watertown

263. Perkins School for the Blind, Blindiana Museum and Library
175 N Beacon St
Watertown, MA 02172

Contact: Keeneth A Stuckey, Research
   Librarian

(617) 924-3434
Hours: Mon-Fri, 8:30-5
Accessible to Public: Yes
Accessible to Scholars: Yes

The collection consists of material, aids
and appliances, pictures, and artifacts
relating to the blind and education of
the blind from early times to the
present, including the largest collection
of print material relating to nonmedical
aspects of blindness. Specific materials
relate to individuals such as Helen Keller, Annie Sullivan Macy (Keller's teach-
er), and Laura Bridgman.

Wellesley

264. Wellesley College, Margaret Clapp Library
Special Collections
Wellesley, MA 02138

Contact: Anne Anninger, Special
   Collections Librarian
(617) 235-0320 Ext 2129
Hours: Mon-Fri, 10-12, 1-5
Accessible to Public: Yes
Accessible to Scholars: Yes
Special Considerations: Two forms of
   identification are required

Juvenile Collection: Consists of 1,000
volumes, including works by Bewick,
Dore, Greenaway, Crane, Caldecott,
Henty, and Alger, along with 370 Big
Little Books.

Postcard Collection: Contains one album of Tubingen, 15 albums of cards
and clippings of the U.S. and Europe,
and a file of cards related to Great
Britain and Europe.

Book Arts Collection: Includes 3,200
volumes covering all aspects of book production, papermaking, printing, illustrating, and bookbinding. Also includes 1,350
fine printing specimens from the late
18th century to the present.

Other materials within the collections include two boxes of embroidered paper
bookmarks (19th and 20th centuries),
two boxes of bookplates, materials related to bookplates, the *Durant Collection* of Victorian books (7,600 volumes),
and major collections related to English
poetry, Jamaica, and Italy.

Wenham

265. Wenham Historical Association and Museum, Inc.
132 Main St, Rte 1A
Wenham, MA 01984

Contact: Eleanor E Thompson, Dir
(617) 468-2377
Hours: Office Hours: Mon-Fri, 11-4; Sat,
  1-4; Sun, 2-5; Library Hours: Mon-Fri,
  9:30-4:30
Accessible to Public: Yes
Accessible to Scholars: Yes
Special Considerations: Some portions of
  the collections are in storage and
  require advance notice for study

The collections include 400 women's
gowns, dresses, and bridal gowns (1790-
1965); 50 items of children's attire
(shoes, hats, underwear, accessories); ice
cutting tools; two shoe shops, one fully
equipped; 5,000 dolls and toys; 500 items
of wood and tinware, pottery, and assorted kitchen utensils; 300 embroidery
block stamps; the *Conant Photo Collection* of images related to Wenham area
(1890-1917); 1,000 books in the research
library with an emphasis on genealogy
and local records; agricultural books in
the *Massachusetts Society for Promoting
Agricultural Library*; paper ephemera,
including Christmas and Valentine cards,
farm and store ledgers, school primers,
and trade cards; quilts, rugs, and textiles;
and the fully furnished *Claflin-Richards
House* of 1000.

Williamstown

266. Chapin Library of Rare Books and Manuscripts
Williams College
Williamstown, MA 01267

Contact: Robert L Volz
(413) 597-2462
Hours: Mon-Fri, 9-12, 1-5
Accessible to Public: Yes
Accessible to Scholars: Yes

Children's Books Collection: Consists
of 500 volumes for children and juveniles, emphasizing fine condition, first
printings, and good illustrations.

Kipling X Collection: Contains 115
volumes of reprints and cheap editions

of writings by Rudyard Kipling, organized as a subsection of a larger Kipling
collection.

Post Movie Collection: Includes 1,500
movie posters, press books, stills, etc.,
organized as a subsection of the *Violet
and Carl Post Performing Arts Collection.*

**Spanish Romanceros and Poesias
Collection:** Includes 265 items of this
popular form of Spanish chapbook literature, chiefly from Madrid, Seville,
Cordoba, and Valencia, and published in
the 18th century.

Ballad Collection: Consists of 150
broadside ballads and verse sheets, mostly in English, of the late 17th and the
18th centuries.

Worcester

267. American Antiquarian Society
185 Salisbury St
Worcester, MA 01609

Contact: Nancy Burkett, Asst Librarian
(617) 755-5221
Hours: Mon-Fri, 9-5; closed legal
  holidays, third Wed in Oct, and Fri
  after Thanksgiving
Accessible to Public: No
Accessible to Scholars: Yes
Special Considerations: Open to adult
  researchers with two forms of
  identification (one with photograph)
  and after an interview with a senior
  staff member. Graduate students may
  gain access by presenting a letter of
  introduction from their supervising
  faculty member.

With holdings numbering close to
3,000,000 books, pamphlets, broadsides,
manuscripts, prints, maps, and newspapers, this Library preserves the largest
single collection of printed source material relating to the history, literature,
and culture of the first 250 years of what
is now the United States. It specializes
in the American period to 1877, and
holds two-thirds of the total pieces
known to have been printed in this
country between 1640 and 1821, as well
as the most useful source materials and
reference works printed since that period. Its files of 18th and 19th century
American newspapers, numbering

2,000,000 issues, are the finest anywhere. The collecting fields in which the holdings are strongest include advertising trade cards, almanacs, amateur newspapers, art catalogs, ballads, Bible and prayer books, bibliography, biography, book catalogs, bookplates, political caricatures, children's literature, city views, cookbooks, circusiana, city directories, graphic arts, genealogy, imprints, institutional publications, learned societies, libraries, literary annuals, literature, manuscripts, maps, municipal documents, newspapers, paper currency, periodicals, portraits, printing and related arts, psalmody, reference works, religion, school books, school catalogs and histories, sheet music, songsters, state and local histories, state documents, United States history (chronological and topical), transportation (roads, railroads, canals, and bridges), trade catalogues, trade directories and year books, and Valentine cards.

MICHIGAN

Alpena

268. Jesse Besser Museum
Johnson St
Alpena, MI 49707

Contact: Dennis Bodem
(217) 356-2202
Hours: Mon-Fri, 9-5; Thur, 7 pm-9 pm; Sat-Sun, 1-5
Accessible to Public: Yes
Accessible to Scholars: Yes
Special Considerations: Noncirculating

Collections include postcards, Valentines, Christmas cards, general greeting cards, quilts, pottery, and baskets.

Ann Arbor

269. University of Michigan, Bentley Historical Library
1150 Beal Ave
Ann Arbor, MI 48109

Contact: Nancy Bartlett, Reference Archivist
(313) 764-3482
Hours: Mon-Fri, 8:30-5; Sept-May, Sat, 9-12:30

Accessible to Public: Yes
Accessible to Scholars: Yes

Important groups of papers include those of James Oliver Curwood (novelist and conservationist, 1878-1927), John and Leni Sinclair (leaders of the counterculture movement in Michigan during the 1960s and 1970s), Arnold Gingrich (founder and editor of *Esquire* magazine), Ivan Henry Walton (Michigan folklorist, 1893-1968), Gerald Lyman Kenneth Smith (founder of the America First Party and outspoken conservative, 1898-1976), and Mike Wallace (including television and newspaper transcripts and files).

270. University of Michigan, Horace H. Rackham Library
Rare Book Room
Ann Arbor, MI 48109-1045

Contact: Special Collections Librarian
None listed
Hours: By appointment
Accessible to Public: Yes
Accessible to Scholars: Yes

Crosby Shakespeare Collectanea: Consists of eleven boxes of the personal collectanea of Joseph Crosby, a 19th century book collector, and includes play programs, reprints, critical essays, travel guides, theater festival guides, academic exercises, "Shakespeare sermons," agenda for reading clubs, and an envelope of "verdure from Shakespeare's grave." Material is cataloged.

271. University of Michigan Library, Department of Rare Books and Special Collections
711 Hatcher Graduate Library
Ann Arbor, MI 48109-1205

Contact: Robert Starring
(313) 764-9377
Hours: Mon-Sat, 10-12; Mon-Fri, 1-5
Accessible to Public: Yes
Accessible to Scholars: Yes

Labadie Collection: Includes 100 comic books of the U.S. counterculture movement (1960s and 1970s) and 500 posters of a radical protest and reform nature (anarchist, labor-related, Vietnam War, women's liberation, etc.) and from many different countries, 1910-present.

Poster Collection: Consists of 500 World War I posters (U.S., France, and Germany, 1914-1918), 37 World War II Posters from the U.S. (1942-1943), 700 election posters (Austria, Canada, France, Germany, and Great Britain, 1919-1957), and 140 U.S. theatrical posters (1880-1910).

Playbill and Theatre Programs: Contains 15,500 items, mostly U.S. and Great Britain, with the bulk dating from the second half of the 19th century, with some later and some earlier.

Henty Collection: Consists of 125 volumes of boys' books by George Alfred Henty.

Hubbard Imaginary Voyages Collection: Includes about 3,000 volumes of imaginary voyages, of which almost half are various editions, translations, adaptations, and imitations of Defoe's *Robinson Crusoe*. The works of Jonathan Swift, especially *Gulliver's Travels*, form another large part.

Dearborn

272. Henry Ford Museum and Greenfield Village, Department of Archives and Library
PO Box 1970
Dearborn, MI 48121

Contact: Jeanine M Head
(313) 271-1620
Hours: Mon-Fri, 8:30-5
Accessible to Public: Yes
Accessible to Scholars: Yes
Special Considerations: It is recommended that researchers make advance appointments, though this is not required

As a museum the collection contains numerous and extensive material objects related to the study of popular culture in areas such as transportation, communication, agriculture, industry, and domestic life. Print and manuscript formats include the following: over 5,000 trade catalogs and brochures, with particular strengths in agricultural machinery, industrial equipment, decorative arts, and women's clothing (18th through 20th century, with most dating after 1850); 2,000 trade cards (strongest collection dates 1880-1900); 600 greeting cards, including Christmas, Valentine, birthday, Easter, and other holidays (1850-1950); 5,000 items of sheet music concerning social and political events and popular tunes (1776-1960, with bulk from 1850-1900); 86 sets of paper dolls, both commercial and handmade (1850-1959); 100 broadsides (18th and 19th centuries, most dated 1850-1890); 1,250 almanacs (18th-20th centuries); 600 children's books (18th-20th centuries); 250 *McGuffey Readers*, including numerous editions; 200 pieces of travel literature, including tour books, maps, brochures, souvenir booklets, and excursion tickets (1835-1975, with most dating 1925-1955); World's Fairs and Exhibitions materials, including 800 items such as brochures, souvenir booklets, and memorabilia (1856-1984); 1,500 historical and decorative prints (mostly 19th century Currier and Ives, with some 18th century items); 20,000 scenic postcards, including 15,000 Detroit Publishing Co. cards (1890-1980); 1,000 posters (1890-1945, with strongest groups in circus posters from 1890-1910 and World War I posters); 30,000 photographic images (19th and 20th centuries), including Daguerreotypes, tintypes, cabinet cards, *cartes de visite*, stereographs, and 25,000 photoprints from the Detroit Publishing Co. (1890-1915); and over 350,000 graphics, of which 300,000 are photographs, including architectural drawings and advertising graphics related to Henry Ford's personal and company interests (1863-1947), and Ford Motor Co. products and activities from 1903-1950, including automotive, aviation, farm tractors, and war production subjects.

Detroit

273. Detroit Institute of Art Archives
5200 Woodward Ave
Detroit, MI 48202

Contact: James L Limbacher; Audley Grossman
(313) 833-1742
Hours: Not yet open to public; by appointment only
Accessible to Public: No
Accessible to Scholars: Yes

This is a new collection and consists of 16mm films, super 8mm films, 8mm films, VHS videotapes, clipping files on movies, and film and television reference books. Inquire as to specific holdings prior to visit.

274. Detroit Public Library, Burton Historical Collection
5201 Woodward Ave
Detroit, MI 48202

Contact: Alice C Dalligan
(313) 833-1483
Hours: Mon-Sat, 9:30-5:30; Wed, 9-9
Accessible to Public: Yes
Accessible to Scholars: Yes

Collections include the *Ernie Harwell Sports Collection*, which contains periodicals, guides, record books, yearbooks, and rule books (18,985 volumes) and the *Edgar DeWitt Jones Abraham Lincoln Library* of 900 volumes.

275. Detroit Public Library, Music and Performing Arts Department
5201 Woodward Ave
Detroit, MI 48202

Contact: Agatha Pfeiffer Kalkanis
(313) 833-1460
Hours: Mon-Tues, 9:30-5:30; Wed, 9-9; Thur-Sat, 9:30-5:30
Accessible to Public: Yes
Accessible to Scholars: Yes
Special Considerations: Photocopying is not available for copyrighted materials; materials not available for interlibrary loan; residents of Michigan may check materials out of the library

Collections include 18,000 titles of popular sheet music.

276. Wayne State University
Purdy/Kresge Libraries
Detroit, MI 48202

Contact: Gloria L Sniderman
(313) 577-4040
Hours: Mon-Thur, 8 am-11 pm; Fri, 8-6; Sat, 9-5; Sun, 12-7
Accessible to Public: Yes
Accessible to Scholars: Yes
Special Considerations: The *Ramsey Collection* is closed to the public and requires 24 hour advance notice for use by scholars; all materials used only under staff supervision

Eloise Ramsey Collection of Literature for Young People: Consists of 8,000 British and American books of the 19th and 20th centuries, including Sunday School Tracts, ABC and Counting Books, Eve Titus manuscripts, and numerous miscellaneous items.

General collections include sources of materials for study and research in children's literature, and a circulating collection of more than 55,000 children's books ranging from preschool to college level for use by student teachers and library science students, mostly from the latter part of the 20th century.

Urban and Ethnic Collection of Literature for Young People: This is a noncirculating examination collection of books about urban and ethnic life in cities.

277. Wayne State University Folklore Archive
448 Purdy Library
Detroit, MI 48202

Contact: Janet Langlois, Dir
(313) 577-4053
Hours: Hours vary by academic semester; generally open two or three days per week; make advance appointment
Accessible to Public: Yes
Accessible to Scholars: Yes
Special Considerations: Advance appointment is best; standard archival procedures are in effect in order to protect the materials

Field Research Collections: Contains approximately 5,000 collections based on interview/participant observation/questionnaire methodologies. Most collections relate to southeastern Michigan and cover a wide range of folklore genres, groups, and subject matter. Collections contain nearly 1,000 audiotapes, 300 slides, 500 photographs, and five videotapes.

Special Collections: This large and varied group includes an international library of African music on phonographs records; a copy of the *Ivan Walton Collection of Michigan Folklore* (originally housed at Bentley Historical Collection of the University of Michigan Libraries) which includes 98 tapes and 12 boxes of xeroxed materials; a copy of the *Michigan State University Collection of Folk*

Narrative (originally housed in Indiana University Folklore Institute Archives) which includes 17 boxes of xeroxed materials; a copy of the *Great Lakes Art Alliance Collection* of 40 interview tapes collected from southern whites in Detroit; 100 tapes of Greek-Americans from different generations in the Greater Detroit area; the *Great Lakes Lighthouse Keepers' Association Oral History Collection* of 26 tapes collected from lighthouse keepers and their families; the *Bruce Harkness Poletown Photograph Collection* of 400 prints of an urban multi-ethnic community that was displaced for the new General Motors plant in Detroit; a collection of 1,500 science fiction magazines dating from the 1940s to the 1970s (index is available); the *Tremain Rock-n-Roll Collection*; and the *Bruno Nettl Archive of Ethnomusicology* that consists of approximately 500 tapes.

Other collections include a pamphlet file on various topics in folklore and oral history, a newsletter file on folklore and archival practices, a small reference collection of published titles in folklore, and 200 phonograph albums related to folklore, many from the Library of Congress Folkways Recordings series.

East Lansing

278. Michigan State University Libraries, Robert Vincent Voice Library
Voice Library, Michigan State
 University
East Lansing, MI 48824-1048

Contact: Maurice A Crane
(517) 355-5122
Hours: Mon-Fri, 8-4:30
Accessible to Public: Yes
Accessible to Scholars: Yes
Special Considerations: Noncopyrighted
 materials will be copied for patrons
 who supply reels or cassettes

The collection houses 40,000 voices, including the entire body of the Science Fiction Oral History Association's collection, the entire Oral History of East Lansing Collection, many conversations with old steam railroadmen, interviews with former inhabitants of three towns in Tombigee County, Alabama, which are now under water and no longer on the map (old photographs of the towns

accompany this collection), recordings in nonwritten languages of the Natchee and Creek Indians, a copy of the taped dictionary/workbook of the nonwritten Chippewa language, and complete runs of the Johnson Foundation's "Voices From Wingspread" and the Stanley Foundation's "Common Ground." The collection is also particularly strong in old radio, political addresses, and sports and show business.

279. Michigan State University Libraries, Russel B. Nye Popular Culture Collection
Special Collections Division
East Lansing, MI 48824

Contact: Jannette Fiore
(517) 355-3770
Hours: Mon-Fri, 9-5; Sat (during
 academic year only), 10-2
Accessible to Public: Yes
Accessible to Scholars: Yes
Special Considerations: Identification
 required; collection does not circulate,
 but photocopies are permitted when
 materials and copyright laws permit

The collections consist of printed materials only and include more than 85,000 items organized into four primary categories as follows: **Comic Art:** includes 40,000 comic books and 3,000 volumes of supporting materials (histories, anthologies, reprints, magazines, and fanzines); **Popular Fiction:** contains juvenile fiction (emphasis on series books, 5,800 volumes), western fiction (more than 3,000 novels, over 1,000 pulp magazine issues), women's fiction (emphasis on Harlequin novels, including over 4,000 novels and over 1,000 issues of confession, romance, and movie magazines), science fiction (8,500 books and periodicals, over 1,500 fanzine issues), and detective/mystery fiction (5,000 novels and magazines); **Popular Information:** includes 5,100 items (almanacs, Haldeman-Julius' Blue Book series, advice books, self-help books, and about 2,000 public school texts; and **Popular Performing Arts:** consists of 3,000 items in popular theater, music, radio, film, television, and tent shows (250 scripts and related items).

The Special Collections also include a growing vertical file of ephemeral support materials (pamphlets, leaflets, clippings, conference papers, off-prints, etc.) for many categories of popular culture research. A recent acquisition related to popular music includes 22,000 items. This latter collection includes 4,500 items of sheet music by Black composers and 1,500 music compositions related to attitudes toward Blacks in America. Artists include Scott Joplin, Jelly Roll Morton, James P. Johnson, Lillian Hardin Armstrong, Fats Waller, and Eubie Blake.

Flint

280. Flint Public Library, Children's Department
1026 E Kearsley St
Flint, MI 48507

Contact: Marcia Carlsten, Head
(313) 232-7111 Ext 234
Hours: Mon-Thur, 9-9; Fri-Sat, 9-6
Accessible to Public: No
Accessible to Scholars: Yes
Special Considerations: Noncirculating

Holdings consist of a quality collection of children's literature, including fiction, picture books, fairy tales, and poetry, and is supported by a reference collection of source books related to children's literature.

Holland

281. Holland Historical Trust, The Netherlands Museum
Third Floor, City Hall
Holland, MI 49423

Contact: John P Luidens
(616) 394-1362
Hours: Thur, 9:30-4; some other times possible by advance appointment
Accessible to Public: Yes
Accessible to Scholars: Yes
Special Considerations: By appointment

This collection documents the lives and roles of Dutch immigrants to the United States, and includes diaries, personal papers, business and government records, newspapers, periodicals, church and school records, and pamphlets. The materials focus on western Michigan. A detailed guide to the collections has been published and is available to researchers.

Kalamazoo

282. Western Michigan University
University Libraries, Reference Dept
Kalamazoo, MI 49008

Contact: Gordon Eriksen
(616) 383-1556
Hours: Mon-Fri, 9-5
Accessible to Public: No
Accessible to Scholars: Yes

Collections include 5,000 rare and special children's books, including several hundred miniatures.

283. Western Michigan University, Harper C. Maybee Music and Dance Library
Dorothy U. Dalton Center
Kalamazoo, MI 49008

Contact: Gregory Fitzgerald, Music Librarian
(616) 383-1817
Hours: Mon-Thur, 8 am-11 pm; Fri, 8-5; Sat, 10-5; Sun, 2-11; hours abbreviated during spring and summer school sessions
Accessible to Public: Yes
Accessible to Scholars: Yes
Special Considerations: Noncirculating

Sheet Music Collection: Consists of 3000 titles, mostly popular vocal music, indexed by title (1890-1960).

Marquette

284. Marquette County Historical Society
213 N Front St
Marquette, MI 49855

Contact: Linda Panian
(906) 226-3571
Hours: Mon-Fri, 9-4:30; closed holidays
Accessible to Public: Yes
Accessible to Scholars: Yes

Collections include 55 children's books; 106 items of sheet music and music books; 86 scrapbooks; 25 boxes of postcards; one box each of Valentines,

Christmas cards, and miscellaneous greeting cards; and two file drawers of trade cards (including advertising art, posters, and calendars).

Marshall

285. American Museum of Magic
PO Box 5
Marshall, MI 49068

Contact: Robert or Elaine Lund
(616) 781-7666, 781-7674
Hours: By appointment
Accessible to Public: No
Accessible to Scholars: Yes
Special Considerations: Availability subject to curators' convenience

Collection consists of approximately 250,000 items related to magic and magicians, and includes apparatus, letters, newspaper clippings, photographs, films, videotapes, audiotapes, record albums, costumes, business cards, scrapbooks, diaries, coins and tokens, figures, programs, posters, sheet music, books and magazines, toys, games, and advertising materials.

Monroe

286. Monroe County Library System
0700 S Custer Rd
Monroe, MI 48161

Contact: Peggy Mawby, Special
  Collections Coord; Marie D Chulski,
  Head of Reference and Information
(313) 241-5277
Hours: Mon-Thur, 9-9; Fri, 9-5; Sat, 10-5
Accessible to Public: Yes
Accessible to Scholars: Yes
Special Considerations: By appointment

George Armstrong Custer Collection: Consists of materials related to Custer and the events surrounding and shaping his life, and includes more than 3,500 items (books, pamphlets, maps, manuscripts, motion pictures, slides, magazines, newspapers, paintings, photographs, sound recordings, and memorabilia).

Rochester

287. Oakland University, Kresge Library
Special Collections
Rochester, MI 48063

Contact: Robert Gaylor, Curator
(313) 370-5355
Hours: Mon-Fri, 9-4
Accessible to Public: Yes
Accessible to Scholars: Yes
Special Considerations: A current
  driver's license is required

Collections include the *Hicks Collection* of 2,000 volumes of material written by and about women (1600-1800) and the *James Collection* of 1,000 volumes of material on folklore of the 19th century.

MINNESOTA

Minneapolis

288. American Swedish Institute
2600 Park Ave
Minneapolis, MN 55407

Contact: Marita Karlisch, Archivist
(612) 871-4907
Hours: Mon-Fri, 12-4
Accessible to Public: Yes
Accessible to Scholars: Yes
Special Considerations: Phone prior to
  visit

Collection includes more than 100 Swedish and Swedish-American postcards as well as other materials related to Swedish-Americans.

289. Bakken Library and Museum of Electricity in Life
3537 Zenith Ave S
Minneapolis, MN 55416

Contact: Elizabeth Ihrig, for Print
  Materials; Albert Kuhfeld, for
  Instruments
(612) 927-6508
Hours: Mon-Fri, 9-5
Accessible to Public: Yes
Accessible to Scholars: Yes

Special Considerations: Call or write in advance for appointment.

Ephemera Collection: Consists of about 200 advertisements, programs, broadsides, brochures, circulars, and instructional pamphlets dealing with alternative electromedical therapies. Most of the materials date from the 1800s.

Trade Catalogs Collection: Includes about 300 trade catalogs and price lists, 1875-1930, which display electrical apparatus, surgical and dental instruments, medical appliances, electrotherapeutic apparatus, and early X-ray machines. The catalogs are mostly from the U.S., but also include some European examples.

Instrument Collection: Contains nearly 2,000 instruments, including electrostatic generators, magneto-electric generators, induction coils, physiological instruments, and recording devices and accessories.

290. University of Minnesota Libraries, Children's Literature Research Collections

109 Walter Library, University of Minnesota
Minneapolis, MN 55455

Contact: Karen Nelson Hoyle
(612) 624-4576
Hours: Mon-Fri, 8-4:30
Accessible to Public: Yes
Accessible to Scholars: Yes
Special Considerations: Users must complete a registration card; materials must be used in reading room

Kerlan Collection of Manuscripts and Illustrations for Children's Books: Consists of 40,000 children's books, including toy books, miniatures, 550 figurines of children's literature characters, and manuscripts and/or illustrations for 5,000 titles. The materials represent 640 authors and 584 illustrators who have donated manuscripts and original art, with an additional 31 translators represented.

Hess Collection: Includes 5,500 series books, 70,300 dime novels, story papers, periodicals, pulps, 550 Big Little Books, 1,200 comic books, and a large collection of series books and dime novels related to author Edward Ellis.

Paul Bunyan Collection: Contains 136 monographs, correspondence, advertising materials, art, and maps that use the Paul Bunyan image.

Edward S. Ellis Collection: Consists of books, dime novels, periodicals, and correspondence by Ellis.

Gustaf Tenggren Collection: Contains books and original illustrations by Tenggren, including his *Poky Little Puppy* work.

291. University of Minnesota Libraries, Music Library

70 Ferguson Hall
Minneapolis, MN 55455

Contact: Katharine Holum, Head of Music Library
(612) 624-5890
Hours: Mon-Thur, 8 am-9 pm; Fri, 8-5; Sat, 10-5; Sun, 1-9
Accessible to Public: Yes
Accessible to Scholars: Yes
Special Considerations: No materials are cataloged

All materials relate to various forms of popular music and include the following: 78 rpm records (7,300), 45 rpm records (300), and LP recordings (400) in popular music, musical comedies, and jazz; 365 square dance recordings (78 rpm); 4,000 items of sheet music (popular songs and musical show sheets, dated from 1848-1970); and a large book collection related to popular music (180 titles), jazz (450 titles), blues (60 titles), and rock (110 titles).

Morris

292. West Central Minnesota Historical Center

University of Minnesota
Morris, MN 56267

Contact: Bert Ahern
(612) 589-6172
Hours: Mon and Wed, 1-5; Tues and Thur, 2-5; Fri, 10-12, 1-3
Accessible to Public: Yes
Accessible to Scholars: Yes

Oral History Collection: Contains numerous tapes of citizens who tell their life histories and relate information of the "Old Days" in and around west central Minnesota. Topics covered include biographies, historical episodes, social events, businesses, schools, and farming, among others.

Saint Paul

293. College of St. Catherine
2004 Randolph Ave
Saint Paul, MN 55105

Contact: Mary William Brady
(612) 690-6553
Hours: Mon-Thur, 8-11, 1-3; closed July and Aug
Accessible to Public: Yes
Accessible to Scholars: Yes
Special Considerations: Identification required

Ruth Sawyer Collection: Consists of 2,225 children's books, including complete runs of Caldecott and Newbery winners, examples of children's books from early times, early pop-up books, toy books, panorama books, correspondence of Ruth Sawyer and Anne Carroll Moore, photographs and memorabilia of Sawyer and Robert McCloskey, book figures, and Kate Greenaway almanacs.

19th Century Women Novelists Collection: Contains 150 novels by and about women, with many first editions in original bindings, and includes nine by Marion Harland, 10 by Ouida, and 11 by Emma Southworth.

294. Minnesota Historical Society, Audio-Visual Collections
690 Cedar
Saint Paul, MN 55101

Contact: Bonnie Wilson
(612) 296-2489
Hours: Mon-Fri, 8:30-5
Accessible to Public: Yes
Accessible to Scholars: Yes

Collections include 6,000 feet of home movies, 5,000 postcards, 15,000 snapshots, and 5,000 stereographs. Additionally, 150,000 photographs (arranged by name, subject, and location), an oral history collection related to Minnesota, 25,000 maps of North America (includes

900 insurance maps of Minnesota towns and cities), a film and videotape collection related to the state, and a large slide collection of Minnesota sites and art work.

295. Minnesota Historical Society Museum
1500 Mississippi St
Saint Paul, MN 55101

Contact: Hilary Toreu
(612) 296-0148
Hours: Mon-Fri, 8:30-5
Accessible to Public: Yes
Accessible to Scholars: Yes
Special Considerations: Researchers should make an advance appointment of one week

The collections include a large volume of Valentines (1870-present), other greeting cards (1880-present), postcards (1880-present), and trade cards (1870-present, with an emphasis on Minnesota). The *Badge and Button Collection* includes 2,000 presidential election buttons (1832-present), more than 200 items related to Minnesota elections, and 4,750 nonpolitical buttons (veteran's organizations, St. Paul Winter Carnivals, Minnesota festivals, commercial and business buttons, and similar items).

Sauk Centre

296. Sinclair Lewis Foundation, Inc.
Sinclair Lewis Interpretive Center/ Museum, PO Box 222
Sauk Centre, MN 56378

Contact: Joyce Lyng, Sec
(612) 352-5201
Hours: Summer: Mon-Sun, 9:30-6; Sept: Mon-Fri, 9:30-5; Oct-Mar: Mon-Fri, 8:30-1; Apr-May: Mon-Fri, 8:30-5
Accessible to Public: Yes
Accessible to Scholars: Yes
Special Considerations: Wheelchair access is available; inquiries to the above address should be in care of the Sauk Centre Chamber of Commerce

Collections consist of a large variety and volume of materials for study of Lewis and his work. All of his novels and several autographed first editions are available for study. Numerous photographs of Lewis and his family, as well as his papers, awards, and manuscripts, are also in the collection. His boyhood home is restored and several other important Lewis sites are located within the community.

Walnut Grove

297. Laura Ingalls Wilder Museum
Box 58
Walnut Grove, MN 56180

Contact: Shirley Knakmuhs
(507) 859-2358
Hours: June-Labor Day: Mon-Fri, 10-7; May, Sept, and Oct: Mon-Fri, 10-5; other times by appointment
Accessible to Public: Yes
Accessible to Scholars: Yes
Special Considerations: Wheelchair ramp

Collections relate to both Wilder and to Walnut Grove history and culture.

MISSISSIPPI

Columbus

298. Mississippi University for Women, J.C. Fant Memorial Library
J. C. Fant Memorial Library, W1625
Columbus, MS 39701

Contact: Patsy McDaniel, Special Collections Librarian
(601) 329-7338
Hours: Mon-Sat, 8 am-10 pm; Sun, 2-10
Accessible to Public: Yes
Accessible to Scholars: Yes

Mississippi Authors Collection: Includes correspondence, scrapbooks, notes, printed matter, and other material relating to the history of Columbus.

Hattiesburg

299. University of Southern Mississippi, McCain Library and Archives
Southern Station Box 5148
Hattiesburg, MS 39406-5148

Contact: Terry S Latour

(601) 266-4345
Hours: Mon-Thur, 8 am-9 pm; Fri, 8-5; Sat, 10-5; Sun, 2-6; when classes not in session, Mon-Fri, 8-5
Accessible to Public: Yes
Accessible to Scholars: Yes
Special Considerations: Some collections may have specific restrictions; most materials do not circulate

The Lena Y. de Grummond Collection of Children's Literature: Contains manuscripts, galleys, illustrations, photographs, and similar materials from more than 1,000 authors and illustrators of children's literature. Individuals represented include Barbara Cooney, Roger Duvoisin, Gail Haley, Marcia Brown, Madeleine L'Engle, Maud and Miska Petersham, Richard Peck, and Lynd Ward. Collection contains 300 original Kate Greenaway illustrations, as well as several pieces of her correspondence and many examples of her greeting cards. More than 24,000 published volumes, dating from as early as 1530, are included, with over 8,000 volumes of children's literature published prior to 1915. Also included are numerous children's periodicals.

Other collections within the library include 250 oral histories conducted by the Mississippi Oral History Program, extensive railroad records dating from 1869, a major Civil War collection, a large collection of Mississippiana (newspaper, magazine, and newsletter files; maps and state documents; a vertical file), substantial resources in genealogy, and a collection of 3,500 editorial cartoons by over 300 cartoonists (1900-present), which is sponsored by the Association of American Editorial Cartoonists.

Laurel

300. Lauren Rogers Museum of Art Library
PO Box 1108
Laurel, MS 39441

Contact: Diane E Clark, Librarian
(601) 649-6374
Hours: Tues-Sat, 10-5; Sun, 1-4
Accessible to Public: Yes
Accessible to Scholars: Yes

The museum's local history collection includes postcards, cookbooks, and yearbooks produced in Laurel, Mississippi.

University

301. University of Mississippi, Blues Archive
Earley Hall
University, MS 38677

Contact: Suzanne Flandreau Steel,
   Archivist
(601) 232-7753
Hours: Mon-Fri, 8-5
Accessible to Public: Yes
Accessible to Scholars: Yes
Special Considerations: Copying is
   restricted on some collections

Collection contains 35,000 sound recordings (albums, 45s, and 78s), plus photographs, posters, videotapes, taped interviews, magazines, and manuscript collections relating to blues music and related musical styles. Special collections
include the *Kenneth S. Goldstein Folklore Collection*, which consists of books,
periodicals, and recordings covering all
aspects of folklore, with a strong emphasis on Southern folklore and music,
with strengths in blues albums and recordings from the late 1950s through the
1970s, and in music-oriented magazines
and periodicals from the same period;
the *B. B. King Collection* of promotional
materials, posters, photographs, and other materials concerning King, as well as
his personal collection of phonograph
records (over 10,000 recordings ranging
from classic blues to big-band jazz and
rock and roll); and the *Living Blues Archival Collection*, with extensive subject
files, photographs, posters, periodicals,
and taped interviews covering all aspects
of the blues (includes 10,000 45s, classic
recordings, and anthologies). Other materials concern all aspects of the blues
and the history of the form and related
styles; documents related to gospel music; and papers and mementoes of blues
artists Percy Mayfield and Lille Mae
Glover (Ma Rainey II). The Archive also
holds the papers of the Red Tops, a
Mississippi dance orchestra. Business
records and recordings of Trumpet
Records/Diamond Record Company, and
a collection of over 1,000 albums recorded by Mississippi-born musicians are
also featured. Several record companies,
including Kent, Malaco, Mr. R & B,
Wolf, and Origin Jazz Library have
donated their current recordings and
promotional materials.

MISSOURI

Cape Girardeau

302. Southeast Missouri State University, Kent Library
900 Normal Ave
Cape Girardeau, MO 63701

Contact: James K Zink, Dir
(314) 651-2235
Hours: Mon-Thur, 7:45 am-11:30 pm;
   Fri, 7:45-6; Sat, 9-5; Sun, 1:30-11:30;
   shortened hours when school not in
   session
Accessible to Public: Yes
Accessible to Scholars: Yes
Special Considerations: The *Regional
   History Collection* is available by
   appointment only

Regional History Collection: Includes
photographs, personal papers of prominent citizens, oral history tapes and
transcriptions, and published materials
on the region.

Columbia

303. Missouri Cultural Heritage Center
Conley House, Conley St and Sanford St
Columbia, MO 65211

Contact: Howard Marshall
(314) 882-6296
Hours: Mon-Fri, 8-5
Accessible to Public: Yes
Accessible to Scholars: Yes
Special Considerations: Advance
   appointment is recommended

**Traditional   Arts   Apprenticeship
Program:** Contains audiotapes, photographs, field notes, and videotapes of
over 30 master craftspeople throughout
the state.

Missouri   Performing   Traditions:
Consists of audiotapes, photographs,
logs, and field notes of over 40 traditional performing groups and performers
from the state.

304. Missouri State Historical Society
1020 Lowry
Columbia, MO 65201-7298

Contact: James W Goodrich
(314) 882-7083
Hours: Mon-Fri, 8-4:30
Accessible to Public: Yes
Accessible to Scholars: Yes

Varied collections include 1,275 titles of sheet music relating to Missouri (sorted by subject, composer, and/or publisher); 1,250 children's books written about Missouri and/or written by Missourians; nearly 100 books of dime novels and other works written about the Younger Brothers and/or Frank and Jesse James; various popular Missouri magazines dating from the 1880s and covering a wide range of subject areas (theater, agriculture, religion, specific regions or cities); printed newsletters, minute books, proceedings, handbooks, yearbooks, etc., for various Missouri patriotic, fraternal, civic, genealogical, religious, and social organizations; a collection of popular Missouri authors' novels, poetry, and historical books; a general reference collection of craft, art, antique, folklore, and period books that may be used to research lifestyles and living habits; 5,000 postcards; 250 *cartes de visite*; and 100 stereopticon cards.

Hannibal

305. Mark Twain Boyhood Home and Museum
208 Hill St
Hannibal, MO 63401

Contact: Henry Sweets, Curator
(314) 221-9010
Hours: Winter: Mon-Sun, 10-4; Summer: Mon-Sun, 8-6
Accessible to Public: Yes
Accessible to Scholars: Yes
Special Considerations: Wheelchair accessible

Collections consist of three historic buildings (Twain's boyhood home, the John M. Clemens Law Office, Grant's Drug Store), 600 books, many periodicals, some manuscript letters, personal belongings of Twain, and photographs, with an emphasis on Twain and Hannibal at the time the Clemens family lived here (1839-1853).

Independence

306. Harry S. Truman Library
Truman Library
Independence, MO 64050

Contact: Benedict K Zobrist
(816) 833-1400
Hours: Mon-Fri, 8:30-5
Accessible to Public: No
Accessible to Scholars: Yes
Special Considerations: Researchers should demonstrate a need to use original material prior to access

Numerous portions of the collections relate to popular culture, especially the "Gifts to the President" file, which includes 24 linear feet of material consisting primarily of correspondence relating to gifts sent (mostly) by ordinary Americans to Truman. Materials include music, newspapers, radio programming materials, magazines, photographs, phonograph records, and materials related to sports, television, motion pictures, art, cartoons, fairs, and museums. Other collections within the library hold materials that reflect popular tastes and interests in a variety of fields. An inquiry prior to visit might assist researchers in determining whether the holdings will be useful.

Kansas City

307. University of Missouri-Kansas City Libraries
5100 Rockhill Rd
Kansas City, MO 64110

Contact: Ted Sheldon
(816) 276-1531
Hours: By appointment
Accessible to Public: No
Accessible to Scholars: Yes
Special Considerations: By advance appointment only

Marr Sound Archives: Consists of over 35,000 sound recordings in a large variety of formats, and constitutes a social history of the 20th century United States in sound.

Kirksville

308. Northeast Missouri State University, Violette Museum

Violette Museum
Kirksville, MO 63501-0828

Contact: George Hartje, Dir
(816) 785-4526
Hours: Mon-Fri, by appointment
Accessible to Public: Yes
Accessible to Scholars: Yes

Collections include 275 posters, mostly political and many British, and all from the 20th century. Other topics include World War I propaganda and labor.

Mansfield

309. Laura Ingalls Wilder/ Rose Wilder Lane Home Association

Box 496, Rocky Ridge Farm
Mansfield, MO 65704

Contact: Irene Lichty-Le Count, Dir
(417) 924-3626
Hours: May 1-Oct 15, Mon-Sat, 9-4
Accessible to Public: Yes
Accessible to Scholars: Yes
Special Considerations: Adults must pay
   $3 fee

Collections in the museum include five original *Little House* manuscripts, first editions of all of Wilder's works, about 40 translations of her books, and many exhibits related to her family and life, including "Pa's fiddle" and contemporary furniture and other artifacts.

Rolla

310. University of Missouri/ State Historical Society of Missouri—Manuscript Collections

Room G-3 Library, University of
   Missouri at Rolla
Rolla, MO 65401-0249

Contact: Mark C Stauter, Assoc Dir
(314) 341-4874
Hours: Mon-Fri, 8-5
Accessible to Public: Yes
Accessible to Scholars: Yes

The collections include the following: five volumes of sheet music for piano and Spanish guitar (1828-1890); materials related to Charles C. Pyle (1882-1939) and his "International Transcontinental Foot Races" of 1928 and 1929; material related to the Marble Hill (MO) String Bands and the Quartette String Band (1875-1902); a collection related to minstrel shows and the Benevolent and Protective Order of Elks assembled by and related to producer Arthur Clinton Draper (1872-1944); other materials related to minstrel shows near Rolla; and records and miscellaneous papers related to various clubs and organizations associated with Rolla and other Missouri communities, including the West Plains Gentleman's Club (1901-1909), the Pickwick Club and Marquis Orchestra (1911-1913), the "Republicans of West Plains" (1912), the Miami Club (1901-1913), the Women's Christian Temperance Union of West Plains (1949-1978), the Springfield Ladies Saturday Club (1921-1928), the Mothers and Patrons' Club of Flat River (1907-1924, 1937), the Flat River Woman's Club (1913-1953), the Potosi Civic League (1921-1961), and the Knights of Labor of Phillipsburg (1888-1896). All materials are made more accessible via detailed "Information Sheets."

Saint Louis

311. Missouri Historical Society, Division of Library and Archives

Jefferson Memorial Building, Forest
   Park
Saint Louis, MO 63112-1099

Contact: Peter Michel, Chief Curator
(314) 361-1424
Hours: Tues-Fri, 9:30-4:45
Accessible to Public: Yes
Accessible to Scholars: Yes

Manuscript collections document the history of the city and the American West in public, private, and family documents. Especially strong are resources related to the fur trade (including the records of the American Fur Company), Civil War, Mexican War, river history and steamboating, Kate Chopin, Sara Teasdale, and the St. Louis World's Fair of 1904. The research collection of the library has 150,000 volumes related to such topics as the 1904 World's Fair, American fur trade, early travel on the Mississippi and Missouri Rivers, family history and genealogy, state and local history, the Veiled Prophet organization, and all aspects of St. Louis and Missouri art, culture, transportation, government, and business. Collections also include many rare maps, atlases, and books related to the West, as well as several runs of early newspapers.

312. St. Louis Sports Hall of Fame
100 Stadium Plaza
Saint Louis, MO 63102

Contact: Carolyn M Possini
(314) 421-3263
Hours: Mon-Sat, 10-5
Accessible to Public: Yes
Accessible to Scholars: Yes
Special Considerations: Researchers should make advance appointment

Collections relate to all aspects of St. Louis sports history, including baseball gloves, bats, balls, uniforms, shoes, socks, photographs, and trophies.

313. University of Missouri at St. Louis, Western Historical Manuscript Collection
8001 Natural Bridge Rd
Saint Louis, MO 63121

Contact: Kenn Thomas
(314) 381-7087 or (314) 553-5144
Hours: Mon-Fri, 8-5; Tues, 8 am-9 pm
Accessible to Public: Yes
Accessible to Scholars: Yes

Chuck Berry Project Research Papers: Includes oral histories, articles, and documents on the career of rock 'n' roll performer Chuck Berry, a native of St. Louis. Contains news clippings and articles on Berry from 1958-1983, the trial transcript from Berry's 1959 arrest, oral histories with his daughter Ingrid and guitarist Billy Peek, and papers and articles by the project directors. There are eight folders and two tapes.

Charlotte Peters Collection (1939-1978): Includes scripts, photographs, videotapes, and correspondence of the first woman on St. Louis television with a daily show.

Other materials held by the library include those related to Dr. Tom Dooley (including 78 tapes of his radio broadcasts), St. Louis suffragists, Black community leaders, riverboat jazzmen, labor leaders, International Women's Year (1977), St. Louis public television station KETC, and numerous St. Louis materials.

314. University of Missouri at St. Louis Women's Center
8001 Natural Bridge Rd
Saint Louis, MO 63121

Contact: Cathy Burack
(314) 553-5380
Hours: Mon-Fri, 8:30-5
Accessible to Public: Yes
Accessible to Scholars: Yes
Special Considerations: Noncirculating to general public; scholars should inquire in advance

Women's Resource Files: Consists of three filing cabinets of topically arranged resource files relating to women's issues and the changing roles of men and family, and includes clippings, journal articles, flyers, brochures, conference materials, and similar materials. Files are constantly growing.

Springfield

315. Springfield-Greene County Library
PO Box 737, J.S.
Springfield, MO 65801

Contact: Michael Glenn
(417) 869-4621
Hours: Mon-Thur, 8:30 am-9 pm; Fri, 8:30-6; Sat, 8:30-5
Accessible to Public: Yes
Accessible to Scholars: Yes

Max Hunter Collection: Consists of audiotapes and manuscripts documenting Ozark folklore. The tapes include fiddle tunes, jokes, sayings, songs, visits, and miscellaneous materials. The tunes, songs, and visits were taped by Hunter in the field in the 1950s and 1960s.

Warrensburg

316. Central Missouri State University, Ward Edwards Library

Ward Edwards Library, Central Missouri
 State University
Warrensburg, MO 64093

Contact: Ophelia Gilbert, Children's and
 Young Adults' Librarian
(816) 429-4508
Hours: Mon-Sun, 7:30 am-11 pm
Accessible to Public: No
Accessible to Scholars: Yes
Special Considerations: Identification
 required for noncirculating materials

Midwest Research Collection in Literature for Children and Young Adults: Consists of 27,000 circulating titles, 5,000 uncataloged titles, 4,000 historical titles (dating from 1788), Mark Twain Award nominees and winners (1970-present), an uncataloged collection of toy and movable books, and manuscripts, video interviews, and correspondence from 148 current authors.

MONTANA

Hamilton

317. Ravalli County Museum

205 Bedford, Old Courthouse
Hamilton, MT 59840

Contact: Erma Owings, Dir
(406) 363-3338
Hours: Winter and Summer: Mon-Fri, 9-4
Accessible to Public: Yes
Accessible to Scholars: Yes

McIntosh Apple Boom Collection: Consists of memorabilia and newspaper articles pertaining to McIntosh apples and includes 150 apple box labels.

Other collections relate to bitterroot, the state flower, and include china and 200 other items depicting bitterroot. Another group of materials includes 200 books on Montana history and 250 books on general history of the American West.

Also includes Bitterroot Valley newspapers, both those still active and those now extinct (*Western News, Bitter Root Times, Northwest Tribune, Ravalli Republic*, and several others).

NEBRASKA

Bellevue

318. Strategic Air Command Museum

2510 Clay St
Bellevue, NE 68005

Contact: Jack L Allen, Dir
(402) 292-2001
Hours: Daily, 8-5; closed Thanksgiving,
 Christmas, and New Year's Day
Accessible to Public: Yes
Accessible to Scholars: Yes
Special Considerations: Inside of aircraft
 open only on pre-announced
 occasions, such as Armed Forces Day

Collection includes 30 aircraft ranging from early World War II bombers and transports through strategic and reconnaissance aircraft still used by the Strategic Air Command; seven tactical and intercontinental ballistic missiles and a large display of World War I era to jet age aircraft engines also available. Large collection of miscellaneous memorabilia includes military uniforms, weapons, radios, bomb sights, and other ephemera from World War II, the Korean conflict, and the Southeast Asia operations.

Boys Town

319. Father Flanagan's Boys' Home Philamatic Center

PO Box 1
Boys Town, NE 68010

Contact: Ivan E Sawyer
(402) 498-1143
Hours: Mon-Sat, 8-4:30; Sun, 9-4:30;
 closed Thanksgiving, Christmas, and
 New Year's Day
Accessible to Public: Yes
Accessible to Scholars: Yes
Special Considerations: Prior request to
 use library

Collections include a worldwide stamp collection of over 200,000 items; a coin and banknote collection with over 6,000 foreign coins and 6,000 banknotes; a U.S. coin collection of primarily the late 19th and 20th centuries; a U.S. coin and banknote collection; and a library of coin, stamp, and banknote-related items.

Crawford

320. Nebraska State Historical Society—Fort Robinson Museum
PO Box 304
Crawford, NE 69339

Contact: Thomas R Buecker, Curator
(308) 665-2752
Hours: Apr 1-Nov 1, daily, 8-5; winter months, Mon-Fri, 8-5
Accessible to Scholars: Yes
Special Considerations: By arrangement with museum office

Collections include a Western Americana collection with Indian ethnology and U.S. military items, Fort Robinson records on microfilm, newspapers of Crawford and Chadron, and the Fort Robinson Medical Library.

Gering

321. Scotts Bluff National Monument
PO Box 427
Gering, NE 69341-0427

Contact: Tamera Leeling or Robert W Manasek
(308) 436-4340
Hours: June-Aug, 8-8; Sept-May, 8-5; closed Christmas and New Year's Day
Accessible to Public: Yes
Accessible to Scholars: Yes
Special Considerations: Items do not circulate

Collections include 2,000 volumes on Oregon and California Trail history, copies of pioneer diaries, issues of *Nebraska Quarterly History* from 1934-1967, and information about the National Park Service and natural science.

Lincoln

322. National Museum of Roller Skating
PO Box 81846
Lincoln, NE 68501

Contact: Michael W Brooslin, Dir
(402) 489-8811
Hours: Mon-Fri, 9-5; closed weekends and holidays
Accessible to Public: Yes
Accessible to Scholars: Yes
Special Considerations: By appointment only

Collections deal with roller skating history, including competitive sports, technological history, and recreational industry/businesses and the personalities involved, 1900-present; also archival collections of national roller skating sports and trade organizations, and several collections of vaudeville roller skating professionals, 1900-1930s.

323. University of Nebraska—Lincoln Libraries, Department of Special Collections
308 Love Library
Lincoln, NE 68588

Contact: Joseph G Svoboda, University Archivist
(402) 472-2531
Hours: Mon-Fri, 8-11:30, 12:30-5
Accessible to Public: Yes
Accessible to Scholars: Yes
Special Considerations: The *Botkin Collection* is not fully organized and is not fully accessible

Benjamin A. Botkin Collection: Consists of 12,000 volumes of cataloged books, Botkin's correspondence, research notes, phonographic records, interviews, and other materials related to Botkin's study of American folklore and popular culture (a total of 200 cubic feet of materials). Only the books are available to researchers at this time.

Harold William Felton Collection: Contains materials relating to Felton's writing, mainly drafts and research notes (3.15 cubic feet). Other materials, consisting of 1.75 cubic feet, include his correspondence, speeches, photographs, phonograph records, tapes, and scrapbooks.

Omaha

324. Joslyn Art Museum Reference Library
2200 Dodge St
Omaha, NE 68102

Contact: Librarian
(402) 342-3300 Ext 47
Hours: Tues-Sat, 10-5; Sun, 1-5
Accessible to Public: Yes
Accessible to Scholars: Yes
Special Considerations: Access by prior appointment; fee to enter museum

Collections include 100 stereographs of views from around the world and 180 old postcards from around the world.

325. National Park Service Midwest Regional Office
1709 Jackson St
Omaha, NE 68102

Contact: Elizabeth Lane
(402) 221-3477
Hours: Mon-Fri, 8-4:30
Accessible to Public: Yes
Accessible to Scholars: Yes
Special Considerations: All materials available for use within the library only; noncirculating, limited access

Collections include 1,600 volumes related to the National Parks, with an emphasis on the Midwest Region. Interests include history, architecture, preservation, scientific data of natural landmarks, parks, and monuments, as well as historic sites.

NEVADA

Las Vegas

326. Liberace Foundation for the Performing and Creative Arts
1775 E Tropicana
Las Vegas, NV 89119

Contact: Dora Liberace, Admin
(702) 798-5595

Hours: Mon-Sat, 10-5; Sun, 1-5; closed Thanksgiving, Christmas, and New Year's
Accessible to Public: Yes
Accessible to Scholars: Yes

Collections include classic automobiles, miniature cars, musical instruments, antique pianos, and miniature pianos, as well as Liberace memorabilia.

327. University of Nevada-Las Vegas Library, Special Collections Department
4505 Maryland Pkwy
Las Vegas, NV 89154

Contact: Susan Jarvis, Special Collections Librarian
(702) 739-3252
Hours: Mon-Fri, 8-5
Accessible to Public: Yes
Accessible to Scholars: Yes
Special Considerations: Items do not circulate

Menu Collection: Over 2,000 award-winning menus, special occasion menus, and menus with unique formats, 1870 to date.

Oral History Collection: Consists of 150 transcribed oral histories reflecting Nevada's history; 500 tapes of reminiscences of early Las Vegas history.

Gaming Collection: Includes 2,500 titles on gambling and its related activities, with the history and economics of gambling and the total spectra of the psychological, sociological, and moral aspects of the gaming phenomena.

NEW HAMPSHIRE

Durham

328. University of New Hampshire Library Special Collections
University of New Hampshire
Durham, NH 03824

Contact: Barbara A White
(603) 862-2714
Hours: Mon-Fri, 8-4:30
Accessible to Public: Yes
Accessible to Scholars: Yes

Collections include accoustical recordings, bookplates, Boston and Maine Railroad memorabilia, movie stills, a New England calendar collection, and New Hampshire postcards.

Franconia

329. New England Ski Museum

Box 267
Franconia, NH 03580

Contact: Arthur F March, Jr, Exec Dir
(603) 823-7177
Hours: Daily, 10-4, Jan-Mar and June-Oct 15
Accessible to Public: Yes
Accessible to Scholars: Yes
Special Considerations: Library and other research use subject to fee

Collection includes ski equipment, clothing, literature, photographs, 16mm film, and ski memorabilia dating from the beginnings of the sport in the U.S. Contact staff for further information.

Also includes the *New England Ski Museum Oral History Archive* of 50 tapes of interviews with ski figures (20 have also been transcribed).

Hanover

330. Dartmouth College Library Special Collections

Dartmouth College
Hanover, NH 03755

Contact: Philip N Cronenwett, Chief of Special Collections
(603) 646-3712
Hours: Weekdays, 8-4:30
Accessible to Public: Yes
Accessible to Scholars: Yes

1926 Collection: Over 2,000 illustrated books and broadsides published in New England, 1769-1869; many examples of primers, temperance tracts, gift annuals, almanacs, and other "ordinary" contemporary publications.

White Mountains Collection: Extensive collection of books, pamphlets, brochures, stereoscopic views, postcards, and other ephemera of New Hampshire's White Mountains and their scenes, trails, hotels, railroads, observatories,

etc.; much 19th and early 20th century material.

Juveniles Collection: Approximately 1,000 books by authors Edward Ellis, Ralph Barbour, William Taylor Adams, Horatio Alger, and others.

Also a dime novel collection and an illustrated books collection.

Laconia

331. Carpenter Museum of Antique Outboard Motors

PO Box 654
Laconia, NH 03247

Contact: Lawrence or Ann Carpenter
(603) 524-7611
Hours: Daily, 9-9, by appointment
Accessible to Public: Yes
Accessible to Scholars: Yes
Special Considerations: Advance appointment required

Personal collection of over 300 restored and excellent condition original antique and special interest outboard motors with related memorabilia, such as advertising signs, accessories, and the like. Restoration always in progress.

Manchester

332. Institut Canado-Americain/Association Canado-Americain

52 Concord St/PO Box 989
Manchester, NH 03105

Contact: Robert A Beaudoin, MD
(603) 625-8577
Hours: Mon-Fri, 9-4:45
Accessible to Public: Yes
Accessible to Scholars: Yes
Special Considerations: Prefer advance notice for research

Collection includes books, documents, manuscripts, theses, etc. on the role of the French in the exploration and colonization of Canada and the U.S. Contains history, sociology, folklore, genealogy, ethnology, and the like dating back to the 17th century; includes French newspapers published in the U.S. from the 1840s to date, plus books by and about Franco-Americans. Also paintings, sculptures, and portraits; knowledge of

French necessary for research, although some holdings are in English.

333. Lawrence L. Lee Scouting Museum and Max I. Selber Scouting Library
PO Box 1121 (Bodwell Rd)
Manchester, NH 03105

Contact: Mr Yvon A J Brunette, Chair
(603) 669-8919 or home phone (603) 627-1492
Hours: July-Aug, daily, 10-4; Sept-June, Sat, 10-4
Accessible to Public: Yes
Accessible to Scholars: Yes
Special Considerations: Unrestricted during regular hours; call for appointment

Lord Robert Baden-Powell Collection: Consists of books, plates, and related artifacts from the Boer War to 1940.

Boy Scout of America Collection: Includes badges, pins, uniforms, equipment, and memorabilia from 1910-present.

World and National Boy Scout Jamboree Souvenir Collection: Contains a wide variety of souvenirs from every World and/or National Boy Scout Jamboree, including Jamboree patches from around the world.

Scouting Library: Includes complete collection of *Boy's Life, Scouting, Annual Reports to Congress, Scout Executive,* and other related periodicals; extensive fiction collection of 850 scouting books, as well as a complete collection of *Boy Scout Handbooks, Scoutmaster Handbooks, Patrol Leader Handbooks,* and *Fieldbooks,* plus braille and visually impaired Boy Scout and Cub Scout books. Complete volumes of *Scoutcraft* by Ernest Thompson Seton, Daniel Carter Beard, and Lord Robert Baden-Powell.

NEW JERSEY

Burlington

334. Delia Biddle Pugh Library, Burlington County Historical Society
457 High St
Burlington, NJ 08016

Contact: M M Pernot, Dir
(609) 386-4773
Hours: Mon-Thurs, 1-4pm; Sun, 2-4; by appointment
Accessible to Public: Yes
Accessible to Scholars: Yes

Collection consists of material about Burlington County history and specializes in genealogy, early maps of the area, and a large photo collection, including over 600 deeds, some dating back to 1600s. Birthplace of James Fenimore Cooper on property, and library holds manuscripts and early editions of his works.

Far Hills

335. United States Golf Association Museum and Library
Golf House
Far Hills, NJ 07931

Contact: Janet Seagle, Librarian/ Museum Curator
(201) 234-2300
Hours: Mon-Fri, 9-5; Sat-Sun, 10-4; closed holidays
Accessible to Public: Yes
Accessible to Scholars: Yes
Special Considerations: Items do not circulate

Collection includes over 8,000 volumes on golf, as well as sheet music, postcards, films, 10,000 photographs, stereoptician cards, toys, games, art work, 2,000 golf clubs, 3,000 golf balls, ceramics, and glassware.

Glassboro

336. Denis Mercier Collection

Communications Department—Glassboro
State College
Glassboro, NJ 08028-1773

Contact: Denis Mercier
(609) 863-7104
Hours: By appointment only
Accessible to Public: No
Accessible to Scholars: Yes
Special Considerations: Must be serious
scholars with permission of Mercier to
use materials

Private collection of Afro-American imagery in American popular culture,
1870s-present; approximately 1,500
items, including sheet music, advertisements, kitsch, toys and games, children's
books, magazine articles, 78 rpm records,
etc.

Newark

337. Newark Public Library, Art and Music Department

5 Washington St—PO Box 630
Newark, NJ O7101-0630

Contact: William J Dane
(201) 733-7840
Hours: Mon, Wed, Thurs, 9-9; Tues, Fri,
9-5:30; Sat, 9-5; Sun, 1-5; summer
hours vary
Accessible to Public: Yes
Accessible to Scholars: Yes
Special Considerations: Some materials
available by appointment only

Shopping Bag Collection: A design
study collection, includes 500 examples
from 1960 on.

Theater Portraits Collection: Consists of 250 autographed glossy photographs of major stars and leading performers of the American Theater from
1910-1930.

Other collections include a Valentine and
greeting card collection of 1,500 items
arranged iconographically, 2,000 trade
cards, 5,000 postcards depicting fine arts
topics, 3,000 song sheets of popular music from 1900 on, 1,500 long-playing reference albums recording major stars and
groups from 1910 to present, 1,200 illustrated books recording the work of illustrators in Europe and America from
the 19th and 20th centuries, and
1,000,000 pictures on all topics.

338. Rutgers University, Institute of Jazz Studies

135 Bradley Hall, Rutgers University
Newark, NJ 07102

Contact: Edward Berger
(201) 648-5595
Hours: Mon-Fri, 9-5
Accessible to Public: Yes
Accessible to Scholars: Yes
Special Considerations: By appointment
only

Archival collection devoted to jazz and
jazz-related topics. Holdings include
60,000 phonograph records, 5,000 books,
an extensive collection of periodicals,
catalogs, research files, sheet music, photographs, and memorabilia. Maintains
oral history program with over 100 interviews on file, most of which are transcribed.

Princeton

339. Princeton University, Gest Oriental Library

317 Palmer Hall—Princeton University
Princeton, NJ 19544

Contact: D E Perushek, Curator
(609) 452-3183
Hours: Mon-Fri, 8:45-5
Accessible to Public: Yes
Accessible to Scholars: Yes
Special Considerations: Prior notice of
arrival and credentials

**Chinese Shadow Figures from Pup-
pet Theater:** Includes hundreds of
shadow figures and shadow theater scenery pieces from north China dating
from the early 20th century.

Somers Point

340. Atlantic County Historical Society

PO Box 301
Somers Point, NJ 08244

Contact: Elizabeth Ehrhardt
(609) 927-5218
Hours: Wed-Sat, 10-4
Accessible to Public: Yes

Accessible to Scholars: Yes

Collections include manuscripts, city directories, and similar documents providing resources for the study of Atlantic County, New Jersey, from the arrival of the first settlers to the present. Materials include family records, photographs and images, nautical records, pamphlets, church and institutional records, newspapers, clippings, and a full range of archival documentation. A guide to the collection is available.

Teterboro

341. Aviation Hall of Fame and Museum of New Jersey
Teterboro Airport
Teterboro, NJ 07608

Contact: H V Pat Reilly, Exec Dir
(201) 288-6344
Hours: Daily, 10-4
Accessible to Public: Yes
Accessible to Scholars: Yes

Collection includes an extensive aeronautical library; collection of photographs pertaining to New Jersey aviation and history; collection of aeronautical and space artifacts; aircraft on display; over 200 aircraft models; film library; and a collection of bronze plaques of 71 AHOF inductees.

Trenton

342. Trenton State College Library
Hillwood Lakes—CN 4700
Trenton, NJ 08650-4700

Contact: Richard Matthews, Librarian
(609) 771-2346
Hours: Mon-Fri, 9-5
Accessible to Public: Yes
Accessible to Scholars: Yes

Historic Textbook Collection: Consists of about 500 19th century elementary school readers, spellers, geography books, arithmetic books, etc.

Historic Children's Books: Consists of about 100 early 20th century boy's stories and novels by such authors as Edward Ellis, Frank Fowler, J. A. Henty, and Victor Appleton.

West Orange

343. Edison National Historical Site
Main St and Lakeside Ave
West Orange, NJ 07502

Contact: Mary B Bowling, Archivist; Dr Edward J Pershey, Supv Museum Curator
(201) 736-0550
Hours: Museum: Tues-Sun, 9-5; Archives and Research Collection: Mon-Fri, 9-4:30, by appointment only
Accessible to Public: Yes
Accessible to Scholars: Yes
Special Considerations: By appointment only for archives, two weeks advance notice required

Artifact Collection: Over 400,000 objects relating to phonographs, motion pictures, electric light and power, and Edison's Victorian mansion, Glenmont.

Sound Recordings: Over 20,000 cylinders and discs.

Archives: Includes over 3,500,000 items, such as 60,000 photographic images; over 2,500 pieces of sheet music; advertising and promotional printed ephemera; fan letters to Edison; and personal, business, and laboratory correspondence of Edison.

NEW MEXICO

Alamogordo

344. Space Center
PO Box 533, Top of NM Hwy 2001
Alamogordo, NM 88311-0533

Contact: Gregory P Kennedy, Exec Dir
(505) 437-2840
Hours: Museum: Daily, 9-6, closed Christmas; Planetarium: Shows at 10, 12, 2, and 4; Fri-Sun also 7 pm show
Accessible to Public: Yes
Accessible to Scholars: Yes
Special Considerations: Appointment recommended

Collections include videoand audiotape oral history of participants in space research and related programs in New Mexico; also include photographs and documents relating to space and rocket programs at White Sands Missile Range and Holloman AFB. Related ephemera such as the Daisy Test Track, Sonic Wind I rocket sled, and other New Mexico space artifacts available.

Albuquerque

345. University of New Mexico General Library, Special Collections Department
University of New Mexico
Albuquerque, NM 87131

Contact: Bill Tydeman, Head; Janet Thompson, Asst Head
(505) 277-6451
Hours: Mon-Fri, 8-4:30; also evenings during academic terms, Tues-Wed, 6: 30-9 pm
Accessible to Public: Yes
Accessible to Scholars: Yes
Special Considerations: Sign register

Collections include cartoons by W. C. Morris; 19th and 20th century travel literature/ephemera for New Mexico, 1881-1951; Civil War cartoons and slogans from Union point of view; and other popular ephemera.

J. W. Kerr Archive/Posters: Consists of four U.S. War Bond posters of Norman Rockwell paintings.

A. R. Seder Dime Novel Collection: Over 2,500 items.

Oral History Collection: Pioneers Foundation Tape Archive, consists of 527 tapes of reminiscences of life and popular culture of early New Mexico.

Donald Day Science Fiction Collection: Also available, as is the **Brazilian Literatura de Cordel Collection** of 1,000 volumes of *Cordel* poetry.

Cimarron

346. Philmont Museum and Seton Memorial Library
Philmont Scout Ranch
Cimarron, NM 87714

Contact: Stephen Zimmer, Dir; Annette Carlisle, Librarian
(505) 376-2281
Hours: Winter: Mon-Fri, 8-12, 1-5; Summer: daily, 8-12, 1-5

Accessible to Public: Yes
Accessible to Scholars: Yes
Special Considerations: Prior notice requested

Collections include Boy Scouts of America uniforms, 1926-present; BSA handbooks, 1910-present; Boy Scout fiction by various authors, 1900-1968, 195 vols; *Boy's Life* from 1934-1985; *Scouting* from 1929-1985; and assorted manuals, books, pamphlets, and correspondence relating to the Boy Scouts of America.

Portales

347. Eastern New Mexico University, Jack Williamson Science Fiction Library
Golden Library—Eastern New Mexico University
Portales, NM 88130

Contact: Mary Jo Walker
(505) 562-2636
Hours: Mon-Fri, 8-5; also by appointment
Accessible to Public: Yes
Accessible to Scholars: Yes
Special Considerations: Most materials do not circulate; some may have copying restrictions

Jack Williamson Science Fiction Library: Contains 8,710 books; 702 magazine titles (9,934 issues); 320 audiotaped oral history interviews; private papers from Williamson, Edmond Hamilton, Leigh Brackett, Forrest J. Ackerman, Piers Anthony, and James Blish, including correspondence, manuscripts, photographs, and memorabilia; and copy-edited manuscripts from *ANALOG*. A depository for the Science Fiction Oral History Association and Science Fiction Writers of America.

Santa Fe

348. Museum of International Folk Art Library
PO Box 2087
Santa Fe, NM 87504-2087

Contact: Judith Sellars, Librarian
(505) 827-8353
Hours: Mon-Fri, 10-12, 1-5; closed Mon during winter

Accessible to Public: Yes
Accessible to Scholars: Yes

Collections include 4,000 postcards, mostly recent, of folk costumes and other material folk culture.

Taos

349. Kit Carson Memorial Foundation
Box XXX
Taos, NM 87571

Contact: Neil Poese, Dir
(505) 758-0505
Hours: Research Center open by appointment
Accessible to Public: Yes
Accessible to Scholars: Yes

Collections are extensive and diverse; properties include the Kit Carson Home, the Blumenschein Home, and the Martinez Hacienda. Each contains articles pertinent to the history and importance of interpretation; research center contains library, photographic, and archeological materials for research.

NEW YORK

Albany

350. Film and Television Documentation Center
SUNYA, Richardson 390C—1400 Washington Ave
Albany, NY 12222

Contact: Vencent Aceto or Fred Silva
(518) 442-5745
Hours: Mon-Fri, 8:30-5
Accessible to Public: Yes
Accessible to Scholars: Yes

Collection consists of a journal collection of 175 film and television titles indexed in **Film Literature Index** from 1973-present. Document delivery service available.

351. Museum of the Historical Society of Early American Decoration
19 Dove St
Albany, NY 12210

Contact: William Jenney
(518) 462-1676
Hours: Wed-Fri, 9:30-4; Sat, 12-3; closed holiday weekends
Accessible to Public: Yes
Accessible to Scholars: Yes
Special Considerations: Use of library is by appointment only

Collection is one of the finest in the world in the areas of ornamental tin, papier mache, and wood, and is supported by a research library.

Ballston Spa

352. National Bottle Museum
Box 621
Ballston Spa, NY 12020

Contact: Joyce Spence, NBM Admin Asst; Richard Beresford, Dir
(518) 885-7589
Hours: Weekdays, 10-4; also open holidays and weekends from June-Sept
Accessible to Public: Yes
Accessible to Scholars: Yes

1890 Apothecary Shop: Contains several hundred medicine bottles, trade cards, stoneware pieces, herbs, and pieces typical of the era.

There is also a permanent doctor's office display, including more bottles, a desk with related material, and a cabinet with doctor's instruments and a doctor's bag. Exhibits include insulators, Hamiltons, Albany Tricentennial, inks, glass canes and chains, Architectural Heritage Year, figurals, Miss Liberty, and Bonney Ink.

Binghamton

353. Broome County Public Library
78 Exchange St
Binghamton, NY 13901

Contact: Mary Brigiotta, Head, Information Svcs Dept
(607) 723-6457
Hours: Mon-Thurs, 9-9; Fri-Sat, 9-5
Accessible to Public: Yes
Accessible to Scholars: Yes
Special Considerations: Restricted to use by serious researchers

Dr. Frederick W. Putnam Collection: Includes scrapbooks from 1926-1933 of clippings, photographs, trivia, programs, advertising booklets, and memorabilia on aspects of Broome County history, including churches, medicine, fraternal groups, clubs, and organizations; 126 vols.

Binghamton and Broome Co. History Pamphlet and Clipping File: Contains clippings and pamphlets related to aspects of Binghamton and Broome County, including history, industries, architecture, biographies, government, organizations, and population.

Other collections include works of local authors and old and rare books.

Bronx

354. Belmont Branch Library—Enrico Fermi Cultural Center
610 E 186th St
Bronx, NY 10458

Contact: Theresa Casile
(212) 933-6410
Hours: Mon, 10-6; Tues-Wed, 12-8;
  Thurs, 12-6; Fri, 1-6; Sat, 10-5; hours
  vary in summer and yearly
Accessible to Public: Yes
Accessible to Scholars: Yes

Italian Heritage Collection: Consists of over 5,000 circulating books in Italian covering all subjects, plus 1,500 Italian heritage reference books in English and Italian on Italian-American immigration and Italian culture. Also available are Italian videotapes, records, newspapers, magazines, and a children's collection of Italian heritage material.

355. Huntington Free Library/Library, Museum of the American Indian
9 Westchester Sq
Bronx, NY 10461

Contact: Mary B Davis, Librarian
(212) 829-7770
Hours: Mon-Sat, 10-4:30
Accessible to Public: Yes
Accessible to Scholars: Yes
Special Considerations: Call for
  appointment

American Indian Newspapers: Current and retrospective American Indian periodicals with current subscriptions to 140 Indian newspapers, ranging from the daily *Navajo Times Today* to the semiannual *American Indian Law Review*. Native publications from Canada and Central and South American countries are also collected.

Brooklyn

356. APM Library of Recorded Sound
502 E 17th St
Brooklyn, NY 11226

Contact: Allen Koenigsberg
(718) 941-6835
Hours: Mon-Fri, 9-5
Accessible to Public: Yes
Accessible to Scholars: Yes
Special Considerations: By appointment
  only

Koenigsberg Collection: Contains 60 antique phonographs; 5,000 cylinder records, 1877-1930; and books, catalogs, manuals, posters, patents, sheet music, journals, logs, and advertisements pertaining to the history of recorded sound.

357. Brooklyn College Televison Center, Whitehead Hall
Bedford Ave and Ave H
Brooklyn, NY 11210

Contact: Jill Berger
(718) 780-5558
Hours: Mon-Fri, 9-5
Accessible to Public: Yes
Accessible to Scholars: Yes
Special Considerations: Must be
  screened at the Museum of
  Broadcasting in New York

Celia Nachatovitz Diamant Memorial Library of Classic Television Commercials: Consists of 69 classic commercials from 1948-1959; a two-hour collection on quadruplex video tape, can be copied for nominal charge (contact office for details). Book by Lincoln Diamant, *Television's Classic Commercials,* contains scripts and background information on the 69 commercials.

358. Brooklyn Historical Society Library
128 Pierrepont St
Brooklyn, NY 11361

Contact: Robert Hawkins or Clara
   Lamers
(718) 624-0890
Hours: Tues-Sat, 10-4:45; closed Sun,
   Mon, and national holidays
Accessible to Public: Yes
Accessible to Scholars: Yes
Special Considerations: Donation $2
   appreciated

Postcard Collection: About 3,000 post-cards, mainly early 20th century to mid-century, of Brooklyn and European scenes.

Collections also include about 30,000 photographs with an excellent collection of turn-of-the-century photos of Coney Island and 25 baseball cards with other Brooklyn Dodgers material, as well as several hundred menus, dinner programs, and other ephemera about 19th and 20th century Brooklyn social life.

359. Brooklyn Museum Libraries
200 Eastern Pkwy
Brooklyn, NY 11238

(718) 638-5000 Ext 308
Hours: Wed-Fri, 1-4:45
Accessible to Public: Yes
Accessible to Scholars: Yes
Special Considerations: Call for
   appointment

Collections emphasize American art and culture, and include over 170,000 volumes on the Americas, Asia, the Middle East, and Africa. Special strengths include decorative arts, costumes and textiles, and paintings and sculpture; collections contain scrapbooks, photographs, and files.

Buffalo

360. Buffalo and Erie County Public Library Music Department
Lafayette Sq
Buffalo, NY 14203

Contact: Norma Jean Lamb, Head,
   Music Dept

(716) 856-7525
Hours: Mon-Wed, Fri, 8:30-6; Thurs, 8:
   30 am-9 pm
Accessible to Public: Yes
Accessible to Scholars: Yes
Special Considerations: Closed stack
   access requires ID and verification of
   institutional or project connection

American and British Sheet Music Collection: Consists of about 81,700 unbound pieces and about 32,000 pieces in 657 volumes, 1790 to date. Includes special sheet music collections: *Jack Yellen Collection* (Buffalo-born lyricist) of 138 items, *World War I Collection* of 560 items, and *Campaign and Presidential Collection* of 260 items.

19th Century Songsters Collection: Over 400 items, including 90 minstrel items housed in Library's Rare Book Room.

Other collections include over 1,500 19th century broadsides and about 17,000 78 rpm phonograph records, many popular.

361. State University of New York at Buffalo, University Archives
420 Capen Hall
Buffalo, NY 14260

Contact: Shonnie Finnegan or
   Christopher Densmore
(716) 636-2916
Hours: Mon-Fri, 9-5
Accessible to Public: Yes
Accessible to Scholars: Yes

Francis H. Striker Papers: Consists of papers from 1929-1961, over 180 volumes plus one box; scripts from the *Lone Ranger* and *Green Hornet* radio programs are featured, as well as numerous other radio scripts authored by Striker.

Historical Manuscripts Collection: Includes records of women's organizations such as the Buffalo Branch of the American Association of University Women and the Camp Fire Girls of Buffalo and Erie County. Other collections are concerned with civil rights and social reform.

Cooperstown

362. New York State Historical Association Library
PO Box 800, Lake Rd
Cooperstown, NY 13326

Contact: Eileen O'Brien, Special
  Collections Librarian
(607) 547-2509
Hours: Mon-Fri, 9-5; Sat, 1-5
Accessible to Public: Yes
Accessible to Scholars: Yes

Collections include the *Louis C Jones
Folklore Archives, Harold W Thompson
Folklore Archives, Cooperstown Graduate
Program Archives, Ephemera Collection,
Broadside Collection, Trade Catalogue
Collection, Postcard Collection,* and *Local
History Collection.*

Corning

363. The Rakow Library, Corning Museum of Glass
1 Museum Way
Corning, NY 14830-2253

Contact: Virginia Wright, Assoc
  Librarian; Norma Jenkins, Head
  Librarian
(607) 937-5371
Hours: Mon-Fri, 9-5; closed Christmas
  week and holidays
Accessible to Public: Yes
Accessible to Scholars: Yes
Special Considerations: Although there
  are no restrictions, an advance phone
  call or letter will enable the staff to
  help the researcher make the most of
  her/his time at the Library

Collections include glass company trade
catalogs, with 3,500 on microfiche. Many
originals were borrowed for filming. All
of the Library's originals are reserved for
use when a publication needing illustrations is in process; "flat work" may be
requested at that time.

Deansboro

364. Musical Museum
Deansboro, NY 13328

(315) 841-8774
Hours: Apr-Dec 31, daily, 10-4
Accessible to Public: Yes
Accessible to Scholars: Yes

Collection includes music boxes, melo-
deons, nickelodeons, grind organs, and
other musical materials. The Old Lam-
plighter Shop at the Museum contains
antique lamps plus other memorabilia.
The Reed Organ Society, Inc. is head-
quartered at the Museum.

Flushing

365. Queens College, Ethnic Materials Information Exchange
Graduate Library School, Kiely Hall, Rm
  215
Flushing, NY 11367

Contact: David Cohen, Dir
(718) 520-7139, 520-7194
Hours: Mon, 9-5; Wed, 9-5; Fri, 9-5
Accessible to Public: Yes
Accessible to Scholars: Yes
Special Considerations: Collections open
  to faculty, students, and local
  residents

Collections include several thousand volumes and audiovisual materials that focus on multiethnic materials, including
works by and about all ethnic and minority groups.

Fredonia

366. SUNY College at Fredonia, Reed Library
Fredonia, NY 14063

Contact: John P Saulitis, Dir of Library
  Svcs
(716) 673-3183
Hours: Mon-Fri, 8:30 am-11 pm; Sat, 11-
  6; Sun, 1-11 pm; hours vary during
  summer and semester breaks
Accessible to Public: Yes
Accessible to Scholars: Yes
Special Considerations: Materials do not
  circulate

Local History Collection: Includes 1,000 postcards of Chautauqua County, New York, 400 trade cards, and 150 novels by Chautauqua County authors, including Grace Richmond, Jean Webster, Harry Castleman, and "Pansy" (Mrs. G. R. Alden).

Music Library: Contains about 2,000 items of popular sheet music from the 1920s-1940s, as well as 200 items of silent film music and 1,500 items of dance band orchestrations of popular music from the 1920s-1940s.

Goshen

367. Trotting Horse Museum, Inc
PO Box 590
Goshen, NY 10924

Contact: Philip A Pines, Dir
(914) 294-6330
Hours: Daily, 10-5; Sun, holidays, 12-5
Accessible to Public: Yes
Accessible to Scholars: Yes

Collections include 175 authentic lithographs, mainly Currier & Ives; materials devoted exclusively to the American trotting horse with reference books from 19th and 20th centuries on same.

Hyde Park

368. Franklin D. Roosevelt Library and Museum
259 Albany Post Rd
Hyde Park, NY 12538

Contact: Raymond Teichman (Archives), Sheryl Griffith (Library), or Alycia Vivona (Museum)
(914) 229-8114
Hours: Weekdays, 9-4:45; closed national holidays, Thanksgiving, Christmas, and New Year's Day
Accessible to Public: Yes
Accessible to Scholars: Yes
Special Considerations: Application form required; under 16, accompanied by adult

FDR's Naval Book Collection: Consists of 150 volumes of 19th century shipwreck narratives, sea chanties, tales of seafaring life, and popular biographies of naval heroes.

Juvenile Book Collection: Includes 650 chapbooks, dime novels, and 18th to early 20th century books.

Other collections include a general book collection of about 500 popular novels, annuals and gift books from the 19th to early 20th centuries, and a collection of 700 scrapbooks, including political cartoons, Christmas cards, major events, and public figures of the Roosevelt period.

Ithaca

369. Ithaca College School of Communications
Ithaca College
Ithaca, NY 14850

Contact: Thomas W Bohn, Dean
(607) 274-3242
Hours: Mon-Fri, 8:30-5; Other hours by appointment
Accessible to Public: Yes
Accessible to Scholars: Yes
Special Considerations: Twilight Zone videotapes (3/4") are available to researchers and the general public during business hours

Rod Serling Archives: Represents the largest collection of Serling material in existence, and consists of items related to all aspects of his career. Nearly all *Twilight Zone* episodes are included (3/4" videotape), kinescopes and/or 16mm prints of other episodes of *Twilight Zone* and *Night Gallery*, interviews with Serling and producer Buck Houghton, original copies of most *Twilight Zone* scripts, and assorted books and items of memorabilia related to Serling.

New York

370. American Bible Society Library
1865 Broadway
New York, NY 10023

Contact: Alexander Plaza
(212) 581-7400
Hours: Mon-Fri, 9:30-4:30
Accessible to Public: Yes
Accessible to Scholars: Yes
Special Considerations: Closed stacks; noncirculating

Includes more than 35,000 Bibles and Testaments in 1,700 languages, dating from Gutenberg to the present.

371. American Irish Historical Society
991 5th Ave
New York, NY 10028

Contact: Damian Doyle
(212) 288-2263
Hours: Mon-Fri, 10-5
Accessible to Public: Yes
Accessible to Scholars: Yes

Collection includes substantial primary source documents, such as the records of the Society, the Society of the Friendly Sons of St Patrick, the Friends of Irish Freedom, the Catholic Club, and the Guild of Catholic Lawyers. There are also records of personal papers of Daniel F. Cohalan and the Rev. Donald M. O'Callahan.

372. Archives of Contemporary Music
110 Chambers St
New York, NY 10017

Contact: David Wheeler; Zach Snow
(212) 964-2296 or (212) 619-3505
Accessible to Public: No
Accessible to Scholars: Yes
Special Considerations: By appointment only

Collection includes 150,000 records, press kits, interviews, literature, and other materials relating to the recording industry. Material also available on-line via modem.

373. Australian Information Service, Australian Consulate-General
636 5th Ave
New York, NY 10111

Contact: Contact Librarian
(212) 245-4000
Hours: Mon-Fri, 9-1, 2-5
Accessible to Public: No
Accessible to Scholars: No
Special Considerations: Report to receptionist at front desk

Collection includes books, maps, newspapers, statistics, etc. on either Australia or by Australians.

374. City College Library, Archives and Special Collections
City College Library
New York, NY 10031

Contact: Barbara J Dunlap
(212) 690-5357
Hours: Mon-Fri, 1-5; by appointment
Accessible to Public: Yes
Accessible to Scholars: Yes

Collections include memorabilia collections of some faculty and alumni; also a collection of albums of travel postcards from about 1900.

375. Columbia University, Alfred I. duPont-Columbia University Awards in Broadcast Journalism
701 Journalism—Columbia University
New York, NY 10027

Contact: Janet West, Assoc Dir
(212) 280-5047
Hours: Mon-Fri, 9-5
Accessible to Public: Yes
Accessible to Scholars: Yes
Special Considerations: Call ahead to reserve tapes

Collection includes a videotape library of award-winning television and radio news and public affairs broadcasts; over 900 programs, 1968-present.

376. Columbia University Oral History Research Office
Box 20, Butler Library
New York, NY 10027

Contact: Ronald J Grele, Dir
(212) 280-4012
Hours: Mon-Fri, 9-5; closed holidays
Accessible to Public: Yes
Accessible to Scholars: Yes
Special Considerations: Some materials may be restricted

Collections include *Popular Arts Project, Radio Pioneers Project, Hollywood Film Industry Project* (in process), *Children's Television Workshop Project, American Cultural Leaders Project, Book-of-the-Month-Club Project, Mercury Theater/ Theater Union Project* (in process), and *New York's Art World Project.*

377. Franklin Furnace Archive Inc
112 Franklin St
New York, NY 10013

Contact: Martha Wilson
(212) 925-4671
Hours: Tues-Sat, 12-6
Accessible to Public: Yes
Accessible to Scholars: Yes
Special Considerations: By appointment only

Largest public archive of its kind in U.S., containing over 18,000 artists' books, periodicals, postcards, cassette tapes, records, pamphlets, broadsides, and other ephemera published as artworks by artists from all over the world.

378. International Count Dracula Fan Club
29 Washington Sq W—Penthouse N
New York, NY 10011

Contact: Dr M Jeanne Youngson, Pres
(212) 533-5018
Hours: By appointment
Accessible to Public: Yes
Accessible to Scholars: Yes
Special Considerations: Please contact Dr Youngson by mail

Vampire and Horror Memorabilia Collection: Includes autographed photos of Bela Lugosi, Boris Karloff, Christopher Lee, Peter Cushing, Lon Chaney Jr, Vincent Price, and others; also Dracula masks and figurines, statuettes, horror records and cassettes, puzzles, candles, buttons, pins, car plaques, wallets, assorted games, make-up kits, jewelry, bats, fangs, selected comic books, fanzines, movie stills, and related horror memorabilia.

379. Italian Cultural Institute
686 Park Ave
New York, NY 10021

Contact: Maria A Gargotta
(212) 879-4242
Hours: Mon-Fri, 9-1, 2-5
Accessible to Public: Yes
Accessible to Scholars: Yes

Collection consists of about 20,000 books on all aspects of Italy and Italian culture, including books on Italian folklore.

380. J. Walter Thompson Company Archives
466 Lexington Ave
New York, NY 10017

Contact: Cynthia G Swank, Archivist
(212) 210-7123
Hours: Mon-Fri, 9-5; by advance appointment only
Accessible to Public: Yes
Accessible to Scholars: Yes
Special Considerations: Users must arrange an appointment in advance

This archive houses advertisements created by the company, 1875-present (bulk are U.S. dating from 1910-present; some are international and date from the late 1920s-early 1930s and from the 1960s-present), and includes 1.3 million items. Also included are radio and television programs produced by the company, 1930-1960 (200 reels of microfilm); 50 microfilm reels of research studies, 1915-1943 (demographics, consumer studies, trade, media); company newsletters, 1916-present (27 cubic feet); and company publications, 1887-present (24 cubic feet).

381. Morris N. and Chesley V. Young Mnemonics Library
270 Riverside Dr, 8C
New York, NY 10038

(212) 227-4714
Hours: By appointment only
Accessible to Public: No
Accessible to Scholars: Yes

Collections on mnemonics are extensive, and include a collection of the *Medieval Art of Memory*; collection of medical aspects of memory, amnesia, and dyslexia; and a *Remembrance Cups and Memory Mementos Collection.* Includes over 1,700 printed monographs on memory, over 2,000 serial articles, and over 500 items of memorabilia, such as posters, engravings, handbills, advertisements, birthday cards, phonograph records, and *Mark Twain's Memory Builder Game.*

382. New York Public Library, Research Libraries
5th Ave and 2nd St
New York, NY 10018

Contact: Faye Simkin, Chief Librarian, Admin Svcs

(212) 930-0583
Hours: Hours vary
Accessible to Public: Yes
Accessible to Scholars: Yes
Special Considerations: Admission card
    required for Special Collections; users
    should be over age 18

Holdings are extensive, and are described in Sam P. Williams' *Guide to the Research Collections of the New York Public Library.*

383. New York Public Library at Lincoln Center, General Library and Museum of the Performing Arts

111 Amsterdam Ave
New York, NY 10023

(212) 870-1627 (Dance/Drama/Arts Admin); (212) 870-1625 (Music); (212) 870-1629 (Records); or (212) 870-1633 (Children's Room)
Hours: Mon, Thurs, 10-8; Tues, 10-7;
    Wed, Fri, 12-6; Sat, 10-6; hours vary
    in summer and yearly
Accessible to Public: Yes
Accessible to Scholars: Yes

Billy Rose Theater Collection: Includes a comprehensive collection of stage plays, screen plays, teleplays, and radio plays in both print and audio formats; extensive clipping files of reviews and articles.

Dance Collection: Consists of books, scores, records, and cassettes on all forms of dance, both theatrical and social; large clipping collection.

Arts Administration Collection: Consists of books, pamphlets, and other materials related to aspects of arts administration and funding.

Video Collection: Consists of VHS videos on the performing arts, as well as a collection of children's and family videos.

Music Collection: Includes many book titles on popular culture, youth culture, and popular and show-biz music. A score collection contains hundreds of largely American popular songs from 1890s to present. Also a collection of Broadway musicals, as well as an extensive clippings file.

Children's Room Collection: Consists of performing arts material for children and adults working with children, and includes material on circus, puppetry, and story-telling in addition to basic material in theater, dance, and music; nearly 10,000 recordings on LP and cassette relating to children. Also a permanent exhibit on Elsie Leslie, popular 19th century child actress. Collection of puppets and toy theaters available.

There is also an extensive record collection (13,000 recordings) of historical and current popular music and traditional and popular folk music, as well as books and periodicals in each area.

384. New York University, Tamiment Institute Library/ Robert F. Wagner Labor Archives

70 Washington Sq S
New York, NY 10003

Contact: Dorothy Swanson, Head
    Librarian
(212) 598-3708
Accessible to Public: Yes
Accessible to Scholars: Yes

Collections include papers of individuals associated with the Left and trade union organizations and the records of labor unions.

385. N.W. Ayer Incorporated Archives

1345 Ave of the Americas
New York, NY 10105

Contact: Annamarie V Sandecki,
    Archivist
(212) 708-5575
Hours: Mon-Fri, 9-5
Accessible to Public: Yes
Accessible to Scholars: Yes
Special Considerations: Prior
    appointment is necessary to use
    collections

The materials in the collection relate to the history of N. W. Ayer Inc., one of the oldest advertising agencies in the nation (founded in 1869). Also includes material related to the history of Newell-Emmett (later Cunningham and Walsh). Items available include advertisements (approximately 150,000), newsletters (six cubic feet), company produced publications, and biographical and client files.

386. Research Foundation for Jewish Immigration
570 Seventh Ave, 16th Fl
New York, NY 10018

Contact: Dennis E Rohrbaugh, Archivist
(212) 921-3871, 921-3873
Hours: Mon-Fri, By Appointment
Accessible to Public: Yes
Accessible to Scholars: Yes
Special Considerations: Written and
telephone appointments and inquiries
are accepted; qualification for use of
collections determined by staff

Archival Collection: Consists of biographical data on 25,000 German-speak-
ing individuals who fled Nazi persecution
in Central Europe during the years 1933-
1945, and their world-wide immigration,
including both published material and
personal information provided by emigres and their relatives.

Oral History Collection: Contains
transcriptions of 275 taped interviews
with German-Jewish emigres to the
United States and their children.

387. Shubert Archive
145 W 45th St—Lyceum Theatre
New York, NY 10036

Contact: Brigitte Kueppers
(212) 944-3895
Hours: By appointment only
Accessible to Public: No
Accessible to Scholars: Yes
Special Considerations: Apply to use
materials

Collections include papers, photographs,
paintings, and memorabilia related to
the Shuberts and their careers as producers and managers in the late 19th
and early 20th century; includes scripts,
legal and financial records, costume designs, and music.

388. Statue of Liberty National Monument—American Museum of Immigration Library and Archives
Liberty Island
New York, NY 10004

Contact: Won H Kim, Librarian; Diana
Pardue, Museum Curator
(212) 363-3279 or (212) 363-3200

Hours: Library: Mon-Fri, 9:30-5;
Museum: Mon-Fri, 9:30-5; Sat-Sun, 9:
30-6; winter hours in effect after Oct
31, Sat-Sun, 9:30-5
Accessible to Public: Yes
Accessible to Scholars: Yes
Special Considerations: By appointment
only; items do not circulate

Book Collection: About 2,000 books,
manuscripts, reports, and studies with
subject emphasis on Ellis Island immigration and the Statue of Liberty National Monument.

Photographic Collection: Consists of
historic photographs and slides of the
Statue of Liberty and Ellis Island, including a collection by Augustus F. Sherman of photographs of immigrants who
passed through Ellis Island between 1892
and 1925 (140 prints).

Oral History Collection: Tapes (about
400) and transcripts that include interviews with immigrants who passed
through Ellis Island between 1892 and
1954.

Also available is a collection of about 50
16mm films about the Statue of Liberty
and Ellis Island immigration. Museum
contains items of Statue of Liberty
memorabilia, as well as passports, immigrant native costumes, household
items brought to America by immigrants, prayer books, sheet music, posters, trade cards, and other ephemera.

389. William E. Wiener Oral History Library of the American Jewish Committee
165 E 56th St
New York, NY 10022

Contact: Muriel Robbins
(212) 751-4000
Hours: Mon-Fri, 9:30-5:30
Accessible to Public: No
Accessible to Scholars: Yes
Special Considerations: By appointment
only

Collections include 1,700 memoirs of
well-known American Jews, as well as
Jews in sports and broadcasting, and
Jews of Lower East Side. Also collections on 250 survivors of the Holocaust
in America, recent Soviet emigres to
America, and a special collection on civil
rights. Transcripts available on site only.

Northport

390. Northport Public Library
151 Laurel Ave
Northport, NY 11768

Contact: Victoria Wallace, Dir
(516) 261-6930
Hours: Mon-Fri, 9-9; Sat, 9-5; Sun, mid-Sept to mid-June, 1-5
Accessible to Public: Yes
Accessible to Scholars: Yes
Special Considerations: Kerouac manuscript can be seen Mon-Fri, 9-5; also by appointment

Oral History Collection: Consists of tapes of Northport and East Northport senior citizens' reminiscences; about 30 interviews.

Manuscript of *The Town and The City* by Jack Kerouac also available.

Oneonta

391. James M. Milne Library Special Collections Center
SUC at Oneonta
Oneonta, NY 13820

Contact: Diane A Clark
(607) 431-3702
Hours: Mon-Fri, 8-4:30
Accessible to Public: Yes
Accessible to Scholars: Yes
Special Considerations: Items do not circulate

Collections include *Early Textbook and Educational Theory Collections, Popular Fiction Collection, Lantern Slide Collection.*

Oswego

392. State University of New York, College at Oswego, Penfield Library Special Collections
State University of New York, College at Oswego
Oswego, NY 13126

Contact: Judith Wellman and Nancy Osborne, Co-coords, Special Collections

(315) 341-3110 or (315) 341-4233
Hours: Mon, Thurs, 1:30-4:30; also by appointment
Accessible to Public: Yes
Accessible to Scholars: Yes
Special Considerations: Preferable for researcher to visit during open hours during semester; appointments also available

Local and Regional History Collections: Consists of printed, manuscript, photographic, and oral records pertaining to the history of Oswego and the surrounding area.

Oral History Program of Oswego County: Consists of oral history tapes pertaining to area.

Owego

393. Tioga County Historical Society Museum
110-112 Front St
Owego, NY 13827

Contact: William Lay, Jr, Curator
(607) 687-2460
Hours: Tues-Fri, 10-12; Tues-Sun, 1:30-4:30; Wed, 7-9pm
Accessible to Public: Yes
Accessible to Scholars: Yes
Special Considerations: Stored material retrieved by staff on request

Collections include "Mischief Cards" and advertising cards from the latter 19th century, greeting cards, postcards, and photographs reflecting life in the late 19th and early 20th centuries, children's books from that era, and oral history tapes containing personal reminiscences of life in Tioga County in bygone days.

Palmyra

394. Historic Palmyra, Inc
PO Box 96
Palmyra, NY 14522

Contact: Richard V Palmer, Exec Dir
(315) 597-6981
Hours: Daily, 9-5, June-mid-Sept; also by appointment
Accessible to Public: Yes
Accessible to Scholars: Yes

Alling Coverlet Collection: Consists of over 200 hand-woven and machine-made coverlets, virtually all 19th century and American-made. There is a related collection of quilts.

Rochester

395. International Museum of Photography at George Eastman House
900 East Ave
Rochester, NY 14607

Contact: David Wooters, Print Archivist
(716) 271-3361
Hours: Tues, 9:30-12, 1:15-4:30
Accessible to Public: Yes
Accessible to Scholars: Yes
Special Considerations: By appointment only

Collection includes over 350,000 photographs for the study of the history of photography; access by photographer's name, not by subject. Materials predominantly 19th century photography.

396. Sibley Music Library, Eastman School of Music
University of Rochester
Rochester, NY 14604

Contact: Charles Lindahl
(716) 275-5789
Hours: Mon-Thurs, 8am-10pm; Fri, 8-5; Sat, 11-5; Sun, 1-9; hours vary during school breaks
Accessible to Public: Yes
Accessible to Scholars: Yes

Popular American Sheet Music Collection: Consists of sheet music from 1790s-1940s, most before 1900; about 75,000 items, including 700 items of Civil War music. Uncataloged.

Collection of about 700 uncataloged piano rolls, 1900-1930, also available.

397. Strong Museum
One Manhattan Sq
Rochester, NY 14607

Contact: William T Alderson, Dir
(716) 263-2700
Hours: Tues-Sat, 10-5; Sun, 1-5; closed Mon, Thanksgiving, Christmas, and New Year's; Library Hours: Tues-Fri, 10-5
Accessible to Public: Yes
Accessible to Scholars: Yes
Special Considerations: Special collections by appointment; for information on specific holdings, contact library

Collections consist of more than 300,000 objects relating to domestic life in middle-class America from 1820-1940; includes household furnishings, accessories, dolls, toys, doll houses, and oriental artifacts, as well as 4,000 trade catalogs and advertising pieces and 8,000 slides.

398. University of Rochester Library, Department of Rare Books and Special Collections
University of Rochester Library
Rochester, NY 14627

Contact: Peter Dzwonkoski, Head
(716) 275-4477 or (716) 275-4494
Hours: Mon-Fri, 9-5
Accessible to Public: Yes
Accessible to Scholars: Yes
Special Considerations: Advance notice preferred

Collections are varied and extensive, including 20,000 photographs, 320 stereo views, 200 prints of 19th century upstate New York, 1,300 postcards, 25 postcard albums, 500 trade cards, 1,500 broadsides, 6,500 theater programs, 300 almanacs, 10,000 dime novels from about 1860-1915, 2,400 children's books, 1,000 filmed books, and 500 textbooks. Collections are strongest in 19th century and New York-area holdings.

399. Victorian Doll Museum
4332 Buffalo Rd
Rochester, NY 14514

Contact: Linda Greenfield
(716) 247-0130
Hours: Tues-Sat, 10-4:30; Sun, 1-4:30; closed Mon, holidays, and month of Jan
Accessible to Public: Yes
Accessible to Scholars: Yes
Special Considerations: Dolls not removed from display settings

Collection includes hundreds of dolls of bisque, china, wood, wax, metal, felt, ivory, and papier mache; includes Kewpie dolls, paper dolls, Schoenhut Dolls and Circus, Noah's Ark, toys, and an action puppet theater. There are dolls representing famous personalities of comics, literature, movies, history, medicine, fashion, and advertising.

Rye Brook

400. Museum of Cartoon Art

Comly Ave
Rye Brook, NY 10573

Contact: Chuck Green
(914) 939-0234
Hours: Tues-Fri, 10-4; Sun, 1-5
Accessible to Public: Yes
Accessible to Scholars: Yes
Special Considerations: By appointment only

Collections are extensive, and include videotaped interviews with famous artists, 60,000 original cartoons in archives, an extensive research library, lectures by famous artists, over 60 hours of cartoons on videotape, a film collection, an extensive comic book collection, and an official Cartoon Hall of Fame.

Saratoga Springs

401. National Museum of Racing, Inc

Union Ave
Saratoga Springs, NY 12866

Contact: Mrs Elaine E Mann, Asst to Pres; Mrs Ann D Genaro, Dir
(518) 584-0400
Hours: Hours vary
Accessible to Public: Yes
Accessible to Scholars: Yes
Special Considerations: Library facilities by appointment only; not available during Aug racing season

Collection includes 200 books on the history of thoroughbred racing as well as the history of the horse in art.

Seneca Falls

402. Seneca Falls Historical Society

55 Cayuga St
Seneca Falls, NY 13148

Contact: Ed Polk Douglas, Exec Dir
(315) 568-8412
Hours: Business: Mon-Fri, 9:30-4:30; Visitors: Mon-Fri, 1-4; Library: same or by appointment
Accessible to Public: Yes
Accessible to Scholars: Yes
Special Considerations: Library on third floor; no handicapped access to second or third floors

Collections include local history items (primarily Seneca County with some overlap into adjoining counties of upstate New York), and a *Women's Studies Collection* containing materials relative to the organizers of the Women's Rights Convention of 1848, and genealogy.

Stony Brook

403. Museum at Stony Brook

1208 Route 25A
Stony Brook, NY 11790

Contact: Lilita Bergs
751-0066
Hours: Wed-Sat, 10-5; Sun, 12-5
Accessible to Public: Yes
Accessible to Scholars: Yes
Special Considerations: Carriage Reference Library and archives open by appointment only

Carriage Collection: Consists of 250 horse-drawn vehicles, including carriages, sleighs for personal and public transportation, trade, fire-fighting, and some children's vehicles, as well as vehicle accessories, tools, harnesses, and luggage; predominantly American, 18th to early 20th century, with some European. 100 vehicles on display; rest by appointment.

Carriage Reference Library: Includes over 2,000 items of rare books, trade catalogs, periodicals, advertising, carriage-related art, original design drawings, and 20th century references.

Art Collection and Archives: Consists of paintings, drawings, and personal papers of 19th century American genre painter William S. Mount; includes works by other 19th century artists such as William M. Davis, Edward Lamson Henry, Edward Lange, and Charles Henry Miller.

Syracuse

404. Syracuse University, George Arents Research Library for Special Collections

Rm 600 Bird Library—Syracuse
  University
Syracuse, NY 13244-2010

Contact: Carolyn Davis, Manuscript
  Librarian
(315) 423-2697
Hours: Mon-Fri, 8:30-5; closed some
  holidays
Accessible to Public: Yes
Accessible to Scholars: Yes
Special Considerations: ID required;
  access forms; advance appointment

Street and Smith Collection: Consists
of predominantly published periodicals,
some novels, late 19th to mid-20th century; some internal records pertaining to
periodical publishing, but collection lacks
editorial and author correspondence.
Also present are radio scripts for *Shadow, Nick Carter, Chick Carter, Doc Savage,* and *Avenger.*

Gertrude Berg Collection: Consists of
about 80 linear feet of radio scripts and
scrapbooks pertaining to Mrs. Berg's career as "Molly" in the program *Molly
and the Goldbergs.*

Utica

405. Munson-Williams-Proctor Institute, Museum of Art

310 Genesee St
Utica, NY 13501

Contact: Christopher Bensch, Asst
  Curator of Decorative Arts
(315) 797-0000
Hours: Tues-Sat, 10-5; Sun, 1-5
Accessible to Public: Yes
Accessible to Scholars: Yes
Special Considerations: Researchers
  should call for advance appointment
  for materials not on display

Photograph Collection: Consists of
Williams and Proctor family photographs from about 1860-1930; over 2,000
photos and 45 bound volumes cataloged
by subject.

Other collections include 800 postcards,
100 stereoscope cards, 150 examples of
central New York stoneware, 70 souvenir
spoons, 125 thimbles, and 120 decks of
playing cards, plus 300 items of silver by
New York silversmiths (primarily
spoons) and a collection of 289 watches
and other timepieces.

Vestal

406. Vestal Museum—Vestal Historical Society

Vestal Pkwy W
Vestal, NY 13850

Contact: Mrs Ann Marie Rose, Pres
(607) 785-8288
Hours: Sat, 1-4; Sun, 2-5
Accessible to Public: Yes
Accessible to Scholars: Yes

Collections include railroad memorabilia,
clothing, furniture, toys, cards, and pictures; also an exhibit on the art of
mourning, among others.

West Sayville

407. Suffolk Marine Museum

PO Box 144
West Sayville, NY 11796

Contact: Ruth Dougherty
(516) 567-1733
Hours: Mon-Sat, 10-3; Sun, 12-4; closed
  on Mon during winter
Accessible to Public: Yes
Accessible to Scholars: Yes
Special Considerations: Library by
  appointment only

Collections include exhibits of seamen's
crafts, shipwreck artifacts, model building, shellfishing, and the lifesaving service. Also includes the William Rudolph
Oyster House containing materials on
the oyster industry and the local Dutch
community. Library contains related
books, clippings, periodicals, and photographs.

NORTH CAROLINA

Bailey

408. The Country Doctor Museum
PO Box 34
Bailey, NC 27807

Contact: Paul Crellin, Curator
(919) 235-4165
Hours: Sun-Thurs, 2-5; also by
    appointment
Accessible to Public: Yes
Accessible to Scholars: Yes

Collections consist of oral history tapes
of old doctors' reminiscences of medicine
in the 19th and early 20th century and
several pharmacy account books of that
era.

Boiling Springs

409. Gardner-Webb College, Thomas Dixon Room
Gardner-Webb College
Boiling Springs, NC 28017

Contact: M S Lynn Carpenter-Keeter,
    Asst to Library Dir
Accessible to Public: Yes
Accessible to Scholars: Yes
Special Considerations: Ask for access

Collection includes hundreds of books
belonging to Thomas Dixon, Jr.; some
include marginalia by this author of *The
Clansman* and co-scriptor of *The Birth
of a Nation,* as well as memorabilia in
the form of offprints, news articles, and
photographs.

Boone

410. Appalachian State University, W. L. Eury Appalachian Collection
University Hall—Appalachian State
    University
Boone, NC 28608

Contact: E J Olson, Librarian
(704) 262-4041
Hours: Mon-Thurs, 8-9; Fri, 8-5; Sat, 9-
    1; Sun, 5-9
Accessible to Public: Yes
Accessible to Scholars: Yes

Collections consist of Appalachian materials relating to highland portions of
Virginia, West Virginia, Kentucky, North
Carolina, Tennessee, South Carolina,
Georgia, and Alabama; include 13,000
volumes of monographs and periodicals,
100 hours of videotape, 500 hours of
audiotape, 800 phonograph records,
1,500 prints and slides, 800 reels of microfilm, 1,200 microfiche, 200 maps, and
100 linear feet of manuscript and vertical files.

Chapel Hill

411. University of North Carolina at Chapel Hill, Music Library
Hill Hall 020-1—University of North
    Carolina
Chapel Hill, NC 27514

Contact: Ida Reed, Music Librarian
(919) 966-1113
Hours: Mon-Thurs, 8-10; Fri, 8-5; Sat, 8-
    5; Sun, 2-10; during breaks and
    summer session: Mon-Fri, 8-5
Accessible to Public: Yes
Accessible to Scholars: Yes

Early American Music Collection:
Consists of 108 volumes of early American imprints, including a strong collection of Confederate imprints.

Folklore Cassette Collection: Contact
Prof Daniel Patterson, Curriculum of
Folklore, UNC-CH, for information.

Protest Song Collection: Available in
the Undergraduate Library, UNC-CH.

Charlotte

412. University of North Carolina at Charlotte, Atkins Library
University of North Carolina at
    Charlotte
Charlotte, NC 28223

Contact: Robin Brabham, Special
    Collections Librarian
(704) 547-2449
Hours: Mon-Fri, 8-5
Accessible to Public: Yes
Accessible to Scholars: Yes

Rare Book Collection: Includes first
editions of songs by Stephen Foster;

mid-19th century American gift books; 19th century American periodicals, especially those for children; and nearly 1,000 volumes of historical children's books, about half of which are early 19th century American publications.

Comic Books: Contains about 700 individual issues from the 1960s, primarily for boys.

Manuscript Collection: Includes small collection of papers of Wilbur Macey Stone, a collector of children's books; papers of Harry Golden, editor of the *Carolina Israelite*, 1944-1968 and best-selling author of the 1950s; and political ephemera, especially of North Carolina since 1940.

Oral History Collection: Consists of tapes of senior citizens recalling life in Charlotte, North Carolina, in early 20th century.

Durham

413. Foundation for Research on the Nature of Man/Institute for Parapsychology
PO Box 6847, College Station
Durham, NC 27708

Contact: R Jeffrey Munson, Public Info Officer
(919) 688-8241
Hours: Mon-Wed, 9-5
Accessible to Public: Yes
Accessible to Scholars: Yes
Special Considerations: By appointment only

Collection includes 2,500 volumes on psychical research, parapsychology, dreams, hypnosis, religion, and philosophy; includes current scientific journals of parapsychology and psychology.

Fayetteville

414. Fayetteville State University, Chestnut Library Archives
1200 Murchison Rd
Fayetteville, NC 28301

Contact: Ellen Anderson
(919) 486-1613
Hours: Weekdays, 9-4:30

Accessible to Public: Yes
Accessible to Scholars: Yes
Special Considerations: Most materials do not circulate; retrieved by staff

Collections include 1,100 books by and about Blacks and 50 titles of Black journals and periodicals.

415. North Carolina Foreign Language Center—Cumberland County Public Library and Information Center
300 Maiden Ln
Fayetteville, NC 28301

Contact: Mr Lee A Krieger
(919) 483-5022
Hours: Mon-Thurs, 9-9; Fri-Sat, 9-6; Sun, 2-6; closed Sun, June-Aug
Accessible to Public: Yes
Accessible to Scholars: Yes
Special Considerations: Materials available through interlibrary loan in some cases

Collections include over 30,000 titles in over 125 languages, emphasizing popular literature in native languages and children's books. Also over 2,700 audio-visual items available, including recordings of traditional, folk, and popular music from around the world, as well as recordings of prose, poetry, and drama in native languages.

Greensboro

416. University of North Carolina at Greensboro, Jackson Library, Special Collections Division
University of North Carolina at Greensboro
Greensboro, NC 27412

Contact: Emilie W Mills, Special Collections Librarian
(919) 334-5246
Hours: Mon-Fri, 8-5
Accessible to Public: Yes
Accessible to Scholars: Yes
Special Considerations: Serious research only

Early Children's Books: Consists of 2,000 volumes of English and American children's books from about 1750-1850;

emphasis on illustrated books that both teach and entertain, and includes chapbooks, toybooks, thumb Bibles, and books with color lithographs.

American Trade Binding Collection: Consists of 1,000 examples of trade bindings produced in North America from the 18th-20th centuries; emphasis on decorated cloth, signed bindings, and includes works of Margaret Armstrong, George Wharton Edwards, Theodore B. Hapgood, and others.

Woman's Detective Fiction Collection: An adjunct to the 5,000-volume *Woman's Collection* of books by, about, and of interest to women, dating from the 1500s to the end of the 19th century. Detective fiction portion consists of about 500 items, beginning with first American work of detective fiction written by a woman, continuing to 1967; works are by female authors or feature female sleuth, and include works by Charlotte and Margaret Armstrong, Mignon Eberhart, Earl Stanley Gardner, Anna Katherine Green, and others.

Girls Books in Series Collection: Consists of about 500 items representing 150 different series, including Bobbsey Twins, Bunny Brown, Campfire Girls, Nancy Drew, Elsie, and Pansy.

Graphic Ephemera Collection: Consists of about 1,000 items, including old Valentines, greeting cards, rewards of merit, postcards of the early 20th century, postage stamps, tobacco labels, broadsides, printing blocks, and miscellaneous printed nonbook materials.

Pinehurst

417. World Golf Hall of Fame, Inc
PO Box 1908
Pinehurst, NC 28374

Contact: Eugene Whittle, Exec Dir; Ray Davis, Curator
(919) 295-6651
Hours: Daily, 9-5; closed Dec 1-Mar 1
Accessible to Public: Yes
Accessible to Scholars: Yes

Collection includes equipment, photos, memorabilia, and other ephemera pertaining to the sport of golf.

Winston-Salem

418. Moravian Music Foundation
20 Cascade Ave
Winston-Salem, NC 27017

Contact: Karoly Kope, Dir; Chi-Chi Messick, Office Coord
(919) 725-0651
Hours: Mon-Fri, 9-4
Accessible to Public: Yes
Accessible to Scholars: Yes

Collections are extensive, including the *Salem Congregation Collection* of 1,500 manuscript compositions dating between 1770-1840 and the *Irving Lowens Collection* of about 1,000 tunebooks and hymnals dating from the 1700s to the early 1900s. Materials pertain to the development of music in early America, especially as it concerns the spread of Moravian music.

419. Old Salem, Inc.
Drawer F, Salem Station
Winston-Salem, NC 27108

Contact: Contact Curator
Not available
Hours: Mon-Fri, 9-5
Accessible to Public: Yes
Accessible to Scholars: Yes
Special Considerations: Write in advance for particulars and for appointment

Collections predate 1840 and include articles made in Salem or vicinity, especially items pertaining to the Moravian Church and early American life.

NORTH DAKOTA

Fargo

420. North Dakota Institute for Regional Studies
North Dakota State University Library
Fargo, ND 58105

Contact: John E Bye
(701) 237-8914
Hours: Mon-Fri, 8-5
Accessible to Public: Yes
Accessible to Scholars: Yes

Special Considerations: Researchers sign formal agreement for use; no material can be photocopied

North Dakota State University Folklore Collection Records, 1978-1985: Collection of 2,394 items includes a wide variety of folklore items reflecting the major genres (superstitions, folk medicine, legends, proverbs, jokes, riddles, folk speech, holiday traditions, weatherlore, folk architecture, cookery, crafts, etc.); bulk of collection consists of single-sheet folklore data forms, which provide a description of the individual item plus important contextual information. Nearly all items collected in North Dakota and western Minnesota.

OHIO

Athens

421. Ohio University, Vernon R. Alden Library
Park Place
Athens, OH 45701

Contact: Contact Special Collections Librarian
(614) 593-2710
Hours: Mon-Fri, 8-5
Accessible to Public: Yes
Accessible to Scholars: Yes

MSS 11: Presidential Campaign Artifacts: Collection of American campaign memorabilia, including cartoons, badges, photographs, and various artifacts.

Children's Literature Collection: Varied collection of children's books from the 19th and early 20th centuries; 2356 volumes.

Other collections include *Almanac Collection* dating from 1771; *Comic Book Collection; Socialist Pamphlet Collection; Ohioana Pamphlet Collection; Americana Pamphlet Collection; Textbook Collection;* and *Fales Collection of Minor Poets.* Collection inventory available.

Bluffton

422. Mennonite Historical Library
Bluffton College
Bluffton, OH 45817

Contact: Delbert Gratz
(419) 358-8015 Ext 271
Hours: By appointment only
Accessible to Public: Yes
Accessible to Scholars: Yes
Special Considerations: By appointment only

Materials relate to the religion, life, and culture of the Mennonites and Amish; includes over 15,000 volumes and 800 periodicals.

Bowling Green

423. Bowling Green State University, Music Library and Sound Recordings Archives
Jerome Library, Third Floor
Bowling Green, OH 43403

Contact: William L Schurk, Sound Recording Archivist
(419) 372-2307
Hours: Mon-Thur, 8 am-10 pm; Fri, 8-5; Sat, 10-5; Sun, 1-10
Accessible to Public: Yes
Accessible to Scholars: Yes
Special Considerations: This is a noncirculating collection; users must request playback of musical selections through a listening booth system; researchers may, with prior arrangement, be permitted to use record covers and ephemeral material; serious scholars may use one of several preview rooms

The collections currently consist of more than 500,000 popular recordings and associated print documentation. This represents the largest collection devoted to popular music available at any academic institution in the United States or Canada. The collections relate to all areas and forms of popular recording (rock, blues, country and western, gospel, jazz, bluegrass, Cajun, sacred, rhythm and blues, soul, classical, folk, big bands, Broadway, motion picture music, television soundtracks, comedy, juvenile, documentary, and spoken word), and holdings represent all formats, from early cylinder recordings through compact discs. Additionally, the archives are careful to catalog and preserve the jackets, sleeves, and covers associated with these items, along with poster art, advertising and promotional material, and assorted ephemera. The library maintains a comprehensive collection of music and sound recording reference books, newsletters, discographies, popular biographies of individuals related to the recording industry, sheet music, song folios, photographs, record company catalogs, scholarly works, and popular music periodicals. Other materials in the collection include hundreds of hours of early radio programs on tape and oral history interviews with scores of important figures in American popular culture. The collection is accessible through a card catalog (by title, performer, author, composer, etc.) and through the OCLC database. There is no better place in the nation in which to pursue the study of popuar music and the recording industry.

424. Bowling Green State University, Popular Culture Library

Jerome Library, Fourth Floor
Bowling Green, OH 43403

Contact: Brenda McCallum, Head
(419) 372-2450
Hours: Mon-Thur, 8 am-10 pm; Fri, 8-5; Sat, 10-5; Sun, 1-10; hours vary when school not in session and during summers
Accessible to Public: Yes
Accessible to Scholars: Yes
Special Considerations: Noncirculating collection; closed stack system; most items are fully accessible through the OCLC data base

Holdings focus on materials relating to the study of 19th and 20th century American culture, including popular fiction, with comprehensive coverage of mystery/detective and science fiction/fantasy literature in particular; the performing arts; comic and poster art; and recreation and leisure, among many other topics. Core holdings consist of over 63,000 cataloged books, 50,000 cataloged periodicals, 35,000 comic books, 50,000 postcards, 7,000 posters, 50,000 items of other visual materials, 8,400 pulp maga-

zines, 3,500 fanzines, and over 3,000 linear feet of literary manuscripts of more than 100 popular authors. Among the numerous special collections, the following are especially notable:

E. T. (Ned) Guymon Detective Fiction Collection: Includes over 3,000 books and 20 linear feet of literary manuscripts, correspondence, photographs, and illustrative materials by and about such figures as Ellery Queen, Raymond Chandler, Vincent Starrett, Craig Rice, Stu Palmer, Arthur Conan Doyle, and many others.

Manuscript Collection: Contains manuscripts by science fiction and fantasy authors Joanna Russ, Alexei and Cory Panshin, Robert Bloch, Joseph Payne Brennan, R. A. Lafferty, Carl Jacobi, and Philip K. Dick; mystery writers Joan Hess, Ruth Rendell, Martha G. Webb, and Dennis Lynds; psychic Suzy Smith; gothic novelist Dorothy Daniels; novelist Norman Daniels; and many, many others who work in various genres and media.

Allen and John Saunders Collection: Consists of more than 20 linear feet of original comic strip artwork ("Mary Worth," "Kerry Drake," "Steve Roper," and others), research files, story outlines, scripts, proof sheets, correspondence, and photographs.

H. James Horvitz Science Fiction Collection: Contains a grouping of 3,500 pulp magazines, including complete runs of *Amazing Stories, Tales of Magic and Mystery*, and *Weird Tales*, among other titles.

Ray Bradbury Collection: Collection is housed in the Center for Archival Collections (fifth floor of the Jerome Library) and consists of more than 1,500 published works by Bradbury, as well as literary manuscripts (books, short stories, scripts, screenplays, and poems), personal letters between Bradbury and author William Nolan, transcripts, posters, photographs, broadsides, periodicals, and notes, all related in some way to Bradbury and his works.

Performing Arts Collection: Includes 3,000 theatrical programs and playbills; tent show, Lyceum, and Chautauqua materials; 300 linear feet of radio, television, movie, and theater scripts; screenplays and teleplays; advertising and promotional materials; 5,000 Hollywood movie posters; thousands of ephemeral items, including press kits, lobby cards, souvenirs, clippings, photographs, political buttons, etc.

Juvenile Fiction Collections: Materials include comprehensive holdings of juvenile fiction series (for example, the *Frank and Dick Merriwell Library*, Horatio Alger, Tom Swift, the Motion Picture Boys, the Hardy Boys, the Bobbsey Twins, Nancy Drew, the Big Little Books, and the Whitman editions, among scores of others).

The Vintage Paperback Collection: Consists of 5,000 paperback books spanning 100 years of publishing history, from the 1860s to the 1960s, and including nickel and dime novels from the houses of Beadle and Adams, Street and Smith, A. L. Smith, and others; European Tauchnitz novels; Charles Boni Paper Books, Mercury Mystery, and other series; rare early American imprints, such as Black Knight Mysteries, Bart House, and Lion Books; and long runs of early issues from virtually all of the major American paperback publishing houses, including Dell Mapbacks and Ace Double Novels, for example. This unique collection represents one of the best resources for the study of paperback publishing in the United States.

A complete guide to the materials within the Popular Culture Library at Bowling Green State University is impossible in a brief entry such as this. There are resources for serious scholarly work in virtually all areas of the field. Numerous guides and resource aids are available to assist in the use of the collections. Any serious student of popular culture should inquire about the availability of materials to assist in her/his project, for the chances are excellent that this collection will be of great importance to research in most topics.

Cambridge

425. Degenhart Paperweight and Glass Museum, Inc
PO Box 186
Cambridge, OH 43725

Contact: Richard Rusnak, Dir
(614) 432-2626

Hours: Apr-Oct: Mon-Sat, 10-5, Sun, 1-5; Nov, Mar: Wed-Sat, 10-5, Sun, 1-5; Dec, Feb: Sat, 10-5, Sun, 1-5; closed Jan
Accessible to Scholars: Yes
Special Considerations: Advance notice in writing required

William F. and Margaret C. Johnston Kruet Collection: Consists of over 500 contemporary paperweights exhibited; also ledgers from the Cambridge Glass Co. and Degenhart's Crystal Art Glass.

Cincinnati

426. Public Library of Cincinnati and Hamilton County, Art and Music Department
800 Vine St—Library Square
Cincinnati, OH 45202-2071

Contact: R Jayne Craven, Dept Head
(513) 369-6954 or (513) 369-6955
Hours: Mon-Fri, 9-9; Sat, 9-6
Accessible to Public: Yes
Accessible to Scholars: Yes
Special Considerations: Library card or proper ID required; many materials only used under staff supervision

Collections include program files of 16,345 music, dance, and theater programs dating from mid-1860s; World War II photographs produced by Dispatch News; the *Langstroth Collection* of items on the development of chromolithography with emphasis on Cincinnati and the U.S.; vertical picture files; Valentines dating from the 1860s-1930s, including German Valentines; a popular sheet music collection; and a circus poster collection of 1,035 posters, mostly Barnum and Bailey.

427. Public Library of Cincinnati and Hamilton County, Department of Rare Books and Special Collections
800 Vine St—Library Square
Cincinnati, OH 45202-2071

Contact: Alfred Kleine-Kreutzmann
(513) 369-6957
Hours: Mon-Sat, 9-5
Accessible to Public: Yes

Accessible to Scholars: Yes

Collections include about 100 volumes of Edgar Rice Burroughs; 245 dime novels in the Dick Merriwell series; 1,400 pieces of fiction related to the Cincinnati and tri-state area; 4,350 postcards, including scenes of Cincinnati as well as U.S. historic sites, and about 100 stereopticon cards.

428. Public Library of Cincinnati and Hamilton County, Education and Religion Department
800 Vine St—Library Square
Cincinnati, OH 45202

Contact: Susan F Hettinger, Head
(513) 369-6940
Hours: Mon-Fri, 9-9; Sat, 9-6
Accessible to Public: Yes
Accessible to Scholars: Yes

Sports Collection: Includes guides, registers, handbooks, encyclopedias, and other reference books, as well as a large collection of circulating books (17,000 volumes) and noncirculating sports periodicals.

429. Public Library of Cincinnati and Hamilton County, Science and Technology Department
800 Vine St—Library Square
Cincinnati, OH 45202-2071

Contact: Mrs Rosemary Dahmann, Dept Head
(513) 369-6936
Hours: Mon-Fri, 9-9; Sat, 9-6
Accessible to Public: Yes
Accessible to Scholars: Yes

Cookery Collection: Consists of approximately 8,000 volumes dating back to 1817, including dictionaries and encyclopedias of gastronomy, histories of cooking, and books on all manner of American and foreign cooking, as well as many specialized cookbooks dealing with particular kinds of dishes, specific foods, cooking for various health conditions, and recipes using special kinds of equipment.

430. Stan Willis Collection of Handcuffs and Badges
6211 Stewart Rd
Cincinnati, OH 45227

Contact: Stan Willis
(513) 271-0454
Hours: By appointment only
Accessible to Public: Yes
Accessible to Scholars: Yes
Special Considerations: Call for appointment

Collection consists of over 500 handcuffs, leg irons, thumbcuffs, and other police-related restraining devices; items are mostly American, 1860-1986, but other countries are also represented. Also a collection of badges and other police memorabilia; mostly Ohio, but also old northern Kentucky, over 400 items in all. Books, catalogs, and other literature available, as well as photos, histories, buttons, nightsticks, lanterns, and other miscellany.

431. University of Cincinnati, Archives and Rare Books Department
Carl Blegan Library, 8th Floor
Cincinnati, OH 45221-0113

Contact: Kevin Grace
(513) 475-6459
Hours: Mon-Fri, 9-5; inquire as to additional availability
Accessible to Public: Yes
Accessible to Scholars: Yes
Special Considerations: Write or phone in advance of visit for specific use guidelines

The Department holds extensive materials for the study of baseball and its place in American culture, including materials on the dynamics of baseball parks, their design and effect on the game, the relationship of baseball parks to the life and economy of urban neighborhoods, baseball history, baseball architecture, economics and business of the sport, geography and baseball, sociology of baseball, and literature related to baseball and baseball figures. Special areas of the collection relate to the sport at the University of Cincinnati. Collections include oral histories, reference and history books, periodicals, research notes, newsletters, programs, scrapbooks, and media guides. The materials are part of a larger collection related to American Urban Studies.

432. University of Cincinnati Libraries, Archives and Rare Books Department
808 Blegen Library ML 113
Cincinnati, OH 45221

Contact: Kevin Grace
(513) 475-6459
Hours: Mon, 12-5; Tues-Fri, 8-5
Accessible to Public: Yes
Accessible to Scholars: Yes
Special Considerations: Photocopying may be restricted for copyright, physical condition, or donor agreement

Baseball Research Collection: Consists of photographs, oral histories, books, periodicals, research notes, biographical files, and other material related to baseball in America, particularly its place in the urban environment.

433. Xavier University Libraries
3800 Victory Pkwy
Cincinnati, OH 45207-1096

Contact: Gary Strawn or Tom Hinders
(513) 745-3881
Hours: Mon-Thurs, 8 am-11:30 pm; Fri, 8-5; Sat, 8-4:30; Sun, 12 pm-11:30 pm
Accessible to Public: Yes
Accessible to Scholars: Yes

Father Francis J. Finn, 1859-1928, Collection: Consists of 598 items, including correspondence, manuscripts, diaries, clippings, photographs, and miscellaneous items of Father Francis J. Finn, a Jesuit author of boys books.

Cleveland

434. Cleveland State University Libraries, Cleveland Press Collection
1860 E 22nd St
Cleveland, OH 44115

Contact: Henry York
(216) 687-2490
Hours: Mon-Fri, 9-12, 3-5
Accessible to Public: Yes
Accessible to Scholars: Yes

Special Considerations: Materials do not circulate

Clipping Collection: Over 2,000,000 clippings from the *Cleveland Press* newspaper from 1878 to 1982, most from 1930 on; arranged by subject or name of individual.

Photograph Collection: Nearly 2,000,000 photos, about half relating to greater Cleveland; arranged by subject or name of individual.

435. Cuyahoga County Public Library—Mayfield Regional
6080 Wilson Mills Rd
Cleveland, OH 44143

Contact: Pat Holsworth
(216) 473-0350
Hours: Mon-Thurs, 9-9; Fri-Sat, 9-5:30
Accessible to Public: Yes
Accessible to Scholars: Yes

Collections vary; include a collection of 900 songsheets, 400 popular songbooks, and 200 piano-vocal scores to musicals, most indexed by title. Also available are clippings files on Cleveland-based artists and architects, as well as Cleveland architecture.

436. Howard Dittrick Museum of Historical Medicine
Historical Division, Cleveland Health Sciences Library—11000 Euclid Ave
Cleveland, OH 44106

Contact: Laurena Hyslop, Collections Mgr
(216) 368-3648
Hours: Mon-Sat, 10-5; closed Sun, holidays, and Fri after Thanksgiving
Accessible to Public: Yes
Accessible to Scholars: Yes
Special Considerations: Tours are by appointment only, $.50 per person; Museum is free otherwise

Major collections are on history of medicine in the Western Reserve during the 19th century; includes the **Cleveland Herbals Project.**

437. Western Reserve Historical Society Library
10825 East Blvd
Cleveland, OH 44106

Contact: Kermit J Pike, Dir
(216) 721-5722
Hours: Tues-Sat, 9-5
Accessible to Public: Yes
Accessible to Scholars: Yes

Special collections include an auto-aviation collection, almanacs, children's books, 19th century textbooks, pulp magazines, and books on costume. Other collections include broadsides, World War I posters, advertisements and advertising cards, postcards, greeting cards and other miscellaneous cards, calendars, sheet music, buttons, medals, ribbons, political items, and bookplates.

Columbus

438. Circus Historical Society
2515 Dorset Rd
Columbus, OH 43221

Contact: Fred D Pfening, Jr
(614) 294-5461
Hours: Not open to public
Accessible to Public: No
Accessible to Scholars: No
Special Considerations: Collections are open by appointment only and only to authors of circus books

Collections include all types of printed material used by American circuses and an extensive number of circus photographs.

439. Ohio State University, Music Library
1813 High St
Columbus, OH 43210

Contact: Head, Music Library
(614) 422-2310
Hours: Special collections only accessible weekdays, 8-5
Accessible to Public: Yes
Accessible to Scholars: Yes

American Sheet Music Collection: Consists of American sheet music used at the ABC Radio studios for live broadcasts, 1930s-40s; total holdings approach 50,000 titles from 1880-1960. Indexing still in progress.

440. Ohio State University Libraries, Latin American Reading Room
1858 Neil Ave Mall, Rm 312
Columbus, OH 43210-1286

Contact: Contact Latin American Bibliographer
(614) 292-8959
Hours: Office: Mon-Fri, 7-4; Reading Room: Mon-Fri, 7:45 am-12 pm; Sat, 8 am-12 am; Sun 11 am-12 am; hours vary between school sessions
Accessible to Public: Yes
Accessible to Scholars: Yes
Special Considerations: Borrowing by interlibrary loan and courtesy card (issue on application and with proper identification) only

The collections include many secondary works on Latin American popular culture and a good selection of Latin chapbooks (from Brazil, etc.). Research supported by a large reference collection and 228 periodical titles.

441. Ohio State University Library for Communication and Graphic Arts
242 W 18th Ave—147 Journalism Bldg
Columbus, OH 43210-1107

Contact: Lucy Shelton Caswell
(614) 422-0538
Hours: Mon-Fri, 8-5
Accessible to Public: Yes
Accessible to Scholars: Yes
Special Considerations: Advance appointments preferred

Collections include materials relating to the arts of the mass media: comic strips, editorial cartoons, posters, illustrations, magazine art, comic books, newspaper journalism, and photographs. Examples of original cartoons by over 500 cartoonists are available, plus over 4,000 books on cartoon art and 3,000 comic books.

442. Ohioana Library
65 S Front St
Columbus, OH 43215

Contact: Kathy Babeaux
(614) 466-3831
Hours: Mon-Fri, 8:30-4:30
Accessible to Public: Yes
Accessible to Scholars: Yes
Special Considerations: Items do not circulate but may be xeroxed

Collections are varied, but include over 4,000 pieces of sheet music, some material of James Thurber, Lulu Teeter, and William Howells, and over 30,000 books by Ohio authors or about Ohio/Ohioans.

Dayton

443. University of Dayton, Archives and Special Collections
317 Roesch Library—University of Dayton
Dayton, OH 45469-0001

Contact: Cecilia Mushenheim
(513) 229-4267
Hours: Mon-Fri, 8:30-4:30; also by appointment
Accessible to Public: Yes
Accessible to Scholars: Yes
Special Considerations: Advance notice preferred

Science Fiction Writers of America Depository Collection: Consists of 698 books selected and deposited with this library by the Science Fiction Writers of America; books do not circulate.

444. Wright State University Library
Colonel Glenn Hwy
Dayton, OH 45345

Contact: Nancy Leggett
(513) 873-2092
Hours: Mon-Fri, 8:30-5; also Tues-Wed, 7-10pm; Sun, 2-5, during school term; no weekend or evening hours during school vacations
Accessible to Public: Yes
Accessible to Scholars: Yes

Rackham Collection: Consists of 250 books illustrated by Arthur Rackham, plus 24 framed prints.

Mary Harbage Collection: Consists of 18 linear feet of *St. Nicholas Magazine,* volumes I-XLV, dating from 1873-1936; 30 linear feet of rare and out-of-print juvenile literature; and approximately 40 figurines, dishes, and other miscellany relating to juvenile literature.

Children's Literature: Consists of about 3,000 children's books.

Hiram

445. Teachout-Price Memorial Library
Hiram College
Hiram, OH 44234

Contact: Joanne M Sawyer, Archivist
(216) 569-5361
Hours: Mon-Fri, 9-12, 1-4, except during school breaks and summer
Accessible to Public: Yes
Accessible to Scholars: Yes
Special Considerations: Write or call for appointment

Harold E. Davis Collection of World War I Propaganda Pamphlets: Consists of 426 pamphlets discussing various aspects of the war; inventory available on request.

Kent

446. Kent State University Library, Department of Special Collections
Kent State University
Kent, OH 44242

Contact: Alex Gildzen, Curator
(216) 672-2270
Hours: Mon-Fri, 8-12, 1-5
Accessible to Public: Yes
Accessible to Scholars: Yes
Special Considerations: Items do not circulate

Collections are extensive, and include *Alternative Theater Collection,* about 500 volumes of Armed Services Editions; children's books; comic books; a *Motion Pictures and Television Performing Arts Collection,* including memorabilia of actress Lois Wilson; newsreels; a science fiction collection; 16 boxes of theater programs; and the *Andy Purman Vaudeville Collection.*

Kings Island

447. National Football Foundation's College Football Hall of Fame
5440 Kings Island Dr
Kings Island, OH 45034

Contact: Sondra L Dorenbusch
(513) 241-5410 or (513) 398-5410

Accessible to Public: Yes
Accessible to Scholars: Yes
Special Considerations: By appointment
only

Collection consists of college football memorabilia, uniforms, press guides, programs, books, movies, and related ephemera.

Lebanon

448. Warren County Historical Society
PO Box 223
Lebanon, OH 45036

Contact: Thomas G Kuhn
(513) 932-1817
Hours: Tues-Sat, 9-4; Sun, 12-4; closed
Mon
Accessible to Public: Yes
Accessible to Scholars: Yes
Special Considerations: Admission
donation $2 for adults; $1 student
through high school

Collections include a Shaker collection; rare books and microfilm records; genealogical collections for many southwestern Ohio families; and oral histories concerning the history of southwestern Ohio.

Maple Heights

449. Maple Heights Public Library/Civic Center
5225 Library Ln
Maple Heights, OH 44137

Contact: William Shea or Ruth Streeter
(216) 475-5000
Hours: Mon-Thurs, 9-9; Fri-Sat, 9-5:30
Accessible to Public: Yes
Accessible to Scholars: Yes
Special Considerations: Ask for
permission

Oral History Collection: Consists of oral histories by residents of Maple Heights, Ohio, recorded on tape.

Marion

450. Wyandot Popcorn Museum
135 Wyandot Ave
Marion, OH 43302

Contact: Phyllis Tomlin
(614) 383-4031
Hours: Daily, 10-9; Sun 12-5; number
above is for office: Mon-Fri, 8-5
Accessible to Public: Yes
Accessible to Scholars: Yes
Special Considerations: Can
accommodate wheelchairs; formal
program by appointment

Collection consists of about 45 fully restored and operational popcorn poppers and peanut roasters; includes 1899 Cretor's No 1 Popcorn Wagon and Peanut Roaster and 1927 Ford Model T Popcorn Truck.

Newark

451. Heisey Collectors of America
PO Box 27
Newark, OH 43055

Contact: Louise Ream or Neila
Bredehoft
(614) 345-2932 or (614) 349-7672
Hours: Daily 1-4; closed holidays
Accessible to Public: Yes
Accessible to Scholars: Yes
Special Considerations: Must be a HCA
member or request permission to use
archives

Collections include over 4,000 iron moulds for making pressed and blown glass, etching plates, mould drawings, factory records, photographs, and advertisements.

North Canton

452. Hoover Historical Center
2225 Easton St NW
North Canton, OH 44720

Contact: Mrs Stacy Krammes, Dir
(216) 499-0287
Hours: Tues-Sun, 1-5; closed Mon and
all major holidays
Accessible to Public: Yes

Accessible to Scholars: Yes
Special Considerations: Ramp for wheelchairs to Tannery and downstairs house only

Vacuum Cleaner Collection: Consists of 99 antique and up-to-date cleaners, beginning with handand foot-operated models as early as 1858 and continuing with early electric; samples of all Hoover models, beginning with Model O in 1908 through current models.

Oral History Collection: Consists of 15 tapes of former Hoover Company employees and townsfolk in North Canton; reminiscences of historical value regarding industry and town.

Oberlin

453. Oberlin College, Phyllis Garfain Folklore Collection
Oberlin College English Dept
Oberlin, OH 44074

Contact: Phyllis Garfain, Dept of English
(216) 775-8577
Hours: By appointment
Accessible to Public: No
Accessible to Scholars: Yes
Special Considerations: Call for appointment

Collection consists of archives based on student collections; includes materials on campus graffiti, family legends, proverbs, college folklore, immigrant narratives, mnemonic devices, games, etc.

Oxford

454. McGuffey Museum—Miami University Art Museum
Patterson Ave—Miami University
Oxford, OH 45056

Contact: David Berreth, Dir
(513) 529-2232
Hours: Hours vary; call for information
Accessible to Public: Yes
Accessible to Scholars: Yes

Maude Blair Collection: Consists of McGuffey Readers, school books, and children's books. Also McGuffey memorabilia.

455. Walter Havighurst Special Collections Library
King Library—Miami University
Oxford, OH 45056

Contact: Helen Ball
(513) 529-3324
Hours: Mon-Fri, 8:30-11:30, 1-5
Accessible to Public: Yes
Accessible to Scholars: Yes
Special Considerations: Items do not circulate

Materials include *King Collection* of children's books and *Covington Collection* of regional history.

Republic

456. Margie Pfund Memorial Postmark Museum
11557 E SCR 24
Republic, OH 44867

Contact: Mrs Bernice Mittower, Curator
(419) 585-7645
Hours: June-Aug, daily 1-5, except Mon; May and Sept, Sat-Sun, 1-5; or by appointment
Accessible to Public: Yes
Accessible to Scholars: Yes
Special Considerations: Staff member must be present when materials used

Willett Thompson Collection: Postmarks from all 50 states, mounted in over 275 binders.

Name Origin Collection: More than 30 volumes holding 20,000 names.

Also collection of postal directories from 1798-present and related books.

Springfield

457. Swanger Collection
2718 Cardinal Rd
Springfield, OH 45502

Contact: Eugene R Swanger
(513) 390-0046
Hours: By appointment
Accessible to Public: No
Accessible to Scholars: Yes
Special Considerations: Call for appointment

Swanger Collection: Private collection consisting of over 700 charms, amulets, and talismans from Japanese popular culture collected since 1975; items are made of paper, clay, wood, rice straw, bronze, plastic, and brocade silk. Collection currently housed at Wittenburg University, Springfield, Ohio.

Toledo

458. Antiques and Historic Glass Foundation
PO Box 7413
Toledo, OH 43615

Contact: Carl U Fauster
(419) 531-5679
Accessible to Public: No
Accessible to Scholars: No

Reference and background material of Libbey Glass, America's oldest glassmaker. Related book published by contact person in 1979.

459. Blair Museum of Lithopanes and Carved Waxes
PO Box 4557
Toledo, OH 43620

Contact: Mr Laurel G Blair, Curator
(419) 243-4115
Hours: By appointment
Accessible to Public: Yes
Accessible to Scholars: Yes
Special Considerations: Groups of minimum 10, maximum 20; $3 per person admission charge, $2 for senior citizens

Lithopanes: Collection consists of over 2,300 used as placques, candle shields, fireplace shields, lampshades, fairy lights, souvenir cups, steins, and similar material from the 19th century.

Wax Carvings: Over 500 in collection, from Egyptian period to present; includes wax pictures and sculptures in the round.

460. Toledo-Lucas County Public Library
325 Michigan St
Toledo, OH 43624-1614

Contact: Paula J Baker
(419) 255-7055 Ext 229
Hours: Mon-Thurs, 9-9; Fri-Sat, 9-5:30
Accessible to Public: Yes
Accessible to Scholars: Yes

Special Considerations: Material access through public index; items retrieved by staff

Sheet Music Collection: Consists of 15 feet of suspended folders of sheet music of popular songs for voice and piano; greatest concentration from 1930s-1950s.

461. University of Toledo, Ward M. Canaday Center
Carlson Library—2801 W Bancroft
Toledo, OH 43606

Contact: Richard W Oram, Dir
(419) 537-4480
Hours: Mon-Fri, 8-5
Accessible to Public: Yes
Accessible to Scholars: Yes

Women's Collection: Consists of 1,000 books and pamphlets, including popular health guides, marriage manuals, cookbooks, and housekeeping manuals, 1820-1940.

Jamie Farr Collection: Consists of about 250 items, including the actor's marked scripts for various movies and his television series, *M*A*S*H*.

Pete Hoffman Collection: Consists of about 2,000 items, including original cartoons from "Jeff Cobb" syndicated cartoon strip, 1954-1978.

Worthington

462. Worthington Historical Society
50 W New England Ave
Worthington, OH 43085

Contact: Jane Trucksis, Curator; Lillian Skeele, Librarian
(614) 885-1247
Hours: Wed, 10-4
Accessible to Public: Yes
Accessible to Scholars: Yes
Special Considerations: Limited borrowing

Collections include a *Doll Collection*, *Lace Collection*, and a collection of local history books, plus pictures.

Wright-Patterson Air Force Base

463. U.S. Air Force Museum

Research Division
Wright-Patterson Air Force Base, OH
45433

Contact: Charles Worman, Chief of
Research Div
(513) 255-3284
Hours: Mon-Fri, 9-4
Accessible to Public: Yes
Accessible to Scholars: Yes
Special Considerations: Use of collection
requires prior notice

Consists of about 200,000 documents relating to the history of the United States Air Force and its predecessor organizations, including books, manuals, magazine articles, diaries, drawings, photographs, test reports, etc. Material is generally related to aircraft and subsystems, but also includes cultural materials.

OKLAHOMA

Claremore

464. J. M. Davis Gun Museum

PO Box 966
Claremore, OK 74018

Contact: Lee T Good
(918) 341-5707
Hours: Mon-Sat, 8:30-5; Sun, 1-5; closed
Thanksgiving and Christmas Day
Accessible to Public: Yes
Accessible to Scholars: Yes
Special Considerations: Some items in
storage

Collections consist of 20,000 firearms and related accoutrements, a 1,200-item stein collection, 70 saddles, Indian artifacts, a collection of 23 items of John Rogers statuary, musical instruments and music boxes, 600 World War I posters, swords and knives, and a research library containing over 1,000 books.

465. Will Rogers Memorial

PO Box 157
Claremore, OK 74018

Contact: Gregory Malak, Mgr

(918) 341-1719
Hours: Daily, 8-5; closed Thanksgiving
and Christmas
Accessible to Public: Yes
Accessible to Scholars: Yes
Special Considerations: Library open
only by appointment

Will Rogers Collection: Consists of materials pertaining to the life and career of Will Rogers; includes scrapbooks, letters, postcards, telegrams, advertisements, photographs, miscellaneous personal items, books, magazine articles, and 40 Will Rogers movies.

Enid

466. Phillips University, Zollars Memorial Library

Box 2400 University Station
Enid, OK 73702

Contact: John B Sayre
(405) 237-4433 Ext 417
Hours: Mon-Thurs, 8-11; Fri, 8-5; Sat, 9-9; Sun, 2-11; holiday and summer hours vary
Accessible to Public: Yes
Accessible to Scholars: Yes
Special Considerations: Items do not circulate

Living Legends: Approximately 200 cassette interviews conducted by students in oral history seminars of longtime Enid and Garfield County residents. Many interviews refer to the Land Run of 1000 (Cherokee Outlet), early life in Enid, Garfield County, and Oklahoma.

Kingfisher

467. Chisholm Trail Museum/Seay Mansion

605 Zellers Ave
Kingfisher, OK 73750

Contact: Glen McIntyre, Curator
(405) 375-5176
Hours: May 1-Nov 1: Tues-Sat, 9-5; Sun, 1-5; Winter: Wed-Sat, 9-5; Sun 1-5
Accessible to Public: Yes
Accessible to Scholars: Yes
Special Considerations: Noncirculating collection

The museum includes 18,000 square feet of display space, largely devoted to American Indian artifacts and the history of Kingfisher, 1889-1939. Research collections include a large number of postcards (1908-1910 and 1920s-1940s), of which early cards depict not only scenery but American holidays; stereopticons and several collections of stereopticon cards; a small collection of children's books; old calendars (1900-1940); old Wards and Sears catalogs; and several hundred pieces of obscure sheet music (1900-1920).

Norman

468. University of Oklahoma, Western History Colections
630 Parrington Oval, Monnet Hall Rm 452
Norman, OK 73019

Contact: Nathan E Bender, Librarian
(405) 325-2904
Hours: Mon-Fri, 8-5; also during fall and spring semesters, Sat, 9-1
Accessible to Public: Yes
Accessible to Scholars: Yes
Special Considerations: Coats and possessions checked upon entry; pencils only

Mr. and Mrs. Robert Fay Collection: St Louis World's Fair memorabilia, exhibit catalogs, stereoscopic views, etc.; approximately 30 cubic feet.

Frank Phillips Collection: Consists of 40,000 volumes on the western frontier and Native American history; topics include cowboy songs and humor, western women, and western fiction, including 120 Buffalo Bill dime novels.

Oklahoma City

469. Amateur Softball Association
2801 NE 50th
Oklahoma City, OK 73111

Contact: Bill Plummer or Gail Peck
(405) 424-5266
Hours: Mon-Fri, 8:30-4:30; open on weekends during softball season, Mar-Oct, 10-4
Accessible to Public: Yes
Accessible to Scholars: Yes
Special Considerations: Items do not circulate

Approximately 700 items on file relating solely to the sport of softball; includes student papers, theses, and dissertations, as well as videocassettes, books, softball guides, souvenir programs, magazine articles, and miscellaneous items such as Hall of Fame nominee scrapbooks, newspaper clippings dating back to the 1930s, tournament bracket books, unpublished papers, and umpire's examinations. Some foreign items available.

470. National Cowboy Hall of Fame and Western Heritage Center
1700 NE 63rd St
Oklahoma City, OK 73111

Contact: A J "Ace" Tytgat
(405) 478-2250
Hours: Daily, 9-5; Summer hours (Memorial Day-Labor Day): Mon-Fri, 8:30-6
Accessible to Public: Yes
Accessible to Scholars: Yes
Special Considerations: Advance notice required

Collection consists of a 7,000-volume western book collection; includes materials on artists, art, folklore, early western development, Indian/cowboy data, etc.

Tishomingo

471. Chickasaw Council House Museum Branch of Oklahoma Historical Society
PO Box 717
Tishomingo, OK 73460

Contact: Beverly J Wyatt, Curator
(405) 371-3351
Hours: Tues-Fri, 9-5; Sat-Sun, 2-5; closed Mon and holidays
Accessible to Public: Yes
Accessible to Scholars: Yes

Collection includes books relative to history of Oklahoma, Indian Territory, and Oklahoma Territory; includes county histories, biographical sketches, Chickasaw Indian records, collection of Indian song and dance music, and microfilm issues of the *Johnston County Capitol Democrat* newspaper.

Tulsa

472. University of Tulsa, McFarlin Library
600 S College
Tulsa, OK 74114

Contact: Sidney F Huttner, Head,
Special Collections
(918) 592-6000
Hours: Mon-Fri, 8-5
Accessible to Public: Yes
Accessible to Scholars: Yes

Collections include dime novels; individual author collections; the *Henneke Archives of Performing Arts,* which includes a circus collection with some 700 items and ephemera; and an *Indian Studies Collection.*

OREGON

Eugene

473. University of Oregon, Randall V. Mills Archives of Northwest Folklore
Department of English—University of Oregon
Eugene, OR 97403-1202

Contact: Tim Miller
(503) 686-3925
Hours: Open Sept 15-June 15; closed summer
Accessible to Public: Yes
Accessible to Scholars: Yes
Special Considerations: Advance notice of research intent appreciated since archivist's schedule varies

The Randall V. Mills Archives of Northwest Folklore: Collection is primarily made up of folklore (from anecdotes to xeroxography), oral history, and regional dialects from the Pacific Northwest, but its holdings include materials from the Orient, various American Indian tribes, Europe, and Africa. Collections include:

Robert Gordon Collection: Extensive collection consists of folksongs, ballads, and folklore from various sources; some concerned with the Civil War era and minstrel days.

Randall V. Mills Collection: Consists largely of correspondence, manuscripts, research material and note cards, printed material, and scrapbooks pertaining to transportation in the Pacific Northwest and folklore.

Other collections include the *Otillie Seybolt Collection* of dialect studies and slides of over 5,000 pieces of folk art collection from around Oregon; slides also document Russian Old Believer community in Woodburn, Oregon.

474. University of Oregon Library
1501 Kincaid
Eugene, OR 97403

Contact: Ken Duckett
(503) 686-3068
Hours: Mon-Fri, 8-5; Sun, 2-5
Accessible to Public: Yes
Accessible to Scholars: Yes
Special Considerations: University ID or borrower's card for circulating materials

Collections vary, and include:

Ernest Haycox Memorial Library: A cataloged, noncirculating collection of the fiction of Western novel writer Ernest Haycox; 100 volumes.

Armed Services Editions: A noncirculating, partially cataloged collection of paperbacks issued by the U.S. Government for soldiers to use in World War II; about 200 items.

Other collections include a **Paperback Collection** of mysteries, westerns, etc.; a collection of papers of authors of formula novels, including Luke Short (Fred Glidden), W. Todhunter Ballard, and William Cox; a **Broadsides Collection,** mainly relating to Pacific Northwest history; a **Popular Sheet Music Collection,** dating from 1852-1976; a **Pulp Collection;** a **Dime Novel Collection;** a **Children's Book Collection;** and an **Oregon Literature Collection.**

Portland

475. Bassist College Library
2000 SW 5th Ave
Portland, OR 97201

Contact: Mrs Norma Bassist, Exec Librarian

(503) 228-6528
Hours: Mon-Fri, 7:30-5:30
Accessible to Public: Yes
Accessible to Scholars: Yes
Special Considerations: Materials do not
   circulate

Contains a comprehensive collection of approximately 3,000 volumes relating to the fashion industry and costume and fashion history. Includes books on constructing period costume and modern-day clothing, plus bibliographies of fashion designers. Further holdings include 2,000 volumes on interior design and furniture, and 70 linear feet of clipping files, which consist of newspaper, periodical and other reference material on various aspects of the apparel industry, fashion design, interior design, and the retail industry.

476. Multnomah County Library, Art and Music Department
801 SW 10th Ave
Portland, OR 97205

Contact: Barbara K Padden or Barbara
   B Rhyne
(503) 223-7201
Hours: Mon-Thurs, 10-9; Fri-Sat, 10-5:
   30; Sun, 1-5, except July-Aug
Accessible to Public: Yes
Accessible to Scholars: Yes
Special Considerations: ID required

Popular Sheet Music Collection: Consists of 54 file boxes and 11 oversize folders of popular sheet music from the 1830s to the present; collection is strongest from 1900-1940.

477. Oregon Historical Society
1230 Park Ave
Portland, OR 97205

Contact: Peggy Haines
(503) 222-1741
Hours: Mon-Sat, 10-4:45
Accessible to Public: Yes
Accessible to Scholars: Yes

Poster Collection: Includes military posters, especially World War I era, political and movie posters, posters advertising organizations and events, and some commercial advertising posters; materials date from 1890-present.

Business—Miscellaneous: Includes advertising cards and blotters, brochures, business cards, menus, and catalogs; materials date from 1860-present.

Manners and Customs—Miscellaneous: Includes scrapbooks; holiday greeting cards; brochures and other ephemera from fairs, expositions and festivals; programs from sporting events; invitations; pictorial calendars; autograph books; and other items that document social life, recreation, and popular taste. Materials date from 1860-present.

Performing Arts—Miscellaneous: Includes programs for concerts, plays, and dance performances; sheet music for popular songs (1875-1945); and scrapbooks. Programs document amateur as well as professional performances from 1870-present.

PENNSYLVANIA

Ambridge

478. Pennsylvania Historical and Museum Commission—Old Economy Village
14th and Church Sts
Ambridge, PA 15003

Contact: Raymond V Shepherd, Jr, Dir
(412) 775-8064
Hours: Tues-Sat, 9-4; Sun, 12-4
Accessible to Public: Yes
Accessible to Scholars: Yes
Special Considerations: Researchers
   should make appointments, especially
   if wishing to view storage items

Old Economy Village was a successful 19th century communitarian venture of the Harmony Society that has been restored by the PHMC. Grounds cover 6.7 acres and include original homes and shops. Approximately 16,000 research items have been cataloged, but may be in storage.

Carnegie

479. National Standard Council of American Embroiderers—NSCAE Library
Carnegie Office Park, 600 Bell Ave
Carnegie, PA 15106

Contact: Lynne Wohleber, Librarian
(412) 629-0299
Hours: Wed or Thurs, 9-3
Accessible to Public: No
Accessible to Scholars: No
Special Considerations: Must be a
  member of the NSCAE or enrolled in
  the Correspondence School

The library collection consists of books
and pamphlets covering all phases of
needlework; includes some rare and out-
of-print books that are for research use
only.

Center Valley

480. Allentown College, Library
Allentown College
Center Valley, PA 18034

Contact: James P McCabe
(215) 282-1100
Hours: Mon-Fri, 8:30-5
Accessible to Public: No
Accessible to Scholars: Yes
Special Considerations: Interview with
  librarian necessary for access

**John Y. Kohl Collection of Theatri-
cal Memorabilia:** Several hundred
playbills from local theaters; late 19th to
early 20th century materials. Some material from New York, Boston, and
Philadelphia; includes some photographs.

Columbia

481. Watch and Clock Museum of the National Association of Watch and Clock Collectors (NAWCC)
514 Poplar St
Columbia, PA 17512

Contact: P Tomes, Registrar; D Summar,
  Librarian
(717) 684-8261

Hours: Mon-Fri, 9-4; Sat, 9-5
Accessible to Public: Yes
Accessible to Scholars: Yes
Special Considerations: Nonmembers
  pay admission for library use; special
  arrangements must be made to study
  museum collection items not on
  exhibit

Items include a 10,000-piece museum
collection of clocks, watches, tools, and
related equipment dating from late 17th
century to present. There is also a
Horological Library of 2,500 books and
21,000 U.S. patents related to horological
development, and issues of the *NAWCC
Bulletin,* a journal of horology, from
1944 to date.

Cresson

482. Allegheny Portage Railroad National Historical Site
PO Box 247
Cresson, PA 16630

Contact: Mr Larry Trombello
(814) 886-8176
Hours: Mon-Sun, 8:30-5
Accessible to Public: Yes
Accessible to Scholars: Yes
Special Considerations: Written request
  required

Collections consist of artifacts relating to
early 19th century railroading in western
Pennsylvania.

Easton

483. David Bishop Skillman Library
Lafayette College
Easton, PA 18052

Contact: Dorothy Cieslicki, Dir
(215) 250-5151
Hours: Mon-Fri, 8:30-10; Sun, 2-10
Accessible to Public: Yes
Accessible to Scholars: Yes
Special Considerations: Available to
  qualified researchers upon application;
  materials do not circulate

**Tinsman and Cnahay Angling Col-
lections:** Collections on the art and
sport of angling, with special emphasis
on Atlantic salmon fishing; includes 600

monographs and serial titles and 800 hand-tied fishing flies.

American Friends of Lafayette Collection: Collection documents the life and times of the Marquis de Lafayette and American fascination with him as the "hero of two worlds"; includes 250 manuscript items, 650 engravings and prints, and 150 pieces of memorabilia.

Gardner Lincolniana Collection: Consists of printed ephemera and pictorial images of Abraham Lincoln.

Huntington

484. Swigart Antique Automobile Museum

PO Box 214 Museum Park
Huntington, PA 16652

Contact: William E Swigart, Jr, Owner/Mgr; Dolly M Brennen, Exec Sec
(814) 643-3000
Accessible to Public: No
Accessible to Scholars: Yes
Special Considerations: By appointment only; value and rarity of the collection requires supervision for research

The Swigart Museum, the oldest car-transportation museum in America, contains an abundance of printed material, supported by large amounts of automobiliana.

Johnstown

485. Johnstown Flood Museum

304 Washington St
Johnstown, PA 15901

Contact: Richard A Burkert
(814) 539-1889
Hours: Tues-Sat, 10:30-4:30; Sun, 12:30-4:30
Accessible to Public: Yes
Accessible to Scholars: Yes

Johnstown Flood Collection: Documents the May 31, 1889, Johnstown flood and popular culture treatment of disaster; consists of bound volumes, newspapers, photographs and negatives, stereographs, sheet music, lantern slides, and memorabilia.

Lancaster

486. Franklin and Marshall College, Shadek-Fackenthal Library, Archives and Special Collections Department

Franklin and Marshall College
Lancaster, PA 17604

Contact: Charlotte B Brown, College Archivist
(717) 291-4225
Hours: Mon-Fri, 9-5
Accessible to Public: Yes
Accessible to Scholars: Yes
Special Considerations: Subject to restrictions of privacy, fragility, etc.

Unger-Bassler Collection of Pennsylvania-German: Includes about 3,500 items: fraktur, manuscripts, monographs, broadsides, newspapers, almanacs, and drawings from about 1730-1925.

Also included are the *Thomas R. Brendle Collection of Pennsylvania-Dutch Folk Music,* the *Alendar Corbett Collection of Theater Memorabilia,* and the *W. W. Griest Collection of Lincolniana.*

487. Pennsylvania Farm Museum of Landis Valley

2451 Kissel Hill Rd
Lancaster, PA 17601

Contact: John L Kraft, Dir
(717) 569-0401
Hours: Tues-Sat, 9-5; Sun, 12-5
Accessible to Public: No
Accessible to Scholars: Yes
Special Considerations: By special arrangement with the Director; materials do not circulate

Collections include three mid-size boxes of trade cards, some old greeting cards, about 15 sale bills/broadsides, about 50 frakturs, and assorted brochures/pamphlets of local activities.

Lebanon

488. Lebanon County Historical Society
924 Cumberland St
Lebanon, PA 17042

Contact: Mrs Christine L Mason, Asst
  Coord
(717) 272-1473
Hours: Sun, Mon, Wed, and Fri, 1-4:30;
  Mon, 7pm-9pm
Accessible to Public: Yes
Accessible to Scholars: Yes
Special Considerations: Fees $2 charge
  for nonmembers; $10 fee for
  correspondence for nonmembers and
  $8 for same for members

Collections include a postcard collection,
including a series of cards from Mt.
Gretna when it was used as a camp by
the Army, a family histories collection
consisting of information pertaining to
families that settled in and around Lebanon County, and the Lehman Diaries
containing information about the Union
Canal and residents of Lebanon County
from 1830 to the 1860s.

Lincoln University

489. Lincoln University
Langston Hughes Memoral Library
Lincoln University, PA 19352

Contact: Ella Forbes, Special Collections
  Librarian
(215) 932-8300 Ext 266, 267
Hours: Mon-Fri, 8:30-5; Mon-Thur, 7
  pm-10 pm; Sat, 1-5; Summer: Mon-
  Fri, 8:30-5
Accessible to Public: Yes
Accessible to Scholars: Yes
Special Considerations: General public
  may not remove materials from the
  library

Although the library maintains no specific popular culture collections, materials in the *African (7,000 volumes), Afro-
American (13,000 volumes),* and *Langston Hughes (4,000 items) Collections*
can be considered to have popular culture interest and information. Inquire as
to specifics prior to visit.

Lititz

490. Candy Americana Museum—Wilbur Chocolate Company
46 N Broad St
Lititz, PA 17543

Contact: Penny Buzzard
(717) 626-1131
Hours: Mon-Sat, 10-5
Accessible to Public: Yes
Accessible to Scholars: Yes

Collection of equipment and other
memorabilia related to candy production.
Includes a 150 piece collection of por-
celain chocolate pots, and ephemera relating to all phases of the candy
industry—manufacturing, processing,
packaging, and advertising included.

Lock Haven

491. Lock Haven University, Archives and Records Centre
Stevenson Library Bldg
Lock Haven, PA 17745

Contact: Prof Charles R Kent,
  University Archivist
(717) 893-2371
Hours: Mon-Fri, 8-1:30pm during
  university term; also by appointment
Accessible to Public: Yes
Accessible to Scholars: Yes
Special Considerations: Usual archive
  restrictions apply (no food, smoking,
  etc.)

Tim Eck Collection: Comic books from
the 1960s-1970s, some in mint condition;
some issues are complete, for example,
Amazing Adventures and *Where Mon-
sters Dwell.* Inventory available on request $5 reproduction and mailing
charge.

Philadelphia

492. American Philosophical Society Library
105 S Fifth St
Philadelphia, PA 19106

Contact: Roy E Goodman, Ref Librarian;
  Beth Carroll-Horrocks, Manuscripts
  Librarian
(215) 627-0716

Hours: Mon-Fri, 9-5
Accessible to Public: Yes
Accessible to Scholars: Yes
Special Considerations: Open to serious
researchers only; photo ID required

Broadsides in Science, Technology, Medicine, and Agriculture: Over 1,500 broadsides and related ephemera encompassing a wide variety of subjects.

UFO Collections: Three separate UFO collections held by the manuscripts department; consists of over 100 linear feet.

493. American Swedish Historical Museum
1900 Pattison Ave
Philadelphia, PA 19145

Contact: Vito Trimarco, Public Relations
(215) 389-1776
Hours: Tues-Fri, 10-4; Sat, 12-4
Accessible to Public: Yes
Accessible to Scholars: Yes
Special Considerations: Some material
encapsulated

John Ericsson Collection: Consists of scale or actual models of all his major inventions, such as elements of USS Monitor, steam fire engines, precision measurement guages, etc.; also personal items and memorabilia.

Immigrant and Pioneer Rooms: Contain artifacts of the daily life of Swedish-American people during their period of Midwestern immigration.

494. Athenaeum of Philadelphia
219 S 6th St
Philadelphia, PA 19106

Contact: K A Kamm
(215) 925-2688
Hours: Mon-Fri, 9-5
Accessible to Public: No
Accessible to Scholars: Yes
Special Considerations: Access by
appointment only

Sawyer Dime Novel Collection: Approximately 1,600 dime novels, chiefly by publishers Beadle and Adams.

495. Balch Institute for Ethnic Studies
18 S 7th St
Philadelphia, PA 19106

Contact: Joseph Anderson, Library Dir
(215) 925-8090
Hours: Mon-Sat, 9-5
Accessible to Public: Yes
Accessible to Scholars: Yes

Ethnic Images in Advertising Collection: Consists of 300 popular advertisements depicting stereotypical images of 25 ethnic groups in America from 1913 to present.

Other collections include *Advertising Ephemera and Trade Cards,* a collection of postcards showing stereotypes and genre scenes of 13 ethnic groups in America, and collections on folkdance and the international folkdance movement in the U.S. and on ethnic radio.

496. Civil War Library and Museum
1805 Pine St
Philadelphia, PA 19103

Contact: Russ A Pritchard, Dir
(215) 735-8196
Hours: Mon-Fri, 10-4
Accessible to Public: Yes
Accessible to Scholars: Yes

Museum contains artifacts and books related to the Civil War and Union Forces. Some Confederate materials also available.

497. Perelman Antique Toy Museum
270 S 2nd St
Philadelphia, PA 19106

Contact: Leon J Perelman, Dir; Harriet
Goldfarb, Curator
(215) 922-1070
Hours: Daily, 9:30-5, except
Thanksgiving and Christmas Day
Accessible to Public: Yes
Accessible to Scholars: Yes

Collections include over 4,000 early American tin and cast-iron toys, the largest collection of mechanical and still banks in the U.S., and a library of 260 books related to toys.

498. Temple University, Paley Library, Audio Collection
Temple University, 13th and Berks Sts
Philadelphia, PA 19122

Contact: Steve Landstreet, Head of
Collections
(215) 787-8205
Hours: Mon-Wed, 9-8; Thurs-Fri, 9-6;
hours vary from semester to semester
and are reduced in Summer
Accessible to Public: Yes
Accessible to Scholars: Yes
Special Considerations: Photo ID
preferred

Audio Collection: Appoximately 14,000
titles on LP, 78, CD, and cassette, spanning all forms of popular music, as well
as classical and spoken word recordings.
Playback equipment is available for use
in room; items do not circulate.

499. Temple University Libraries, Special Collections Department
Philadelphia, PA 19122

Contact: Thomas M Whitehead, Head,
Spec Collections
(215)787-8230
Hours: Mon-Fri, 9-5
Accessible to Public: Yes
Accessible to Scholars: Yes
Special Considerations: Materials do not
circulate

Collections are extensive, and include
pulps, posters, folk art—especially relating to the Black experience in
America—and media photography, with
some TV news film from 1947 to date.
Less extensive collections include comic
books, trade cards, children's books,
dime novels, stereoptician cards, and
sheet music. *Contemporary Culture Collection* concerns social and political protest.

500. University of Pennsylvania, Annenberg School of Communications
410 Logan Hall
Philadelphia, PA 19104-6387

Contact: Sandra Grilikhes, Dir
(215) 898-8721
Hours: Mon-Fri, 9-5
Accessible to Public: Yes
Accessible to Scholars: Yes
Special Considerations: Call in advance
for appointment

Television Script Collection: Contains
the largest, most comprehensive collection of television scripts in the United
States, and perhaps the world, including
more than 24,000 scripts in every format
and genre. Includes more than 95 per-
cent of what the American public has
seen on prime-time television since 1976.
The collection increases by more than
1,500 scripts each year. Scripts are organized and indexed by title, genre, subject, and topic. A detailed and custom-
made thesaurus of subject headings has
evolved and is available to researchers.

501. University of Pennsylvania, Archive of Folklore and Folklife
417 Logan Hall 6304
Philadelphia, PA 19104

Contact: Camille Bacon-Smith, Archivist
(215) 898-7353
Hours: Varies with each semester
Accessible to Public: Yes
Accessible to Scholars: Yes
Special Considerations: Materials may be
copied but do not circulate

The Wortman Collection: Collection
of 30 scrapbooks of baseball newspaper
clippings collected during the 1960s; on
indefinite loan.

Columbia Race Recordings: 250 of
the 689 releases of the Columbia Phonograph Company's "Race" series on
reel-to-reel tape.

The Birdwhistell Collection: Includes
48 bound volumes of commercially produced books of popular American humor
from the mid-1800s to after the turn of
the century.

**The Jean Curley Folksong Collec-
tion:** Lyric sheets to approximately 300
songs written about science fiction, fantasy, and the science fiction community.

**The Niles C. Geerhold Popular Mu-
sic Collection:** Approximately 2,000
record albums of popular and rock music
from the 1950s to the 1980s; an extensive clipping file is included in this collection.

502. University of Pennsylvania, Van Pelt Library Special Collections
University of Pennsylvania
Philadelphia, PA 19104-6206

Contact: Georgianna Ziegler, Asst Curator
(215) 898-7088 or (215) 898-7552
Hours: Mon-Fri, 9-4:45 (9-4:15 July-Aug); open first Sat of Oct-Nov and Feb-May, 10-4:45
Accessible to Public: Yes
Accessible to Scholars: Yes
Special Considerations: Advance notice appreciated; ID needed after 1 and on Sat

Collections in the Rare Book Dept include:

Theater Collections: Contain materials on Philadelphia theater, American theater and circus posters, and actors and actresses, as well as other materials.

American Juvenile Literature Collection: Literature from 1900-1930.

Broadside Ballad Collection: About 750 British and American broadsides (18th and 19th century).

Furness Memorial Library of Shakespeariana: Includes playbills, programs, photographs, and other materials related to productions of Shakespeare plays.

Pittsburgh

503. Carnegie Library of Pittsburgh, Music and Art Department
4400 Forbes Ave
Pittsburgh, PA 15213

Contact: A Catherine Tack
(412) 622-3105
Hours: Winter: Mon-Wed, Fri, 9-9; Thurs and Sat, 9-5:30, Sun 1-5; summer hours same but closed Sun
Accessible to Public: Yes
Accessible to Scholars: Yes
Special Considerations: Materials only circulate to those with Carnegie Library of Pittsburgh cards; otherwise, all materials may be used in the library

Collections vary, and include:

Cyrus Hungerford Cartoons: Cartoons from the *Pittsburgh Post-Gazette,* December 9, 1941, to December 11, 1954; includes news clippings.

Other collections include the *C. Valentine Kirby Bookplate Collection;* a miscellany of cards; a picture file; a scrap-

book of trade cards; an extensive slide collection; and assorted Valentines.

504. Carnegie Mellon University Libraries, Special Collections
Hunt Library—Schenley Park
Pittsburgh, PA 15213

Contact: Mary Catharine Johnsen, Spec Collections Librarian
(412) 268-6622
Hours: Mon-Fri, 1-4:30 or by appt
Accessible to Public: Yes
Accessible to Scholars: Yes
Special Considerations: Appointments appreciated as collection not entirely cataloged

Anne Lyon Haight Collection: Over 400 editions and versions of "Twas the Night Before Christmas" by Clement C. Moore, mostly illustrated.

505. National Flag Foundation
Flag Plaza
Pittsburgh, PA 15219

Contact: George F Cahill, CAE, Pres
(412) 261-1776
Hours: Mon-Fri, 9-5; by appointment
Accessible to Public: Yes
Accessible to Scholars: Yes
Special Considerations: Appointments preferred, especially for group tours

Collections include materials related to American symbols, such as the eagle and the American flag as it has changed over time. There is a bicentennial collection that includes salutes by prominent Americans (for example, Lucius Clay and John Wayne), as well as a collection of cartoonists' depictions of the American bicentennial and flag.

506. University of Pittsburgh Libraries, Special Collections Department
363 Hillman Library
Pittsburgh, PA 15260

Contact: Charles E Aston, Jr
(412) 648-8191
Hours: Mon-Fri, 8:30-5
Accessible to Public: Yes
Accessible to Scholars: Yes

Archive of Popular Culture: Includes over 2,000 paperback science fiction novels, 14 journal titles, and a collection of science fiction fanzines; also included are over 11,000 inventoried comic books, plus collections of fanzines and pulp magazines.

Selinsgrove

507. Dr. John Charles Cooper, Private Collection

Dept of Philosophy and Religion,
   Susquahanna University
Selinsgrove, PA 17870

Contact: Dr J C Cooper
(717) 374-0101 Ext 4163
Hours: Mon-Fri, 9-3
Accessible to Public: Yes
Accessible to Scholars: Yes

Dr Cooper's collection includes materials on new religions and social movements; 16 file drawers of materials. Materials contain information on cults and radical movements, including "Moonies," faith healing, televangelists, exorcism, witchcraft, neo-fundamentalists, neo-Nazis, KKK, White power groups, Aryan Nation, terrorists, and student movements (especially 1960s), as well as anti-war movements and death of God theology.

Swarthmore

508. Friends Historical Library of Swarthmore College

Swarthmore College
Swarthmore, PA 19081

Contact: J William Frost, Dir
(215) 328-8496
Hours: Mon-Fri, 8:30-4:30; Sat, 9-noon
   when college in session; closed all of
   Aug, and hours may vary with school
   year
Accessible to Public: Yes
Accessible to Scholars: Yes
Special Considerations: Some materials
   may be restricted

Collections are extensive and include materials by and about the Society of Friends, as well as Quaker activity in literature, science, business, education, government, reform efforts in peace, Indian rights, women's rights, and abolition of slavery.

509. Swarthmore College Peace Coalition

Swarthmore College
Swarthmore, PA 19081

Contact: Curator
(215) 328-8557
Hours: Mon-Fri, 8:30-4:30; Sat, 9-noon
   during college session; closed all of
   Aug, and hours may vary with school
   year
Accessible to Public: Yes
Accessible to Scholars: Yes
Special Considerations: Some collections
   are restricted

Collections include miscellaneous graphics on subject of war and peace (two document boxes of cartoons, graphics, and postcards); approximately 4,000 posters, 1,000 buttons, and 200 bumper stickers on peace, war, and related issues.

University Park

510. Pennsylvania State University, Fred Waring Collection

220 Special Services Building
University Park, PA 16802

Contact: Peter Kiefer, Coord
(814) 863-2911
Hours: Inquire for hours
Accessible to Public: Yes
Accessible to Scholars: Yes

Fred Waring's America: This special collection consists of Waring memorabilia that span his career of 60 years. Materials included consist of 7,500 pages of scrapbook clippings (1922-1984); 6,000 photographs (1916-1984); 10,000 recordings of the Waring Radio Shows (1933-1949); Waring Television Shows and Specials (1949-1984, including scripts, rundowns, program listings, and production notes); 6,400 song titles in the Waring Pennsylvanians music library; 500 cartoons for Waring by the nation's finest cartoonists; his business and personal correspondence (1920s-1980s); and items of memorabilia.

511. Pennsylvania State University, Pattee Library, Rare Books and Special Collections
W342 Pattee Library, Pennsylvania
State University
University Park, PA 16802

Contact: Charles Mann
(814) 865-1793
Hours: Mon-Fri, 8-5
Accessible to Public: Yes
Accessible to Scholars: Yes

Science Fiction Collection: Consists of 3,300 English language volumes, including reference and critical works; also pulps and digests, 4,500 issues.

Warren

512. Warren County Historical Society
PO Box 427
Warren, PA 16365

Contact: Chase Putnam, Exec Dir
(814) 723-1795
Hours: Mon-Fri, 9-5
Accessible to Public: Yes
Accessible to Scholars: Yes
Special Considerations: Materials do not circulate

Special collections include greeting and business cards, postcards, and invitations; children's books and school books; theater and concert programs; club and organizational materials; sheet music; autograph books, almanacs, and recipe and cook books. Most materials relate to Warren County by origin or use.

513. Warren Library Association
205 Market St
Warren, PA 16365

Contact: Ann Lesser, Dir
(814) 723-4650
Hours: Mon-Fri, 9:30-9; Sat, 9-5; in June-Aug, 9-1
Accessible to Public: Yes
Accessible to Scholars: Yes
Special Considerations: Materials do not circulate

Robertson Music Collection: Contains 3,590 titles of sheet music, including popular show tunes from 1834 to 1955;

indexed by title, composer, stage show, or movie in which the tune was featured.

West Chester

514. West Chester University, Music Library
Swope Hall, West Chester University
West Chester, PA 19382

Contact: Paul Emmons, Music Librarian
(215) 436-2430
Hours: Mon-Thurs, 8am-11pm; Fri, 8-5; Sun, 2-9
Accessible to Public: Yes
Accessible to Scholars: Yes
Special Considerations: Those outside the university wishing to borrow materials should make arrangements with the administration or the circulation department of the F. H. Green Library, West Chester University

Music collection is primarily classical, but includes about 500 recordings of popular materials, as well as 200 scores of jazz and musical comedy.

Williamsport

515. Little League Baseball Museum
PO Box 3485
Williamsport, PA 17701

Contact: Jim Campbell, Dir; Marc G Pompeo, Curator
(717) 326-3607
Hours: Mon-Sat, 10-5; Sun, 1-5; Memorial Day through Labor Day, Mon-Sat, 10-8; Sun, 1-5
Accessible to Public: Yes
Accessible to Scholars: Yes
Special Considerations: Files and records available upon permission from museum's director or curator

Collections include over 500,000 rosters of Little League Baseball teams from 1954 to present, a complete collection of *Little Leaguer* magazine and *This Is Little League,* along with a complete collection of Little League World Series programs from 1947 to present. There is also a small collection of hardback books pertaining to the sport of baseball and Little League, as well as numerous pamphlets, booklets, rule books, literary articles, and assorted records tracing the growth and development of Little League. A film and videocassette library features full length treatments and highlights of past Little League World Series Games (1947-present), plus training films and special films related to the Little League.

York

516. Hake's Americana and Collectibles
PO Box 1444
York, PA 17405

Contact: Theodore L Hake
(717) 848-1333
Hours: Mon-Fri, 10-5
Accessible to Public: No
Accessible to Scholars: Yes
Special Considerations: Handled by individual circumstances; in some cases, a fee per picture may apply

For 20 years Hake's Americana and Collectibles has specialized in artifacts of popular culture, with a special emphasis on character and personality items. A negative file is maintained, with an estimated 100,000 items available; in addition to a large number of objects on hand, specialties include comic characters, Disneyana, western heroes, space heroes, and radio/TV/movies.

RHODE ISLAND

Newport

517. International Tennis Hall of Fame and Tennis Museum
194 Bellevue Ave
Newport, RI 02840

Contact: Jan Armstrong, Curator
(401) 849-6378
Hours: May-Oct, open every day from 10-5; Nov-Apr, open daily from 11-4
Accessible to Public: Yes
Accessible to Scholars: Yes
Special Considerations: Appointment required for serious research

Materials are varied and in the process of being cataloged: all relate to tennis

and its history in this country. Contact the curator for further information.

Providence

518. Brown University, John Hay Library
Box A, Brown University
Providence, RI 02912

Contact: Jennifer B Lee, Curator of Printed Books
(401) 863-1511
Hours: Mon-Fri, 9-5, during fall and spring semesters; also Wed-Thurs, 7pm-9pm
Accessible to Public: Yes
Accessible to Scholars: Yes
Special Considerations: Valid ID only, preferably with picture

Holdings are extensive, and include:

Manuscript Collections: Contains a variety of collections, including the *William Kelley Papers* with film and TV scripts, the *Davis Publications* with copies of Isaac Asimov's *Science Fiction Magazine* and other science fiction and mystery magazines, and the *William Chauncey Langdon Papers* with material relating to pageants in the first quarter of the 20th century.

Book and Periodical Collections: Include the *Harris Collection of American Poetry and Plays*, a comprehensive collection of material from 1609 to present with virtually all published radio, film, and TV scripts, and the *Dashiell Hammett Collection.*

Sheet Music Collection: Consists of about 500,000 items.

Broadsides Collection: Also includes ephemeral items, such as Christmas and other holiday cards, as well as rewards of merit issued by schools. Includes a World War I and II poster collection, slip ballads, carriers' addresses, the *Rider Collection* of broadsides, and a postcard collection.

Other collections include stamp collections, the *A. S. K. Brown Military Collection,* and the *Brown University Archives.*

519. Providence College, Phillips Memorial Library Archives

Providence College
Providence, RI 02918

Contact: Matthew J Smith, College
   Archivist
(401) 865-2377
Hours: Mon-Fri, 9-6
Accessible to Public: Yes
Accessible to Scholars: Yes

Rhode Island Football Officials' Association Collection: Includes material from 1929-present on Rhode Island interscholastic football league rules, events, members, etc.

Providence College Archives: Includes material from 1919-present, especially on the Physical Education and Athletics Department, with scrapbooks, game programs, pictures, publicity, clippings, and the like.

520. Providence Public Library

150 Empire St
Providence, RI 02903

Contact: Lance J Bauer, Special
   Collections Librarian
(401) 521-7792
Hours: Mon-Fri, 9:30-5; closed all day
   Wed and holidays
Accessible to Public: Yes
Accessible to Scholars: Yes
Special Considerations: Researchers
   should try to contact department in
   advance to confirm hours

Collections are extensive and varied, and include:

Hanes Checker Collection: An unusual collection of materials dating from 1650 to the early 20th century devoted to board games, with special emphasis on checkers.

Harris Collection of Civil War and Slavery: Materials dealing with the Civil War period include books, pamphlets, and periodicals, as well as Civil War broadsides, political tracts and ballads, manuscripts, and newspapers.

Percival Magic Collection: Materials from the reference library of a practicing magician.

Williams Collection: Contains materials on Irish culture, literature, history, and folklore.

521. Rhode Island Historical Society Library

121 Hope St
Providence, RI 02906

Contact: Joyce M Botelho, Graphics
   Curator or Denise J Bastien, Asst
   Curator
(401) 331-8575
Hours: Sept-May, Wed-Sat, 9-6; June-
   Aug, Mon, 12-9, Tues-Thurs, 9-6
Accessible to Public: Yes
Accessible to Scholars: Yes
Special Considerations: Researchers
   must follow the Library's policy on
   conditions for use of materials.
   Discuss with contact person.

Graphics Collection: Collection includes 250,000 images of Rhode Island people, places, and events from 17th century to present, especially 1880-1930, contained in photographs, prints, engravings, oral history, musical recordings, film, videotape, and other ephemera.

522. University of Rhode Island Library, Rhode Island Oral History Collection

Special Collections, University of Rhode
   Island Library
Providence, RI

Contact: Mr David Maslyn
(401) 792-2594
Hours: Mon-Fri, 9-5
Accessible to Public: Yes
Accessible to Scholars: Yes

RI Textile Workers: Oral History Memories: 60 interviews with workers in Rhode Island textile mills. Includes management as well as mill workers. Interviewees are from towns around Rhode Island; considerable data on social conditions of workers outside and inside the mills.

SOUTH CAROLINA

Charleston

523. Macaulay Museum of Dental History
171 Ashley Ave
Charleston, SC 29425

Contact: Anne K Donato, Curator
(803) 792-2288
Hours: Mon-Fri, 8:30-5, and by
appointment
Accessible to Public: Yes
Accessible to Scholars: Yes
Special Considerations: Public and/or
researchers must check with staff of
Waring Historical Library next door
for access to Museum

Collection contains materials relating to
the history of dentistry in the U.S., and
includes a series of dental chairs. Also
some trade cards and advertisements.

Clemson

524. Clemson University Libraries, Special Collections Libraries
Clemson University
Clemson, SC 29634-3001

Contact: Michael Kohl
(803) 656-5176
Hours: Mon-Fri, 8-4:30; Tues, 8am-9pm
when school in session
Accessible to Public: Yes
Accessible to Scholars: Yes

Collections include about 30 books of
Pogo comic strips, 500 World War II
American propaganda posters, and about
300 programs for Clemson's football and
basketball teams.

Greenville

525. Bob Jones University, Collection of Sacred Art
Wade Hampton Blvd
Greenville, SC 29614

Contact: Mrs Joan C Davis
(803) 242-5100 Ext 1050
Hours: Tues-Sun, 2-5; closed Mondays,
Dec 20-25, New Year's Day, and July
4

Accessible to Public: Yes
Special Considerations: Dress code
observed

Collections pertain to religious art and
Bible studies.

SOUTH DAKOTA

Sioux Falls

526. Center for Western Studies
Box 727j
Sioux Falls, SD 57197

Contact: Harry F Thompson, Archivist
(605) 336-4007
Hours: Mon-Fri, 8-5
Accessible to Public: Yes
Accessible to Scholars: Yes
Special Considerations: Appointments
appreciated for major research
projects; registration required of those
using special collections

Collections include eight photographic
collections; 200 manuscript collections;
two oral history collections on Sioux
Falls and early pioneers in South Dakota; 30,000 books, including dime novels, popular and classic literature; 180
periodicals, including popular magazines
and regional periodicals.

For further information on collections,
see *The Archives and Manuscript Collections of the Center for Western Studies,*
Harry F. Thompson, ed., 1984.

Spearfish

527. Leland D. Case Library for Western Historical Studies
Box 9511, College Station, 1200
University
Spearfish, SD 57783-1797

Contact: Miss Dora Ann Jones, Special
Collections Librarian
(605) 642-6361 or (605) 642-6883
Hours: Mon-Fri, 9-12, 1-4, during
academic sessions
Accessible to Public: Yes
Accessible to Scholars: Yes

Special Considerations: Completion of application for admission and issuance of ID card by the Special Collections Librarian

Collections still being processed, but contents cover all aspects of western history and culture, with many popular culture materials included.

Vermillion

528. American Indian Research Project/South Dakota Oral History Project
17 Dakota Hall, University of South Dakota
Vermillion, SD 57069

Contact: Dr Herbert Hoover, Dir; Ben Kitto, Asst Dir
(605) 677-5946
Hours: Mon-Fri, 8-12, 1:30-4:30; Sat-Sun by appointment
Accessible to Public: Yes
Accessible to Scholars: Yes

American Indian Research Project: Collection includes materials on Indian culture, religion, and history in South Dakota, Minnesota, Wisconsin, Montana, Idaho, Washington, and Canada. Includes the *Jurrens Collection of American Indian Music,* as well as 1,144 oral history tapes.

South Dakota Oral History Project: Consists of materials relating to White culture, religion, pioneer experiences, and history of South Dakota; includes 2,256 oral history tapes.

529. Shrine to Music Museum and Center for Study of the History of Musical Instruments
414 E Clark St
Vermillion, SD 57069

Contact: Dr Andre P Larson, Dir; Dr Margaret Downie Banks, Curator
(605) 677-5306
Hours: Mon-Fri, 9-4:30; Sat, 10-4:30; Sun, 2-4:30
Accessible to Public: Yes
Accessible to Scholars: Yes
Special Considerations: By appointment only for research

Musical Instrument Collection: Consists of 4,500 items, strong in all areas, including West European, American, and non-Western. Includes the *Arne B. Larson Collection, W. Wayne Sorensen Collection,* and the *Witten-Rawlins Collection.*

Sound Recordings Archive: Around 8,000-10,000 items, classical and popular, all forms of recordings.

Sheet Music Collection: Consists of about 6,000 items, popular and classical.

Collections also include an historic photographs archive—particularly strong in American bands of the Midwest—and a musical instrument maker/manufacturer sales catalog collection.

TENNESSEE

Clarksville

530. Austin Peay State University, Felix G. Woodward Library
Austin Peay State University
Clarksville, TN 37044

Contact: F Richard Vaughan
(615) 648-7914
Hours: Mon-Thur, 8am-10pm; Fri, 8-4:30; Sat, 10-5; Sun, 3-10; hours vary in summer
Accessible to Public: Yes
Accessible to Scholars: Yes
Special Considerations: Materials do not circulate

Dorothy Dix Collection: Includes papers, correspondence, photographs, scrapbooks, travel diaries, and other materials of Dorothy Dix, aka Elizabeth M. Gilmer, American advice columnist and author.

Harrogate

531. Lincoln Memorial University, The Abraham Lincoln Museum
Lincoln Memorial University
Harrogate, TN 37752

Contact: Judy Johnson, Dir of Program and Resource Development

(615) 869-3611
Hours: Mon-Fri, 9-4; Sat, 11-4; Sun, 1-4
Accessible to Public: Yes
Accessible to Scholars: Yes

Collections include 225,000 books, manuscripts, photographs, medallions, coins, musical scores, oil paintings, and sculptures of and about Lincoln, plus other Civil War Era artifacts.

Humboldt

532. Humboldt Strawberry Festival and Historical Museum
War Memorial Building
Humboldt, TN 38343

Contact: Jess Pritchard
(901) 784-3771
Hours: Tues, 2-5; Fri, 2-5; Sat, 10-2
Accessible to Public: Yes
Accessible to Scholars: Yes
Special Considerations: Phone contact available anytime

The collections relate to the history and development of the Strawberry Festival (celebrated for more than 50 years) and the history and development of Humboldt, and include numerous relics, artifacts, photographs, antiques, fashions, etc.

Johnson City

533. East Tennessee State University, Archives of Appalachia
Box 22450A, East Tennessee State University
Johnson City, TN 37614-0002

Contact: Marie Tedesco
(615) 929-5339
Hours: Mon-Fri, 8-4:30
Accessible to Public: Yes
Accessible to Scholars: Yes
Special Considerations: Researchers must fill out a "Researcher Registration" form

Rogersville Card and Label Company: Includes two boxes of tobacco product labels from various manufacturers, 1929-present, as well as two boxes of non-tobacco labels, 1929-present.

Burton-Manning Collection: Papers and tapes; mostly taped folklore and/or interviews with mountain people.

Broadside Television Collection: 139 videotapes on social, political, and religious life in Southern Appalachia.

Other collections include: *Kenneth Maynard Murray Photograph Collection, the Richard Blaustein Collection* on the history of country music, *Old Time Radio Reunion, and Homefolks Festival, Appalachian Preaching Mission Records,* and the *East Tennessee Medicine Company Collection.*

Jonesborough

534. National Association for the Preservation and Perpetuation of Storytelling
PO Box 309
Jonesborough, TN 37659

Contact: Jimmy Neil Smith
(615) 753-2171
Hours: Mon-Fri, 9-5
Accessible to Public: Yes
Accessible to Scholars: Yes
Special Considerations: By appointment only

A collection of audio and video recordings of contemporary storytelling available for research in Jonesborough.

Memphis

535. Memphis State University, Special Collections Department
Memphis State University Library
Memphis, TN 38152

Contact: Delanie Ross
(901) 454-2210
Hours: Mon-Fri, 8-4:30
Accessible to Public: Yes
Accessible to Scholars: Yes
Special Considerations: Researchers should be post-high school age

Mississippi Valley Collection: Includes several collections, such as the *Baldwin Collection* of children's books; the *Circus Collections*; an *Oral History Collection*; a *Sheet Music Collection* that includes Civil War, World Wars I and II, and ragtime; postcard collections; and photographic collections.

536. National Ornamental Metal Museum
374 W California Ave
Memphis, TN 38106

Contact: James Wallace, Dir
(901) 774-6380
Hours: Tues-Sun, 12-5
Accessible to Public: Yes
Accessible to Scholars: Yes
Special Considerations: Admission charge or pre-arranged meeting with staff members; materials do not circulate

Collections include the Julius Blum Collection and the Abe Sauer Collection of books, portfolios, and catalogs for metal art and industry; some date from 18th century. Also a slide library of contemporary metalwork from the U.S. and abroad, and a permanent collection of contemporary and historic metalwork with special emphasis on architectural ironwork.

Nashville

537. Country Music Foundation Library and Media Center
4 Music Square E
Nashville, TN 37203

Contact: Charlie Seemann, Deputy Dir for Collections and Research
(615) 256-1639
Hours: Mon-Fri, 9-5
Accessible to Public: Yes
Accessible to Scholars: Yes
Special Considerations: By appointment only; materials do not circulate

Roy Acuff Collection: Consists of print and nonprint materials relating to Acuff's career to date.

Extensive collections of recordings, books, photographs, sheet music, songbooks, videotapes, audiotapes, and films relating to country, folk, and gospel music.

538. F. Marion Crawford Memorial Society—Bibliotheca Crawfordiana
Saracinesca House, 3610 Meadowbrook Ave
Nashville, TN 37205

Contact: John C Moran
(615) 292-9695
Hours: By appointment
Accessible to Public: Yes
Accessible to Scholars: Yes
Special Considerations: Access to materials by appointment only

Bibliotheca Crawfordiana: The private library of the F. Marion Crawford Memorial Society consists of an extensive collection of first editions of the works of Crawford and many reprints. Also inludes microfilms of all Crawford's correspondence to his publishers (Macmillan, New York, and Macmillan, London) and other materials relating to Crawford.

Other collections include a collection of 1,000 paper-bound volumes of fantastic and imaginative literature, 1960-1975, and approximately 400 records of dance orchestras, 1920-1950, especially the Jan Garber Orchestra and the Xavier Cugat Orchestra. Includes many John McCormack original records.

539. The International Rock'N'Roll Music Association
PO Box 50111
Nashville, TN 37215

Contact: Bernard Walters
(615) 297-9072
Accessible to Public: No
Accessible to Scholars: No
Special Considerations: Materials accessible only by prior written request

Collection of various rock'n'roll related publications dating from the early 1960s, specializing in English rock music; 1,000 sound recordings; approximately 2,000 slides and photographs.

540. Museum of Tobacco Art and History
800 Harrison St
Nashville, TN 37203

Contact: David R Wright, Museum Mgr
(615) 242-9218
Hours: Tues-Sat, 10-4; closed major
holidays
Accessible to Public: Yes
Accessible to Scholars: Yes
Special Considerations: For major
research or photography, please
contact in advance

Museum of Tobacco Art and History/United States Tobacco Company: Extensive collection of fine tobacco-related antiques totalling about 600 items on display; includes cigar store figures, pipes from all parts of the world, extensive collection of meerschaum pipes, tobacco containers, snuff boxes, and advertising art, pre-historic to present; most of collection is European.

541. Public Library of Nashville and Davidson County, Children's International Education Center
222 8th Ave N
Nashville, TN 37203

Contact: Diane McNabb, Coord of
Children's Services
(615) 244-4700 Ext 60
Hours: Mon-Sat, 9-5
Accessible to Public: Yes
Accessible to Scholars: Yes
Special Considerations: Materials may be
checked out on adult library card; also
available through interlibrary loan

The Children's International Education Center is a constantly expanding collection of books (currently 2,000), music, and artifacts, including children's original art, relating to children from all over the world.

542. Public Library of Nashville and Davidson County, The Nashville Room
8th Ave N and Union
Nashville, TN 37203

Contact: Mary Glenn Hearne, Dir
(615) 244-4700 Ext 68
Hours: Mon-Fri, 9-7; Sat, 9-5; Sun (Oct-
May), 2-5
Accessible to Public: Yes
Accessible to Scholars: Yes

The Nashville Room contains several collections relating to Nashville. Includes *Nashville Authors Collection, Oral History Collection,* and postcard and sheet music collections. Also includes the *Naff Collection* of photographs, posters, and programs of performances held in Ryman Auditorium from 1920-1968.

543. Tennessee State Library and Archives
403 7th Ave North
Nashville, TN 37219

Contact: Fran Schell
(615) 741-2764
Hours: Mon-Sat, 8-8; Sun, 12:30-9
Accessible to Public: Yes
Accessible to Scholars: Yes

Collections include *Rose Music Collection* of music books and sheet music between 1850-1950; over 100 scrapbooks of Tennessee and Southern history, culture, and geography; photographs; broadsides; and *Fair Brochures Collection* of county, state, and local fairs from 1870s to present.

544. Vanderbilt University, Heard Library, Vanderbilt Television News Archive
Vanderbilt University, 419 21st Ave S
Nashville, TN 37240-0007

Contact: James P Pilkington
(615) 322-2927
Hours: Mon-Fri, 8-5
Accessible to Public: Yes
Accessible to Scholars: Yes

A comprehensive collection on videotape of the evening news telecasts of ABC, CBS, and NBC from August 5, 1968, to present, as well as news special broadcasts; currently 14,000 hours of materials. Evening newscasts indexed in detail in publication *Television News Index and Abstracts.*

TEXAS

Arlington

545. Bauder Fashion College Library
508 S Center St
Arlington, TX 76010

Contact: Kevin Park
(817) 277-6666 Ext 47
Hours: Mon-Thurs, 8am-9pm; Fri, 8-5;
Sun, 5-9
Accessible to Public: No
Accessible to Scholars: Yes
Special Considerations: By appointment
only

Collections include 3,000 current and
retrospective titles dealing with the areas
of fashion design, fashion merchandising,
and interior design; also includes periodicals dealing with the fashion areas.

Austin

546. Austin Public Library, Austin History Center
PO Box 2287
Austin, TX 78768

Contact: Audray Bateman Randle,
Curator
(512) 473-4280
Hours: Tues-Thurs, 9-9; Fri-Sat, 9-6;
Sun, 12-6; closed Mon
Accessible to Public: Yes
Accessible to Scholars: Yes
Special Considerations: Closed stacks

Greeting Card Collection: About 300
cards sorted by type, 1800s-present.

Urbantke Papers: Two scrapbooks
containing about 250 holiday and birthday postcards, 1900-1920.

Preston Collection: Consists of Valentines, 1890-1915.

O. Henry Collection: Includes over 200
scattered issues of literary magazines,
1890s-1920s, in which O. Henry's short
stories made their first appearance.

Collections also include an *Oral History
Collection* of 800 tapes and an *Austin
Authors Collection.*

547. University of Texas-Austin, Harry Ransom Humanities Research Center
PO Box 7219
Austin, TX 78713-7219

Contact: Office of the Librarian
(512) 471-9119
Hours: Mon-Fri, 9-5; Sat, 9-12
Accessible to Public: Yes
Accessible to Scholars: Yes
Special Considerations: Photo ID;
application form must be completed to
use manuscript materials

Collections are extensive, including a
*Dime Novel Collection; Popular Imagery
Collection; Little Blue Books Collection;
L. W. Currey Science Fiction and Fantasy Collection; World War I Poster Collection; Chess Collection; FDR Collection*
of memorabilia related to Franklin Dela-
no Roosevelt; *Spanish Comedias Sueltas
Collection* dating from the late 17th century to the early 20th; and an *Ellery
Queen Collection,* among others. Also a
Theater Arts Library containing additional relevant collections, including an
MGM Collection and the David O. Selz-
nick Film Archives.

548. University of Texas-Austin General Libraries, Eugene C. Barker Texas History Center
Sid Richardson Hall 2101
Austin, TX 78713

Contact: Dr Don E Carleton, Dir; Ralph
Elder, Head, Reference Unit
(512) 471-5961
Hours: Mon-Sat, 8-5
Accessible to Public: Yes
Accessible to Scholars: Yes
Special Considerations: Photo ID; read
and sign rule sheet

Texas Film Collection: Includes promotional materials (lobby cards, broadsides, press kits, posters, etc) and scripts
documenting films with a Texas setting
or theme.

Texas Music Collection: Disc and
taped recordings of all varieties of Texas
vernacular music (blues, country, rock,
ethnic), Texas studios and artists; also
sheet music and materials, including
posters, broadsides, and other ephemera
documenting the Texas music scene.

Ephemera Collection: Assorted ephemeral items, including posters, broadsides, invitations, programs, leaflets, menus, calendars, advertisements, business cards, and bumper stickers documenting Texas and Texans.

Canyon

549. Panhandle-Plains Historical Museum
Box 967, WT Station
Canyon, TX 79016

Contact: Claire R Kuehn, Librarian
(806) 655-7191
Hours: Sept-May, Tues-Sat, 10-5; June-Aug, Mon-Sat, 10-6, Sun, 2-6
Accessible to Public: Yes
Accessible to Scholars: Yes

Pioneer Town: Reconstruction of life in a small community in 1900, with stores, shops, homes, and a school.

Bob Wills Memorial Archive of Popular Music: Includes phonograph records, books, articles, discographies, and other information relating to contemporary music.

This is the oldest and largest state-supported museum in Texas, so collections are extensive. Includes a photographic archive, a manufacturer's trade literature collection, and collections of greeting cards, postcards, and stereopticon cards.

College Station

550. Texas A&M University Library, Special Collections
Texas A&M University
College Station, TX 77843

Contact: Dr Donald H Dyal
(409) 845-1951
Hours: Mon-Fri, 8-5
Accessible to Public: Yes
Accessible to Scholars: Yes

Collections include four filing cabinet drawers of materials on the Ku Klux Klan, including membership cards, sheet music, robes, hoods, patches, and pamphlets; postcards, calendars, labels, and the like utilizing the work of 50 illustrators of the West, such as Remington, Russell, Beeler, and Borein; 10,000 prints extracted from *Harper's, Gleason's, Cen-*

tury, and *Scribners*; and 150 posters, most of Michael Moorcock, British fantasy author, but some World War II.

Dallas

551. American Fan Collector Association & Antique Fan Museum
The Fan Man, 4606 Travis
Dallas, TX 75205

Contact: Kurt House
(214) 559-4440
Hours: Mon-Sat 10-6; closed national holidays
Accessible to Public: Yes
Accessible to Scholars: Yes
Special Considerations: By appointment only

Collections are maintained as a part of a retail business that specializes in antique fans and other mechanical American antiques. Extensive collection of all types of mechanical fans, including ceiling fans from 1880s-present, electrical desk fans, and water-powered fans. Museum has hundreds of examples of American ingenuity applied to cooling devices. Also literature and catalogs of major American electrical appliance companies.

552. Southern Methodist University, DeGolyer Library
PO Box 396
Dallas, TX 75275

Contact: Dawn Letson
(214) 692-3231
Hours: Mon-Fri, 8:30-5
Accessible to Public: Yes
Accessible to Scholars: Yes
Special Considerations: Call the library in advance

Collections include a *Western Novel Collection* (1,500 volumes); a *Railroad Model Collection*, O and HO scale, of about 1,500 items; a *Photograph Collection*, including prints, slides, and glass plates on the West as well as American and foreign railroads; and railroad timetables, menus, and other ephemera cataloged by the name of the railroad.

Denton

553. Texas Woman's University, Blagg-Huey Library
PO Box 23715
Denton, TX 76204

Contact: Metta Nicewarner, Special
   Collections Librarian
(817) 898-3751 or (817) 898-3747
Hours: Mon-Fri, 8-6
Accessible to Public: Yes
Accessible to Scholars: Yes
Special Considerations: Most materials
   do not circulate; rare materials used
   under supervision

Cookbook Collection: Consists of 8,442
cookbooks, some dating back to the 17th
century; most are American or British,
some international; also some 18th century hand-written examples.

Cookbooklet Collection: Around 2,000
recipe booklets issued by food/appliance
companies, governmental departments/
agencies, private organizations, personal
authors, and magazine/newspaper publishers. Some date from 1800s.

Menu Collection: Approximately 1,500
menus from restaurants around the
world; some date from early 1900s.

El Paso

554. University of Texas-El Paso, Institute of Oral History
University of Texas-El Paso
El Paso, TX 79968

Contact: Contact Chairman, Department
   of History
(915) 747-5508
Hours: Tues and Thurs, 9-5
Accessible to Public: Yes
Accessible to Scholars: Yes

Oral History Collection: Collection of
750 taped interviews with transcripts;
centers on personalities, history, and
current issues relating to the U.S.-Mexi-
co border; one-third of the interviews are
in Spanish.

Houston

555. Houston Public Library, Fine Arts and Recreation
500 McKinney
Houston, TX 77002

Contact: John Harvath, Mgr, Fine Arts
   and Recreation
(713) 236-1313
Hours: Mon-Fri, 9-9; Sat, 9-6; Sun, 2-6
Accessible to Public: Yes
Accessible to Scholars: Yes
Special Considerations: Houston Public
   Library card necessary to check out
   materials

**Nineteenth Century American Sheet
Music Collection:** Includes 527 pieces
of sheet music from the 19th century; all
are documented and cataloged.

556. Houston Public Library, Special Collections
500 McKinney
Houston, TX 77002

Contact: Donna Grove
(713) 236-1313 ext 293
Hours: Mon-Fri, 9-6
Accessible to Public: Yes
Accessible to Scholars: Yes
Special Considerations: Materials used
   under staff supervision and do not
   leave special collections department

JIS Collection: Includes 1,497 children's books showing trends and development of early children's popular literature.

Norma Meldrum Collection: Contains
5,475 children's books showing changing
patterns, styles, and trends in the best of
children's literature appropriate for 15-
year-olds; includes all important literary
award winners.

Comic Book Collection: 602 comic
books, includes Batman, Superman,
Superboy, and Tarzan.

Other collections include *Mad Magazine
Collection, Pop-ups Collection, Chapbooks and New England Primers Collection, Travel and Promotional Pamphlets
Collection,* and the *Harriet Dickson
Reynolds Collection* of specialized children's books.

557. Texas Southern University Library, The Heartman Collection

3100 Cleburne
Houston, TX 77004

Contact: Dorothy H Chapman
(713) 527-7149
Hours: Mon-Fri, 8 am-10 pm; Sat, 9-5; Sun, 2-8
Accessible to Public: Yes
Accessible to Scholars: Yes
Special Considerations: Noncirculating collection

Materials include 25,000 volumes and 24 legal size drawers of vertical files related to Black culture.

Irving

558. The National Museum of Communications, Inc

Four Dallas Communications Complex, Ste 123, Lock Box 55, 6305 N O'Connor Rd
Irving, TX 75039-3510

Contact: William J Bragg
(214) 556-1234
Hours: Mon-Fri, 10-4
Accessible to Public: Yes
Accessible to Scholars: Yes
Special Considerations: Museum personnel must be present during use of printed items and photographs

Dilled as the world's largest collection of antique and modern broadcast and communications-related artifacts—21 moving vans full in all. Personal items belonging to such greats as Thomas A. Edison, Walter Cronkite, Elvis Presley, Buddy Holly, Bill Haley, and others. Also a library containing over 40,000 sound recordings, films, video tapes, books, drawings, and pictures.

Panhandle

559. The Carson County Square House Museum

PO Box 276
Panhandle, TX 79068

Contact: Don L Markham
(806) 537-3118
Hours: Mon-Fri, 9-5:30
Accessible to Public: Yes

Accessible to Scholars: Yes
Special Considerations: Special permission for use of archives

Historical artifacts from the Texas Panhandle, including weapons, tools, apparel, and transportation from stone age to present. Archives contain photographs, documents, and correspondence from the bison hunters and plains Indians of the late 1700s to present.

Prairie View

560. Prairie View A&M University, W. R. Banks Library Archives

Prairie View, TX 77446

Contact: Ruth Wachter-Nelson, Archivist/Special Collections Librarian
(409) 857-3119 or (409) 857-2012
Hours: Mon-Fri, 8-12, 1-5; closed holidays; appointments recommended
Accessible to Public: Yes
Accessible to Scholars: Yes
Special Considerations: Some materials restricted and accessible only with special permission; materials do not circulate

Campus Photographic Collection: More than 200 photographs depicting campus life at one of the nation's historic Black land grant colleges, 1884-present.

Negro Agricultural Extension Service Photographic Collection/NAES Record Collection: Consists of more than 1,500 photographs and negatives depicting rural Black Texan farm families and work done by NAES, 1919-1960s.

Dr E. B. Evans Veterinary Medicine Collection: Includes materials used by this rural Black veterinarian when making calls to area farms, 1918-1930.

Richardson

561. The University of Texas-Dallas Library, Department of Special Collections

PO Box 830643
Richardson, TX 75083-0643

Contact: Dr Larry D Sall

(214) 690-2570
Hours: Mon-Thurs, 9-6; Fri, 9-5
Accessible to Public: Yes
Accessible to Scholars: Yes
Special Considerations: Materials do not circulate

History of Aviation Collection: Includes juvenile literature, toys, and other aviation-related artifacts, and is part of a collection covering the entire spectrum of aviation and space development.

Temple

562. SPJST Czech Heritage Museum
PO Box 100
Temple, TX 76503

Contact: Otto Hanus; Thelma Bartosh
(817) 773-1575
Hours: Mon-Fri, 8-12, 1-5
Accessible to Public: Yes
Accessible to Scholars: Yes

Collections include 18,000 Czech-language books, including fiction; collection of about 75 svabach Bibles; microfilms of early Czech newspapers of 1900s; and a museum of artifacts brought to America from Czechoslovakia and materials used by Czechs to make their living in America—about 2,000 artifacts in all.

Waco

563. Baylor University, Crouch Music Library
Box 6307
Waco, TX 76076

Contact: Dr Avery T Sharp; Gregg S Geary
(817) 755-1366
Hours: Mon-Thurs, 8am-12:45am; Fri, 8-5; Sat, 1-6; Sun, 2pm-12:45am
Accessible to Public: Yes
Accessible to Scholars: Yes
Special Considerations: Materials contained in special collections available only on Mon-Thurs, 8am-9pm and on Fri, 8-5

Frances G. Spencer Collection of American Printed Music: Consists of about 30,000 individual items of sheet music, including musical comedy items, songs about Texas, and presidential and political items, dating 1790-1955.

Travis and Margaret Johnson Collection of Rare Music: Includes American song books, songsters, and tune-books.

O'Neal Purchase: This extensive collection, contains many copies of American popular songs dating 1910-1970, is currently being processed.

UTAH

Logan

564. Ronald V. Jensen Living Historical Farm
Utah State University
Logan, UT 84322

Contact: Dr Jay Allan Anderson
(801) 245-4064
Hours: Tues-Sat, 8-4
Accessible to Public: Yes
Accessible to Scholars: Yes

Collection of books, articles, journals, and realia on living history (historical simulation). The most extensive collections of living history in North America, compiled by Jay Allan Anderson, author of *Time Machines* and *The Living History Sourcebook*.

Provo

565. Brigham Young University, Harold B. Lee Library
Brigham Young University
Provo, UT 84602

Contact: Elizabeth Pope; Merle Lamson
(801) 378-6735 or (801) 378-6730
Hours: Mon-Sat, 7am-11pm
Accessible to Public: Yes
Accessible to Scholars: Yes
Special Considerations: Some items are not available for browsing but can circulate

Science Fiction/Fantasy Collection: Approximately 7,000 items, including fiction, reference works (bibliographies, history and criticism, etc.), and periodicals titles. Collection also contains supernatural and horror works.

566. Brigham Young University, Harold B. Lee Library, Archives and Manuscripts
Brigham Young University
Provo, UT 84602

Contact: James V D'Arc, Curator
(801) 378-3514
Hours: Call for hours
Accessible to Public: Yes
Accessible to Scholars: Yes
Special Considerations: Call for
  restrictions

Arts and Communications Archives:
Contains a number of collections pertaining to popular culture and communications. Cinema collections include papers and correspondence of Bosley Crowther, Cecil B. DeMille, Andy Devine, Paul Fix, Gordon Jump, May Mann, James Stewart, and others. Also included are collections on the National Association of Theater Owners, Republic Pictures, and a motion picture and television script collection. Materials are numerous.

567. McCurdy Historical Doll Museum
246 North 100 East
Provo, UT 84601

Contact: Shirley B Paxman, Dir
(801) 377-9935
Hours: Tues-Sat, 12-6
Accessible to Public: Yes
Accessible to Scholars: Yes
Special Considerations: Admission
  charged; adults, $2.00, children under
  12, $1.00

Library of Doll and Toy Books: 100
volumes used for reference.

Doll Collection: Contains 4,000 items, including many types of dolls, such as story book dolls, international dolls, women of the Bible, wives of U.S. presidents, American Indian dolls, Black dolls, Shirley Temple dolls, American folk dolls, Russian nesting dolls, and some modern dolls.

Also collections of antique teddy bears, toys, and paper dolls dating from 1810; Noah's Arks; wooden toys, games, and miniatures.

Salt Lake City

568. Museum of Church History and Art
45 N West Temple
Salt Lake City, UT 84150

Contact: Contact Curator
(801) 531-3310
Hours: Weekdays, Sat
Accessible to Public: Yes
Accessible to Scholars: Yes

Collections consist of hundreds of Mormon journals, some original, some transcribed, describing early members' experiences as pioneers, outcasts, and early Salt Lake society, 1830-1900s. There is also a children's museum with early frontier toys.

VERMONT

Manchester

569. The American Museum of Fly Fishing
PO Box 42
Manchester, VT 05254

Contact: John H Merwin, Exec Dir
(802) 375-9256
Hours: Except major holidays: May 1-
  Oct 31, daily, 10-4; Nov 1-Apr 30,
  Mon-Fri, 10-4; weekends by
  appointment only
Accessible to Public: Yes
Accessible to Scholars: Yes
Special Considerations: Museum
  members have free access to the
  galleries and to the libraries by
  appointment

Collections are extensive, including more than 1,000 rods, 400 reels, thousands of flies, and other items and memorabilia related to the history of fly fishing.

Rutland

570. Norman Rockwell Museum
RR 3 Box 7209 Rt 4 East
Rutland, VT 05701

Contact: Fred Brinckerhoff
(802) 773-6095

Hours: Daily, 9-5
Accessible to Public: Yes
Accessible to Scholars: Yes
Special Considerations: Token admission

This collection of 2,200 pieces includes Norman Rockwell magazine covers, advertising pieces, novel and short story illustrations, movie and war posters, calendars, greeting cards, postage stamps, memorabilia, and other published works dating from 1912-1978.

VIRGINIA

Alexandria

571. Public Broadcasting System Program Data and Analysis Department
1320 Braddock Pl
Alexandria, VA 22314

Contact: Glenn Clatworthy, Program
   Data Specialist
(703) 739-5014
Hours: Contact by phone during normal
   business hours, Mon-Fri, 9-5:30
Accessible to Public: No
Accessible to Scholars: No
Special Considerations: Printed
   resources may be used by the general
   public/scholars in special
   circumstances

PBS holds an archival oneor two-inch video tape copy of virtually every program broadcast by the network since its inception in the early 1970s, and also houses many films and tapes distributed by its predecessor, National Educational Television; descriptive materials for most of the programs from both eras are also available. However, as PBS has no screening facilities for materials, only costly dubbed viewing copies can be obtained through PBS with written permission from a program's owner. Scholars interested in specific programs may wish to contact their local public television stations first, and should call directly with specific inquiries.

Arlington

572. Chesapeake and Ohio Historical Society, Inc.
PO Box 7082
Arlington, VA 22207

Contact: Randolph Kean, Archivist
None available
Hours: Advance appointment
Accessible to Public: Yes
Accessible to Scholars: Yes
Special Considerations: Membership may
   be required; dues are currently $13 per
   year

The Society maintains collections of archival materials, including manuscripts, tapes, publications, images (both photographic negatives and prints), diagrams, maps, and similar materials that are available to researchers, writers, historians, rail fans, and modellers. All of the materials relate in some manner to the Chesapeake and Ohio Railway and its predecessors and successors.

Charlottesville

573. University of Virginia Library, Manuscripts Department and University Archives
University of Virginia Library
Charlottesville, VA 22903-2498

Contact: Curator of Manuscripts
(804) 924-3025
Hours: Mon-Fri, 9-5; Sat, 9-1
Accessible to Public: Yes
Accessible to Scholars: Yes
Special Considerations: Accession
   numbers for specific collections should
   be used during inquiries; materials in
   the Rare Book and Manuscript
   collections may be used under the
   supervision of staff members

Collections at this Library are extensive, and many popular culture materials, such as postcards, Christmas cards, cookbooks, and sheet music are mixed in with other collections.

(2531) **Frederick Otto Seibel Collection:** Includes many original cartoons by this cartoonist for the *Richmond Times-Dispatch* (1886-1969), plus research files.

(6442) **Bernard M. Meeks Collection:** Consists of original cartoons and drawings c. 1860-1945 by Thomas Nast, Walt Disney, Al Capp, Rube Goldberg, Charles Dana Gibson, and others.

(10493) **Kevin Barry Pardue Archive of Traditional Music:** Consists of records, tapes, texts, and scores from Angloand Afro-American traditional music c.1940 to present. Includes recordings of early hillbilly and "race" music.

(123) **Winston Wilkinson Collection:** Consists of traditional Virginia ballads, folk songs, and dance tunes collected between 1932 and 1941 and folk music collected by the WPA in Kentucky, 1938.

(9829) **Arthur Kyle Davis Collection (1897-1972):** Consists of materials collected by this University of Virginia professor. Included are proofs of his books, plus correspondence and other material on ballads, ballad collecting, folk festivals, and traditional Virginia folk music.

(9919) **Naomi Hintz Papers (1936-1972):** Includes correspondence, drafts, and manuscripts of many "true stories" by this writer for confession and ladies magazines such as *Modern Romance.* (NUCMC MS77-1225)

In addition to Ms. Hintz's papers, the library also has correspondence and manuscripts of hundreds of American authors, including S. S. Van Dine, in the Clifton Waller Barrett Library and Virginia Writers Collections.

Chincoteague

574. Oyster Museum
PO Box 4—Maddox Blvd
Chincoteague, VA 23336

Contact: Nicki West
(804) 336-6191
Hours: Memorial Day through Labor Day, daily, 10-5; weekends, spring and fall
Accessible to Public: Yes
Accessible to Scholars: Yes

Collections include live marine exhibits, materials on the seafood and oyster industries, and material relating to marine biology and the history of the area.

Danville

575. National Tobacco-Textile Museum
614 Lynn St
Danville, VA 24541

Contact: Samuel W Price, Dir
(804) 797-9437
Hours: Mon-Fri, 10-4
Accessible to Public: Yes
Accessible to Scholars: Yes

Advertising Art Collection: Consists of materials dating from 1860 to present on tobacco products; includes point of sale colored lithographs on cigars, loose leaf, cigarettes, pipe, and chewing tobacco. Also includes 12 notebooks of advertising premiums inserted in cigarette packs, 1900-1940s, 1,500 cards; 5,300 examples of novelty cigarette pack art, 1886-1970s; and about 100 novelty advertising items, such as tobacco tins and plug cutters.

Pipe Collection: Unique collection of 400 pipes, includes briar, meerschaum, and clay. Also includes authentic "Indian Peace Pipe" and personal pipes from former President Gerald Ford, former British Prime Minister Harold Wilson, and the late Egyptian President Anwar Sadat.

Cigarette Lighter Collection: Consists of approximately 3,100 lighters from the most primitive to the modern day disposable lighters.

The museum also has three operating textile machines and a reference library containing more than 1,100 volumes.

Fairfax

576. Fenwick Library, Special Collections and Archives
George Washington University
Fairfax, VA 22030

Contact: Ruth Kerns
(703) 323-2251
Hours: Mon-Fri, 8:30-5
Accessible to Public: Yes
Accessible to Scholars: Yes

The Library of Congress Federal Theater Project Collection: Contains the records of the Federal Theater Project, 1935-1939. Includes playscripts, set and costume designs, photographs, negatives, posters, production bulletins, playbills, and other related materials—525,000 items in all.

Alexander Haight Civil War Collection: Consists of materials relating to the Civil War and the Haight family, owners of Sully Plantation, a Fairfax County Park Authority Historical Site. Includes Indian artifacts.

Ollie Atkins Photographic Collection: Contains over 15,000 negatives, contact sheets, and photographs, and over 250 matted photographs dating from 1946 to 1968, and includes files on Dwight D. Eisenhower, John and Robert Kennedy, and Lyndon Johnson.

Northern Virgina Oral History Project: Series One of this project consists of about 80 interviews, conducted between 1962 and 1981, documenting community and family life in the Fairfax area. Series Two consists of about 16 interviews, conducted in 1982-83, documenting changes in the Northern Virginia area since World War II.

McLean

577. Robert E. Lee Memorial Library, Arlington House
Turkey Run Park
McLean, VA 22101

Contact: Agnes Mullins, Curator
(703) 557-0613
Hours: Oct-Mar, 9:30-4:30; Apr-Sept, 9: 30-6
Accessible to Public: Yes
Accessible to Scholars: Yes
Special Considerations: By appointment only

M. C. Ewing Collection: Consists of three document boxes of the Alexandria Canal Papers, 1843-1845.

Library collections include three document boxes of 19th century sheet music, 1830-1870.

Newport News

578. Christopher Newport College
50 Shoe Ln
Newport News, VA 23606-2988

Contact: Dr C W Brockett
Hours: Tues, Thurs, 9-12, 1-5
Accessible to Public: Yes
Accessible to Scholars: Yes
Special Considerations: Advance notice by letter or telephone recommended but not required

American Music Archive: Consists of materials relevant to various aspects of popular music, including popular vocal music and piano music.

579. War Memorial Museum of Virginia
9285 Warwick Blvd, Huntington Park
Newport News, VA 23607

Contact: John V Quarstein
(804) 247-8523
Hours: Mon-Sat, 9-5; Sun, 1-5
Accessible to Public: Yes
Accessible to Scholars: Yes
Special Considerations: Objects on exhibit and in storage are available for scholastic review by appointment only

Collections consist of about 60,000 3-D objects relating to U.S. military history since 1775 and include, one of the largest—4,000 items—collections of propaganda posters as well as paintings and illustrations by such artists as Walter Whitehead and Herbert Morton Stoops; a collection of 3,000 different firearms, including rifles, handguns, destructive devices, artillery, and bladed weapons, spanning the period of 1600-1980; U.S. military and militia uniforms, 1800-1980, and foreign military uniforms, 1900-1970 (2,000 items); 10,000 items of accoutrements and equipment, both U.S. and foreign, primarily 1800-1970; 15,000 U.S. and foreign insignias, 1860-1970; a U.S. and foreign military history research library containing 20,000 items, 1600-1980; a U.S. and foreign military history film collection consisting of 500 items, 1914-1975; and archives and photographs of U.S. and foreign military history numbering about 15,000 items, 1600-1985.

Paeonian Springs

580. American Work Horse Museum Library

PO Box 88
Paeonian Springs, VA 22129

Contact: Dr Henry L Buckardt
(703) 338-6290
Hours: Apr-Oct, Wed, 9-5; other times
by appointment
Accessible to Public: Yes
Accessible to Scholars: Yes

Collections consist of 800 books, pamphlets, circulars and pictures about the work horse in America, dating from 1850. Also included is a complete set of USDA Yearbooks, 1900-1985.

Richmond

581. Edgar Allen Poe Museum

1914-16 E Main St
Richmond, VA 23223

Contact: Dr Bruce V English, Pres, Poe
Foundation, Inc
(804) 648-5523
Hours: Tues-Sat, 10-4; Sun-Mon, 1:30-4;
closed Christmas Day
Accessible to Public: Yes
Accessible to Scholars: Yes
Special Considerations: By appointment
only for scholarly research; collection
used under supervision of staff

Collection includes books, manuscripts and other archival materials, paintings, and furniture. The museum presents the life and career of Poe, documenting his legend with pictures, relics, and verse, and focusing on his years in Richmond.

582. Museum of the Confederacy

1201 E Clay St
Richmond, VA 23219

Contact: Elizabeth S Lux, Dir; David
Hahn, Curator of Collections; Guy R
Swanson, Curator of Manuscripts and
Archives
(804) 649-1861
Hours: Mon-Sat, 10-5; Sun, 1-5; closed
for major holidays
Accessible to Public: Yes
Accessible to Scholars: Yes

Special Considerations: Scholars wishing
to use the museum's library or
examine specific objects must arrange
an appointment

The Museum of the Confederacy houses the largest collection of objects associated with the Confederate States of America (1861-1865); its library contains a collection of several thousand manuscripts, other printed and written sources, and over 5,000 photographs related to this time. Of primary interest are materials related to the only president of the Confederacy, Jefferson Davis, and his family. Located next to the Museum is the White House of the Confederacy, the Davis family's wartime residence in Richmond, with related furnishings and objects. The Museum's collections also contain materials associated with the Confederate memorial period, 1865-1920. Extensive uncataloged and fragile ephemera collections consist of many collage materials made by private citizens during the period 1860-1890 as memorials to the "Lost Cause." There also is a collection of veterans magazines published 1900-1925.

583. Virginia Commonwealth University, James Branch Cabell Library

901 Park Ave, Box 2033
Richmond, VA 23284-0001

Contact: Katherine Bachman, Betsy
Parkin, Archivists
(804) 257-1108
Hours: Mon-Fri, 8-5
Accessible to Public: Yes
Accessible to Scholars: Yes

Richmond Oral History Association and Related Oral History Collections: Richmonders discuss their lives and the history of Richmond.

Fred Otto Seibel Collection: Includes Seibel's papers and correspondence, 34 original cartoons, and sketchbooks. Complete set of unpublished cartoons from *Knickerbocker Press* and the *Richmond Times-Dispatch.*

Chick Larsen Collection: 240 original cartoons and drawings and an incomplete set of published cartoons.

C. H. "Bill" Sykes Collection: 160 original editorial cartoons.

John L. Clarke Jazz Collection: Consists of 2,900 recordings, including those of Paul Whiteman, Artie Shaw, Benny Goodman, Miles Davis, Louis Armstrong, Duke Ellington, and other lesser known ensembles, such as the Dutch Swing College Band and the Jazz Club Mystery Jivers.

Other partial collections of cartoons and caricatures from known artists/cartoonists include work by Hank Ketcham, Rube Goldberg, Perry Barlow, Glenn Bernhardt, Jeff McNelly, and many others.

584. Virginia State Library, Picture Collection
11th St at Capitol Square
Richmond, VA 23219-3491

Contact: Jane Sumpter, Librarian; Ann L Tuttle, Asst
(804) 786-8958
Hours: Tues-Fri, 8:15-5
Accessible to Public: Yes
Accessible to Scholars: Yes
Special Considerations: Advance notice by letter or telephone recommended but not required

Works Progress Administration Historical Inventory of Virginia Collection: Consists of 19,000 black-and-white photographs of houses and buildings with accompanying narrative histories.

Harry C. Mann Collection: Consists of 2,418 black-and-white photographs of the Norfolk, Virginia, area (1906-1924).

Hampton Roads Port of Embarkation, 1941-1945: Collection of black-and-white photographs cover events and military personnel in the area (uncataloged).

Additional collections consist of 88,000 black-and-white photographs and prints, e.g., lithographs, engravings, and sketches, as well as 3,000 broadsides and 4,500 pieces of sheet music relating to Virginia or Virginians.

Williamsburg

585. Abby Aldrich Rockefeller Folk Art Center, The Colonial Williamsburg Foundation
PO Box C
Williamsburg, VA 23187

Contact: Anne Watkins, Registrar/Librarian
(804) 229-1000 Ext 2186
Hours: Mon-Fri, 8:30-5
Accessible to Public: Yes
Accessible to Scholars: Yes
Special Considerations: By appointment only; materials do not circulate

The Abby Aldrich Rockefeller Folk Art Center houses a collection of folk art, one of the finest such collections in the nation.

586. Colonial Williamsburg Foundation, Department of the Library
PO Box C
Williamsburg, VA 23187

Contact: Susan Berg
(804) 220-7423
Hours: Mon-Fri, 8-5; Sat, 9-1
Accessible to Public: Yes
Accessible to Scholars: Yes
Special Considerations: Advance notice of visit preferred

Special collections include items on area history, 5,000 volumes of 17th and 18th century printed books, and 500 items of 18th century music.

WASHINGTON

La Conner

587. Skagit County Historical Museum
PO Box 818
La Conner, WA 98257

Contact: David J Van Meer, Curator/Librarian
(206) 466-3365
Hours: Mon-Thurs, 10-4
Accessible to Public: Yes
Accessible to Scholars: Yes

Special Considerations: Archives accessible by appointment only; calls should be 24 to 48 hours in advance

Collections are varied and include 169 popular sound recordings from 1905 to the 1930s, some of which are Edison cylinder recordings; 87 pieces of sheet music and 77 children's books published between 1880 and 1920; 345 popular periodicals published between 1880 and 1950; 243 oral history transcripts of interviews with Skagit County "old timers" who describe everyday life as they remember it from 1890 through the 1930s; 328 stereopticon cards covering the 1880s through the early 1900s; and more than 8,000 photographs taken between 1880 and the early 1920s.

Pullman

588. Washington State University, Rare Books Collection
Holland Library
Pullman, WA 99164

Contact: John Guido
(509) 335-4558
Hours: Mon-Fri, 8-5
Accessible to Public: Yes
Accessible to Scholars: Yes
Special Considerations: Closed stacks; materials may not be photocopied or removed from rare book room

Comix Collection: Over 30,000 underground, new wave, and small press comics. Also includes related items such as posters, articles, and postcards.

589. Washington State University Libraries
Manuscripts, Archives, and Special Collections
Pullman, WA 99164-5610

Contact: Leila Luedeking, Curator, Modern Literary Collections
(509) 335-6272
Hours: Mon-Fri, 8-5
Accessible to Public: Yes
Accessible to Scholars: Yes
Special Considerations: Visitors from out of town are requested to inquire in writing prior to visit

Counter Culture Comix Collection: Consists of approximately 3,000 underground, new wave, and small press "comix."

Seattle

590. University of Washington, Henry Art Gallery
Henry Art Gallery, DE-15
Seattle, WA 98195

Contact: Judy Sourakli, Curator of Collections
(206) 543-2281, 543-1739
Hours: Tues-Fri, 9-5
Accessible to Public: Yes
Accessible to Scholars: Yes
Special Considerations: Access to collections is by prior appointment only

Collections are diverse and include fans, bags, hats, shoes, weaving tools, and related items from throughout the world.

Henry Art Gallery Textile Collection: This multifaceted collection emphasizes hand-woven and hand-decorated costumes and textiles, both functional and decorative, dating from 1500 to the present, and totals 14,600 objects. Ethnographic materials cover India, East Asia, Central and South America, Eastern Europe, and the Middle East and Central Asia. Materials in the *Western Textile and Dress* division include more than 1,000 lace pieces; brocades, velvets, and ecclesiastical pieces from France, Italy, Spain, and Russia; nine major 17th through 18th century tapestries; women's and children's clothing, 19th century to the present; 20th century designer fashions; and over 1,000 period costumes, coverlets, quilts, and household linens from the United States, 18th century to date. Western dress collection includes accessory collection of handbags, fans, parasols, shoes, laces, and underwear. The Gallery also has a collection of several hundred ethnic dolls.

591. University of Washington Libraries, Special Collections and Preservation Division
Suzzallo Library, FM-25
Seattle, WA 98195

Contact: Gary L Menges

(206) 543-1929
Hours: Mon-Fri, 10-5; Sat, 9-5
Accessible to Public: Yes
Accessible to Scholars: Yes

Historical Children's Literature Collection: Contains 2,000 17th-20th century children's books, including illustrated books, chapbooks, miniatures, primers, and textbooks; substantial collection of Hans Christian Andersen titles in various languages, including original Danish.

Frank Richardson Pierce Collection of Pulp Magazines: 1,500 pulp magazines from 1900-1950 containing stories by Pierce.

Mount Saint Helens Collection: A comprehensive collection of nonscientific materials produced after the Mt. St. Helens eruption. Collection contains published materials resulting from the eruption, including disaster agency responses; examples of realia, such as bumper stickers, t-shirts, postcards, and ash samples; manuscripts of poems inspired by the eruption, personal narratives; recordings of songs about the eruption; tapes of radio and television coverage of the disaster and public response; and other unique materials stemming from the eruption.

Photographs and Graphic Collection—Postcard Collection: Contains approximately 62,000 items, ca. 1895 to present, from throughout the world.

Pacific Northwest Collection: Includes westerns and detective novels set in the Pacific Northwest.

Spokane

592. Gonzaga University, Crosby Library
E 502 Boone Ave
Spokane, WA 99258-0001

Contact: Mary M Carr, Head of Technical Services
(509) 328-4220 Ext 3137
Hours: Mon-Thurs, 8am-midnight; Fri, 8am-9pm; Sat, 9-9; and Sun, 11am-midnight during the academic year; Mon-Fri, 9-5 between sessions; summer hours vary
Accessible to Scholars: Yes
Special Considerations: Items must be paged; collections listed below are part of the Rare Book Collections

Hewitt-Dempsey Playbill Collection: Consists of between 500-1,000 playbills published in the twentieth century. Collection is new, so access may be limited while it is being organized.

Fox Collection: Consists of around 300 items, mostly books, concerning radical labor history. Some of the items belonged to Jay Fox, best-known as the editor of *The Agitator* (later *The Syndicalist).* This collection also includes Fox's unpublished, unfinished manuscript.

Crosbyana Collection: Books and memorabilia concerning Bing Crosby, for whom the library is named. Part of the collection, including his gold and platinum records and his Oscar, are on permanent display in the Crosbyana Room. Other items are housed in the Rare Book Room.

Tacoma

593. Bing Crosby Historical Society
PO Box 216
Tacoma, WA 98401

Contact: Ken Twiss, Pres
(206) 627-2947
Hours: Mon-Fri, 11-3
Accessible to Public: Yes
Accessible to Scholars: Yes
Special Considerations: Appointments can be scheduled by telephone outside regular hours

Collections consist of records (LPs, 78, and 45 rpm), books, videotapes, audiotapes, photo albums, and memorabilia relating to the life and career of entertainer Bing Crosby.

594. Tacoma Public Library, Special Collections
1102 Tacoma Ave S
Tacoma, WA 98402

Contact: Gary Fuller Reese
(206) 591-5622
Hours: Mon-Thurs, 9-9; Fri-Sat, 9-6
Accessible to Public: Yes
Accessible to Scholars: Yes
Special Considerations: City library card needed to circulate materials; special collection materials do not circulate

Menu Collection: Consists of three manuscript boxes of menus from local and other restaurants.

Poster Collection: Consists of around 2,000 World War I posters and pre-1960 travel posters of the American West.

Oral History Collection: 100 oral history tapes of North and West European settlers in the Pacific Northwest.

Collections also include 5,000 local and nonlocal postcards; 15,000 35mm slides, mostly of Pacific Northwest subjects; a photographic collection of 25,000 prints of local subjects; and five manuscript boxes of popular sheet music printed before 1960.

Yakima

595. Yakima Valley Museum
2105 Tieton Dr
Yakima, WA 98902

Contact: Ray Swenson, Curator; Frances Hare, Archivist
(509) 243-0747
Hours: Tues, open to research but closed to public; Wed-Fri, 10-5; Sat-Sun, 12-5
Accessible to Public: Yes
Accessible to Scholars: Yes
Special Considerations: Appointment recommended due to limited space

Collections consist of large regional archives that include out-of-print book material, a *William O Douglas Collection,* 3,000 pieces of sheet music, and 30,000 photographs.

WEST VIRGINIA

Hillsboro

596. Pearl S. Buck Birthplace Foundation, Inc.
Box 126
Hillsboro, WV 24946

Contact: Dr Robert Bober
(304) 653-4430
Hours: Apr 15 to Nov 15, 9-5
Accessible to Public: Yes
Accessible to Scholars: Yes

Includes a complete collection of Pearl Buck books, as well as the original manuscripts, which are currently housed at West Virginia Wesleyan College.

WISCONSIN

Appleton

597. Institute of Paper Chemistry, Dard Hunter Paper Museum
1043 E South River St
Appleton, WI 54911

Contact: Hardev S Dugal, Dir, Information Services Division
(414) 738-3399
Hours: Mon-Fri, 8-4; closed holidays
Accessible to Public: Yes
Accessible to Scholars: Yes
Special Considerations: Groups over five should make arrangements about one month in advance

Dard Hunter Collection: Contains approximately 10,000 items, including paper specimens, tools, wood blocks, molds, and equipment documenting the history and craft of hand papermaking from its discovery in 105 A.D. in China. Manuscripts, correspondence, models, watermarks, and rare books from almost every country depict the history of papermaking.

Baraboo

598. Circus World Museum Library and Research Center
415 Lynn St
Baraboo, WI 53913

Contact: Robert L Parkinson, Research Ctr Dir
(608) 356-8341
Hours: Mon-Fri, 8-12 and 1-5
Accessible to Public: Yes
Accessible to Scholars: Yes
Special Considerations: Advance consultation by letter or telephone recommended; inspector on premises

Collections are extensive, including 7,000 original circus lithographs, 400 circus route books, 1,200 circus books, 1,600 circus heralds and couriers, 1,200 circus programs, 50,000 circus photographs, 20,000 circus negatives, 12,000 circus newspaper ads, journals, business records, and other materials. The library houses a Ringling Bros. & Barnum & Bailey Circus Archive, and also has statistical records, circus movies, a circus music library, and materials relating to Wild West Shows.

Beloit

599. Beloit Historical Society, Lincoln Center
845 Hackett St
Beloit, WI 53511

Contact: Evelyn Wehrle
(608) 365-7835
Hours: Tues-Fri, 9:30-3
Accessible to Public: Yes
Accessible to Scholars: Yes
Special Considerations: Access by
  appointment only

Collections center around history of Beloit, and include approximately 100 scrapbooks, diaries, letters of correspondence, and several privately printed books of pioneer reminiscences of early Beloit and Wisconsin, 1840-1930. Also includes a Hall of Fame of local sport figures who achieved some national recognition; high school yearbooks, 1916 to present; stereopticon cards; postcards; oral history tapes; centennial (1936) and sesquicentennial (1986) issues of the *Book of Beloit;* and manuscripts of local civic plays and pageants staged at various moments of the city's history.

Kenosha

600. Harmony Foundation, Inc., Old Songs Library
6315 3rd Ave
Kenosha, WI 53140-5199

Contact: Ruth Marks
(414) 654-9111
Hours: Mon-Fri, 8-12 and 1-5
Accessible to Public: Yes
Accessible to Scholars: Yes

Collection consists of approximately 600,000 titles of sheet music from the late 1700s to the present.

601. University of Wisconsin-Parkside, Area Research Center
Box 2000
Kenosha, WI 5314-2000

Contact: Archivist
(414) 553-2411
Hours: Mon-Fri, 8am-12 noon
Accessible to Public: Yes
Accessible to Scholars: Yes

Horlick's Corporation Collection: Records from 1873-1974 (six boxes, two reels of microfilm) of a Racine, Wisconsin, company that produced Horlick's Malted Milk. Collection consists largely of promotional materials, including advertisements and testimonials of explorers who carried the product on expeditions.

La Crosse

602. University of Wisconsin-La Crosse, Murphy Library, Special Collections Department
University of Wisconsin-La Crosse
La Crosse, WI 54601

Contact: Edwin L Hill
(608) 785-8511
Hours: Mon-Fri, 9-5, Sat, 1-4, during
  academic year; Mon-Fri, 1-4, during
  summer
Accessible to Public: Yes
Accessible to Scholars: Yes
Special Considerations: Advance inquiry
  recommended; materials do not
  circulate

Skeeters Collection: 1,000 volumes of early science fiction, horror, fantasy, and gothic novels, particularly those published between 1900 and 1940.

Oral History Collection: About 800 reels of reminiscences, interviews about local social life and customs, work, education, and family life.

Photographic Collections: About 30,000 images, from the 1880s-1950s, of domestic and family life, farming, business, work, play, and also river scenes. Copy prints may be purchased in most cases.

Madison

603. University of Wisconsin-Madison, Department of Environment, Textiles, and Design
1300 Linden Dr
Madison, WI 53706

Contact: Blenda Femenias, Curator
(608) 262-1162
Hours: Mon-Fri, 9-4
Accessible to Public: Yes
Accessible to Scholars: Yes
Special Considerations: Advance
  appointment required

Helen Louise Allen Textile Collection: Consists of over 12,000 items, including personal and household accessories, of daily life (doilies, towels, blankets, pin cushions, articles of clothing, bags, etc.) and supporting research library materials.

604. University of Wisconsin-Madison, Mills Music Library
728 State St
Madison, WI 53706

Contact: Jean Bonin, Tams-Witmark
  Proj Coord
(608) 263-1884

Tams-Witmark/Wisconsin Collection: Consists of 37,000 items, representing some 1,600 titles of musical stage materials to include opera, operetta, and musical comedy. Comprises full scores, piano-vocal scores, orchestral parts, and choral parts, as well as extensive script materials. A repertory of particular interest is from the popular stage of the 1880s to the 1920s, including music of Julian Edwards, Edward Solomon, Ludwig Englander, Edmond Audran, Leo Fall, John Philip Sousa, and others.

605. Wisconsin State Historical Society Research Collections
816 State St
Madison, WI 53706

Contact: Janice L O'Connell, Dir, Mass
  Communications History Center
(608) 262-9561

Hours: Library: Mon-Thur, 8 am-9 pm;
  Fri-Sat, 8-5; Between University
  Sessions: Mon-Sat, 8-5; Archives:
  Mon-Fri, 8-5; Sat, 9-4; Visual and
  Sound Reading Room: Mon-Fri, 8-5
  (Film Viewing Mon-Fri, 10-5 only)
Accessible to Public: Yes
Accessible to Scholars: Yes
Special Considerations: Some
  restrictions apply to use of specific
  materials

The collections represent a major resource for the study of American history, and contain books, periodicals, maps, manuscripts, and the archives for the state of Wisconsin. Current holdings include 1,000,000 printed items and over 700,000 microforms on all aspects of the history of the United States and Canada, including such related areas as genealogy, archeology, folklore, philately, and numismatics. The holdings are especially rich in pamphlets and ephemeral materials (many of which are related to the study of popular culture), newspapers, dissertations, family and local history materials, information on radical and reform movements, military history, labor and economic history, and the history of religious groups and churches. The *Visual and Sound Archives* include more than 1,000,000 photographs, cartoons, lithographs, portraits, posters, albums, and related ephemera. A special area of strength is pictures of rural and small-town life in the Upper Midwest from about 1880 to the mid-1920s. Also in the holdings are sound recordings including oral histories, historical motion pictures and television news film and videotapes. Visual holdings of the *Wisconsin Center for Film and Theater Research* include hundreds of motion picture and television films of Warner Brothers and RKO Studios, and motion picture, television, and theater-related still photographs. Several excellent guides are available, especially in the areas of film, television, and mass communications research.

Milwaukee

606. Marquette University, Memorial Library Department of Special Collections and University Archives
1415 W Wisconsin Ave
Milwaukee, WI 53233

Contact: Charles B Elston, Archivist
(414) 224-7256
Hours: Mon-Fri, 8-5; evenings and
  weekends by appointment
Accessible to Public: Yes
Accessible to Scholars: Yes

Don McNeill Collection, 1928-1969:
Consists of records relating to McNeill's
nationally broadcast radio program *The
Breakfast Club* (1933-1968) and *Don
McNeill's TV Club* (1950-1951). Includes
correspondence, scripts, advertising and
publicity material, photographs, tape recordings, and kinescopes.

607. Milwaukee Public Library
814 W Wisconsin Ave
Milwaukee, WI 53233

Contact: Kathleen M Raab, Asst City
  Librarian
(414) 278-3023
Hours: Mon-Thurs, 8:30am-9pm; Fri-
  Sat, 8:30-5:30; Sun, 1-5
Accessible to Public: Yes
Accessible to Scholars: Yes

Historic Photo Collection: Consists of
photographs of people, buildings, and
street scenes of the Milwaukee area (24
verticle file drawers arranged by subject).

Children's Room: Approximately 1,000
children's folk and fairy tale books from
the titles found in *Index to Fairy Tales*
and supplements. Also around 350 children's poetry books; 5,000 volumes of
children's books published between 1850-
1940 consisting of readers (some
German-language) and many series titles;
and a collection of children's books by
Wisconsin authors.

Reedsburg

608. Museum of Norman Rockwell Art
227 S Park St
Reedsburg, WI 53959

Contact: Joyce E Devore
(608) 524-2123
Hours: Apr 1 through Oct 31, daily, 9:30-
  5; otherwise by appointment
Accessible to Public: Yes
Accessible to Scholars: Yes

Collection includes over 3,000 original
covers, illustrations, advertisements,
postcards, catalogs, posters, and other
materials, spanning the 65-year career of
Norman Rockwell. The exhibit is on display in a small brick church.

Stevens Point

609. University of Wisconsin-Stevens Point Library, Special Collections
University of Wisconsin-Stevens Point
Stevens Point, WI 54481

Contact: John S Walters
(715) 346-2308
Hours: Tues, Thurs, Fri, 9-4:30; Mon,
  Wed, 9-8:30
Accessible to Public: Yes
Accessible to Scholars: Yes
Special Considerations: Materials do not
  circulate

Assassination Collection: Consists of
a number of materials relating to the
assassinations of John F. Kennedy, Robert F. Kennedy, and Martin Luther
King, including about 400 hours of
audiotapes (radio and television talk
shows and documentaries) and approximately 30 hours of videotapes (on a national symposium on assassinations held
at UWSP in 1976). This collection is one
of the most extensive of its kind.

The library also houses a Native American Indian Collection consisting of federal documents and other materials pertaining to Indian affairs.

Superior

610. University of Wisconsin-Superior, Jim Dan Hill Library
University of Wisconsin-Superior
Superior, WI 54880

Contact: Bob Carmack, Librarian; Leo J Hertzel, Curator
(715) 394-8465 or (715) 394-8346
Hours: Daily, 9-5
Accessible to Public: Yes
Accessible to Scholars: Yes
Special Considerations: Access available after consultation with either of the contact persons named above

Literary Guild Collection: Contains papers from the editorial work of John W. R. Beecroft, editor of the Literary Guild from the middle 1930s through the early 1960s. During Beecroft's time as editor, the Literary Guild became the largest book club in American publishing history. The collection also includes nearly a complete collection of *Wings,* the monthly magazine mailed to all Guild members for the period of Beecroft's tenure, as well as a copy of every Guild selection (and book dividend) chosen during this time.

WYOMING

Cheyenne

611. Wyoming Archives, Museums and Historical Department
Barrett Bldg
Cheyenne, WY 82002

Contact: John Langellier, Head of Museums Division
(307) 777-7022
Hours: Mon-Fri, 8-5
Accessible to Public: Yes
Accessible to Scholars: Yes
Special Considerations: Access with assistance from research staff only

Library of Wyoming History and Western Americana: Contains scholarly journals and academic periodicals published by other historical research agencies; microfilm of Wyoming news-papers, 1867-present; microfilm on early Wyoming military posts, Indian agencies, and Department of Interior papers, plus microfilm of privately generated historical materials; maps, plates, and unpublished manuscripts; primary source documents, letters, ledgers, diaries, and census records; oral history library and folklore materials; historical photographs; and artifacts and objects.

Laramie

612. University of Wyoming, American Heritage Center
PO Box 3924
Laramie, WY 82071

Contact: Gene M Gressley
(307) 766-4114 or (307) 766-4925
Hours: Mon-Fri, 8-12 and 1-5
Accessible to Public: Yes
Accessible to Scholars: Yes
Special Considerations: Restrictions may be imposed on individual collections

Collections consist of literary donations from over 50 authors, including Erma Bombeck, John Jakes, and Owen Wister, as well as music donations from more than 150 musicians, including Paul Anka, Ray Conniff, and Maurice Jarre.

Popular Culture Collections in Canada

ALBERTA

Calgary

613. Canadian Music Centre—Prairie Region Association
911 Library Tower, 2500 University Dr NW
Calgary, Alberta T2N 1N4

Contact: Mr Clare D Richman
(403) 220-7403
Hours: Mon-Fri, 8:30-4:30
Accessible to Public: Yes
Accessible to Scholars: Yes

Imperial Oil McPeek Pops Library:
Consists of arrangements of popular Canadian music, including folk, jazz, rock, popular songs, film scores, and music from radio shows and TV commercials; 64 titles.

614. St. Vladimir's Ukrainian Orthodox Cultural Centre Library and Archives
404 Meredith Rd NE
Calgary, Alberta T2E 5A6

Contact: Mr Mykola Woron, Librarian
(403) 264-3434 or (403) 277-6269
Hours: Sun, 10-2; also by appointment
Accessible to Public: Yes
Accessible to Scholars: Yes

Collections concerning Ukrainian life and culture are extensive; included are a 5,900-volume book collection, a periodical collection, 321 calendar/almanacs, 790 greeting/holiday/postcards with Ukrainian themes, 794 programs for Ukrainian events, photographs, portraits, maps, videocassettes, materials pertaining to Chernobyl, archives of Ukrainian organizational life, materials on Ukrainian participation in the Olympic Games, and related items.

615. University of Calgary Library
2500 University Dr NW
Calgary, Alberta T2N 1N4

Contact: K Zimon
(403) 220-5971
Hours: Mon-Thur, 8:30-8; Fri, 8:30-4:30; Sat-Sun, 12-4
Accessible to Public: Yes
Accessible to Scholars: Yes
Special Considerations: Closed stack system; items must be retrieved by staff

Fine Arts Clippings and Pamphlets Files: Consists of over 50,000 items and includes newspaper clippings, theater programs, press releases, exhibition catalogs, exhibition announcements, photographs, floor plans, and other ephemeral material relating to theater, radio, television, film, dance, design, photography, crafts, fine arts, and architecture. Though the scope of the material is worldwide, the emphasis is on the arts in Canada, and especially in the province of Alberta.

Edmonton

616. Consulate-General of Japan

#2600, 10020-100 St
Edmonton, Alberta T5J 0N4

Contact: Pauline Jones; Tomiko Ohuchi
(403) 422-3752
Hours: Mon-Fri, 9-4:30
Accessible to Public: Yes
Accessible to Scholars: Yes

Collections include over 1,500 books and 1,100 slides, films, and VHS and Beta videotapes pertaining to Japanese history, culture, politics, economy, arts, and craft; both English and Japanese materials.

BRITISH COLUMBIA

Burnaby

617. Simon Fraser University, WAC Bennett Library Special Collections, Contemporary Literature Collection

Simon Fraser University
Burnaby, British Columbia V5A 1S6

Contact: Eugene E Bridwell
(604) 291-4626
Hours: Mon-Fri, 12:30-4:30
Accessible to Public: Yes
Accessible to Scholars: Yes
Special Considerations: Materials do not circulate; application to examine manuscripts required

Contemporary Literature Collection: Consists of post-World War II modern and post-modern poetry, comprising 13,000 volumes of monographs, including a large collection of titles by Jack Kerouac, Allen Ginsberg, William Burroughs, and other writers of the "beat generation."

Contemporary Magazine Collection: Includes American, Canadian, and British little magazines, plus literary magazines and journals, but also including "underground" newspapers and magazines of the 1950s and 1960s to the present; consists of 1,300 titles, with 186 continuing subscriptions.

Michael McClure Archive: Includes manuscripts, correspondence, notebooks, and ephemera from the American poet's career, 1955-present; includes materials related to American social history, the youth and drug cultures, etc.

Other collections include World War I and II propaganda pamphlets, leaflets, and posters, with a strong grouping of World War II materials concerning the Vichy government; over 3,500 items.

Tappen

618. Comic Research Library

Comic Research Library
Tappen, British Columbia V0E 2X0

Contact: Doug Kendig
(604) 835-8529
Hours: By appointment only
Accessible to Public: No
Accessible to Scholars: Yes
Special Considerations: By appointment only

Collections include newspaper comic strips, 1910-1950s; Big Little Books; over 1,000 comic books from 1930-1950s; reference books; and fanzines.

Vancouver

619. Canadian Music Centre/ Centre de Musique Canadienne—BC Regional Office

1007 W 4th Ave
Vancouver, British Columbia V6J 1N3

Contact: Calin Miles, Regional Dir
(604) 734-4622
Hours: Mon-Fri, 9-5; also by appointment
Accessible to Public: Yes
Accessible to Scholars: Yes

Canadian Music Collection: Includes 9,000 music scores by Canadian composers; also a reference collection of about 3,000 records, cassettes, books, periodicals, biographical files on Canadian composers, and information files about the music.

620. University of British Columbia Library, Special Collections Division
1956 Main Hall
Vancouver, British Columbia V6T 1Y3

Contact: Anne Yandle
(604) 228-4879
Hours: During University term, Mon-Fri, 8:30-5; Sat, 12-5; remainder of year, Mon-Fri, 9-5
Accessible to Public: Yes
Accessible to Scholars: Yes
Special Considerations: Materials do not circulate

Children's Book Collection: Consists of 1,500 children's books, mainly before 1930; many Lewis Carroll items.

Science Fiction Pulp Magazine Collection: Consists of 30 titles; limited mainly to 1930s and early 1940s material.

Oral History Collection: Interviews with British Columbia pioneers.

Also a photograph collection and a Robert Burns collection.

Victoria

621. University of Victoria, McPherson Library Special Collections
Box 1800
Victoria, British Columbia V8W 3H5

Contact: Howard Gerwing
(604) 721-8257
Hours: Mon-Fri, 9-5
Accessible to Public: Yes
Accessible to Scholars: Yes
Special Considerations: Proper ID required

Popular Magazines and Journals Collection: Includes the *Comic Almanack, Criterion, Horizon, Lilliput, Floating Bear, Golden Book, Plexus, Tiger's Eye, Yellow Book,* and *New Worlds Science Fiction.*

Children's Literature Collection: Over 1,000 volumes, including comic papers, comic books, and *Big Little Books* such as *Boy's Friend, Bubbles, Butterfly, Comet Crackers, Jingles, Tip Top,* and others.

Local British Columbia Newspapers and Weeklies Collection: Includes *Monday Magazine, Georgia Straight, Pacific Tribune, The Western Gate, Octopus, Islander, Off Beat,* and others.

Other collections include a poster collection of World War I, art galleries, and local events posters, plus an oral history collection of materials on Canadian military history, old soldiers, local educators, and citizens.

MANITOBA

Winnepeg

622. University of Winnepeg Library
515 Portage Ave
Winnepeg, Manitoba R3B 2E9

Contact: Coreen Koz, Asst Chief Librarian
(204) 786-9802
Hours: Mon-Fri, 8am-10:45pm; Sat-Sun, 10-8:45
Accessible to Public: Yes
Accessible to Scholars: Yes

Mamie Pickering Thomson Children's Literature Collection: Consists of about 1,000 books representing children's reading in western Canada in the last 150 years; includes textbooks, boys' and girls' series books, and Sunday School novels.

NEW BRUNSWICK

Doaktown

623. Miramichi Salmon Museum, Inc.
PO Box 38
Doaktown, New Brunswick E0C 1G0

(506) 365-7787
Hours: Jun 1-Sept 30, daily; hours vary by month
Accessible to Public: Yes
Accessible to Scholars: Yes
Special Considerations: Access for handicapped

Collections include salmon and trout fly fishing data, photographs, artifacts, VHS videotapes, cassette tapes, manuscript collection, and mounted fish and animals; over 2,500 items.

Moncton

624. Universite de Moncton, Centre d'Etudes Acadiennes

Universite de Moncton
Moncton, New Brunswick E1A 3E9

Contact: Ronald LeBlanc, Librarian; Ronald Labelle, Folklorist
(506) 858-4085
Hours: Mon-Fri, 8:30-4:30; Tues, 7-10pm
Accessible to Public: Yes
Accessible to Scholars: Yes
Special Considerations: Use of some material permitted only with approval of depositors

Folklore Archive: Contains 2,300 tapes of interviews with French-speaking inhabitants of the Maritime provinces, classified according to eight main subject headings: language and oral history; folktales; folksongs; legends and beliefs; games and pastimes; customs and social life; weather lore and folk medicine; and material life.

Catherine Jolicoeur Special Collection: Consists of 1,100 tapes of Acadian traditional legends from the Maritime provinces and the state of Maine.

Saint John

625. University of New Brunswick, Ward Chipman Library

PO Box 5050
Saint John, New Brunswick E2L 4L5

Contact: Dennis Abblitt
(506) 648-5703
Hours: Mon-Thurs, 8:30am-11pm; Fri, 8:30-5; Sat, 12-6; Sun, 1-10
Accessible to Public: Yes
Accessible to Scholars: Yes
Special Considerations: Only rare and/or fragile books not available; magazine stories and articles photocopied

Science Fiction and Fantasy Collection: Includes books, journals, comics, phonodiscs, cassettes, calendars, manuscripts, galley proofs, letters, fanzines, and other items related to science fiction/fantasy.

NEWFOUNDLAND

Saint John's

626. Memorial University of Newfoundland, Folklore Language Archive

Memorial University
Saint John's, Newfoundland A1C 5S7

Contact: Dr Peter Narvaez, Assoc Dir
(709) 737-8409 (message: 8402)
Hours: Mon-Fri, 9-1, 2-5
Accessible to Public: No
Accessible to Scholars: Yes
Special Considerations: Serious research project

Collections include over 4,000 items relating to folklore (especially children's games, folk festivals, mummery, and the like), language, and oral history of Newfoundland and Labrador, as well as some of eastern Canada; manuscripts, sound recordings, photographs, artifacts, and miscellaneous documents. Also a collection of broadcast materials pertaining to the development of popular culture in Newfoundland.

627. Provincial Archives of Newfoundland and Labrador

Colonial Bldg, Military Rd
Saint John's, Newfoundland A1C 2C9

Contact: David J Davis
(709) 753-9380; also 9390 and 9398
Hours: Mon-Fri, 9-5; Wed-Thurs evenings, 6:30-9:45pm
Accessible to Public: Yes
Accessible to Scholars: Yes

Collections include *Private Papers Collections* and *Still and Moving Images Collections* depicting popular culture as it was recorded in Newfoundland and Labrador.

628. Provincial Reference and Resource Library, Newfoundland Collection

Arts and Culture Centre
Saint John's, Newfoundland A1B 3A3

Contact: Mona Cram, Provincial Ref
  Librarian
(709) 737-3955
Hours: Mon-Thurs, 10-9:30; Fri-Sat, 10-
  5:30; Summer: Mon-Thurs, 10-8:30;
  Fri, 10-5:30
Accessible to Public: Yes
Accessible to Scholars: Yes

Newfoundland Postcard Collection:
Over 630 postcards showing Newfoundland scenes, events, people, etc.

NOVA SCOTIA

Baddeck

629. Alexander Graham Bell National Historic Park—Bell Museum
PO Box 159
Baddeck, Nova Scotia B0E 1B0

Contact: Miss Aynsley MacFarlane
(902) 295-2069
Hours: July 1-Sept 30, daily, 9-9; Oct 1-
  Jun 30, daily, 9-5
Accessible to Public: Yes
Accessible to Scholars: Yes
Special Considerations: Exhibit areas
  accessible to public; reserve collection
  and archival material accessible only
  by advance appointment

Bell Collection: Includes works done by
Alexander Graham Bell and his asso-
ciates between 1885-1922; includes items
in medicine, aerodynamics, and water
transportation (hydrofoil craft), as well
as some items of Bell's work on the
telephone, plus personal memorabilia,
with a total of over 2,000 artifacts.

Halifax

630. Nova Scotia Sport Heritage Centre
1496 Lower Water St—Suite 300
Halifax, Nova Scotia B3J 1R9

Contact: Bill Robinson, Exec Dir
(902) 421-1266
Hours: Mon-Fri, 8:30-4:30; Sat-Sun, 10-3
Accessible to Public: Yes
Accessible to Scholars: Yes

**Nova Scotia Sport Heritage Collec-
tion, 1890-present:** Includes photographs, artifacts, scrapbook collections,
and a library dealing with the sport heritage of Nova Scotia.

ONTARIO

Delhi

631. Ontario Tobacco Museum
Box 182
Delhi, Ontario N4B 2W9

Contact: Mike Lipowski
(519) 582-0278
Hours: Nov 1-Mar 31, Mon-Fri, 8:30-4:
  30; Apr 1-Oct 30, daily, 8:30-4:30
Accessible to Public: Yes
Accessible to Scholars: Yes

Oral History Collection: Cassette
taped interviews dealing with immigrant
experiences, folk culture, and country of
origin (Hungary, Poland, Lithuania,
Ukraine, Yugoslavia, and Belgium) in
early 20th century; also some southern
Ontario, North Carolina, and Virginia,
with materials referring to tobacco growing in Canada and the "old country."
Approximately 350 interviews from 30
minutes to 7 hours; 25% transcribed,
most in English.

Photograph and Film Collection:
Consists of 200 photos and 30 hours of
film on immigration and early tobacco
production.

Also a library of materials related to tobacco production and immigration; about
1,000 items.

Kingston

632. Queen's University, Douglas Library, Special Collections
Queen's University
Kingston, Ontario K7L 5C4

Contact: Barbara Teatero, Curator
(613) 545-2528
Hours: Mon-Fri, 9-5; Mon-Thurs, 7pm-
  10pm; Summer: Mon-Fri, 8:30-4:30
Accessible to Public: Yes

Accessible to Scholars: Yes

Canadian Programme Collection: Includes 14,430 pieces, mainly musical and dramatic, relating primarily to Ontario and Kingston.

Canadian Broadside and Poster Collection: Consists of 3,423 items dating from 1792.

Historical Canadian Picture Postcard Collection: Consists of 2,570 items arranged by province, subdivided by place.

Also a collection of 993 pieces of Canadian sheet music.

Mount Hope

633. Canadian Warplane Heritage
PO Box 35
Mount Hope, Ontario L0R 1W0

Contact: Anna M Bradford, Curator
(416) 679-4141
Hours: Daily, 10-4; closed Christmas and New Year's
Accessible to Public: Yes
Accessible to Scholars: Yes
Special Considerations: Access to library and archives by appointment only

Collections include books, periodicals, and photographs related to vintage and modern aviation.

Niagara Falls

634. Niagara Falls Museum
PO Box 960, 5651 River Rd
Niagara Falls, Ontario L2E 6V8

Contact: J Sherman
(716) 285-4898, (416) 356-2151
Hours: Summer: Mon-Sun, 8:30 am-11 pm; Winter: Sat-Sun, 8:30 am-11 pm
Accessible to Public: Yes
Accessible to Scholars: Yes
Special Considerations: Admission fee; discounts and possible free admission for researchers who schedule visit in advance

The collection consists of memorabilia related to the men and women who have challenged Niagara Falls, and includes original devices used, explicit photographs, detailed articles related to the daredevils, and an accurate time line of stunts performed on the Niagara River. Collection consists of three barrels, one rubber ball, one section of tight rope, 30 photographs, and 14 articles on display.

North York

635. North York Public Library, Canadiana Collection
35 Fairview Mall Dr
North York, Ontario M2J 4S4

(416) 495-3427
Hours: Tues, 9-8:30; Wed, 12-8:30; Thurs-Sat, 9-5
Accessible to Public: Yes
Accessible to Scholars: Yes
Special Considerations: Materials do not circulate

Pulps Collection: Includes 730 volumes published in Canada between 1942-1952.

Souvenir Albums Collection: Consists of 140 souvenir albums of Canadian places, published between 1890-1950.

Ottawa

636. Canadian Ski Museum
457A Sussex Dr
Ottawa, Ontario K1N 6Z4

(613) 233-5832
Hours: Winter: Tues-Sat, 12-4; Summer: Tues-Sat, 11-4
Accessible to Public: Yes
Accessible to Scholars: Yes
Special Considerations: Usually limited to members; access for students

Collection consists of books, periodicals, memorabilia, and other artifacts related to skiing.

637. Indian and Northern Affairs Canada, Departmental Library
Ottawa, Ontario K1A 0H4

Contact: Mgr, Client Svcs Unit
(819) 997-0799
Hours: Mon-Fri, 8:30-4:30
Accessible to Public: Yes
Accessible to Scholars: Yes

Collections include materials on Inuit social life and customs, plus materials on the social life and customs of Indians of Canada.

Saint Catharines

638. Brock University, Popular Music Archive
Brock University
Saint Catharines, Ontario L2S 3A1

Contact: Barry Grant
(416) 688-5550
Hours: Mon-Fri, 9-5; inquire as to additional hours
Accessible to Public: Yes
Accessible to Scholars: Yes

This is a new collection and is constantly growing. Please contact Mr. Grant as to holdings that might be related to specific research projects.

Sudbury

639. Universite de Sudbury, Archives du Department de Folklore
Universite de Sudbury
Sudbury, Ontario P3E 2C6

Contact: Jean-Pierre Pichette, Dir
(705) 673-5661 Ext 305
Hours: By appointment only
Accessible to Public: No
Accessible to Scholars: Yes
Special Considerations: Knowledge of French

Collections include about 200 items of oral literature (stories, legends, songs, proverbs, etc.) of Ontario, especially items in French; also, between 6,000-8,000 plays, plus some manuscripts.

Toronto

640. Academy of Medicine, Toronto, Museum of the History of Medicine
288 Bloor St W
Toronto, Ontario M5S 1V8

Contact: Mrs Felicity Nowell-Smith, Curator
(416) 922-0564
Hours: Mon-Fri, 9:30-4
Accessible to Public: Yes
Accessible to Scholars: Yes

Dr T. G. H. Drake Collection: Consists of ceramics, furniture, glass, textiles, coins, stamps, metals, and prints relating to child welfare and popular health care from the ancient world to 19th century Europe; about 6,000 objects and images.

641. Canada's Sports Hall of Fame
Exhibition Place
Toronto, Ontario M6K 3C3

Contact: J Thomas West, Curator; Chery Rielly, Asst Curator
(416) 595-1046
Hours: Galleries: daily except Mon, 10-4: 30; Library: only by appointment
Accessible to Public: Yes
Accessible to Scholars: Yes
Special Considerations: Library by appointment only

John Davies Library: Contains material relating to Canada's sport heritage, especially materials on the Olympic Games; biographical files are maintained on over 330 Honoured Members of the Hall of Fame, as well as files on many prominent Canadian athletes. Photographic collection includes 30,000 negatives from the *Turofsky/Alexandra Studios Collection.* Also over 3,000 artifacts on exhibition and in storage, plus some video material concerning great moments in Canadian sports (2 1/2 hours).

642. Canadian Broadcasting Corporation Music Library
PO Box 500, Station A
Toronto, Ontario M5W 1E6

Contact: Jan Cornish
(416) 975-5858
Hours: Mon-Fri, 9-5
Accessible to Public: Yes
Accessible to Scholars: Yes
Special Considerations: Advance appointment preferred

Popular Sheet Music and Song Folios Collection: Over 50,000 song titles in collection, cataloged by title only.

Also over 10,000 titles of stock orchestrations for dance bands.

643. Metropolitan Toronto Reference Library, Arts Department
789 Yonge St
Toronto, Ontario M4W 2G8

Contact: Ms Isabel Rose
(416) 393-7017
Hours: Special Collections Room: Mon, Wed, 1-9pm; Tues, Thurs, 12-4
Accessible to Public: Yes
Accessible to Scholars: Yes
Special Considerations: Restricted hours and some restricted photocopying

Music Collection: Includes about 6,500 pieces of American and British historical sheet music, with songs and solo piano "parlour" items, from 18th century-present; 2,500 pieces of Canadian sheet music with topical songs and piano pieces from the 19th and 20th centuries; about 700 Canadian LPs of popular songs by Canadian artists; and ephemera relating to early Canadian piano and organ manufacturers, including trade cards, calendars, and other promotional items.

644. Metropolitan Toronto Reference Library, Business and Social Sciences Department
789 Yonge St
Toronto, Ontario M4W 2G8

Contact: Mr A Salam
(416) 393-7179
Hours: Mon-Thurs, 10-9; Fri-Sat, 10-6; Oct 16-Apr 30, Sun, 1:30-5
Accessible to Public: Yes
Accessible to Scholars: Yes

Current Data File: Includes newspaper clippings and pamphlets on popular culture subjects such as holidays, ethnic groups in Canada, lotteries, women's studies, and others.

645. Metropolitan Toronto Reference Library, Fine Arts Collection of Arts Department
789 Yonge St
Toronto, Ontario M4W 2G8

Contact: Mr A Suddon
(416) 393-7077
Hours: Mon-Sat, 10-9; Oct 16-Apr 30, Sun, 1:30-5

Accessible to Public: Yes
Accessible to Scholars: Yes
Special Considerations: ID required; use of materials supervised

Fine Art Collection: Includes 56,588 postcards of the 20th century, scenic and special occasion, with Canadian emphasis; 19th and 20th century greeting cards (3,000 in number); about 15,000 advertising cards, many 19th century and with Canadian emphasis; and 4,000 trade catalogs emphasizing manufacturing, wholesalers, and retailers of consumer goods produced in Canada or available in Canada, 19th and 20th century. Also materials on art appreciation, interior decoration, handicrafts, needlework, and other items.

646. Metropolitan Toronto Reference Library, General Information Services Division
789 Yonge St
Toronto, Ontario M4W 2G8

Contact: Ms S DeAthe; Ms Darina McFadyen
(416) 393-7131 (Ms DeAthe) or (416) 393-7188 (Ms McFadyen)
Hours: Mon-Sat, 10-9; Oct 16-Apr 30, Sun, 1:30-5
Accessible to Public: Yes
Accessible to Scholars: Yes
Special Considerations: ID required

Popular Magazine Collection: Consists of materials preand post-1900; primarily popular Canadian magazines, with over 50 titles.

Canadian Catalogue: A bibliographic and biographic file of Canadian authors, books, publishers, and periodicals from the 1920s-present.

647. Metropolitan Toronto Reference Library, History Department
789 Yonge St
Toronto, Ontario M4W 2G8

Contact: Mr David Kotin
(416) 393-7155
Hours: Mon-Sat, 10-9; Oct 16-Apr 30, Sun, 1:30-5
Accessible to Public: Yes
Accessible to Scholars: Yes

Baldwin Room Broadside Collection:
Over 25,000 items of printed ephemera,
including political and commercial posters and advertising, programs, menus,
tickets, and trade cards; Canadian, with
special emphasis on the Toronto area.
Materials date from 18th century-
present.

Manuscripts Collection: Consists of
original letters, diaries, and account
books from 18th century to the present;
especially strong on Toronto.

**Canadian Historical Picture Collec-
tion:** Includes 3,000 postcards with
views of Metro Toronto, plus 15,000
paintings, drawings, and prints, and
50,000 photographs.

648. Metropolitan Toronto Reference Library, Language and Literature Department
789 Yonge St
Toronto, Ontario M4W 2G8

Contact: Ms B Gunther
(416) 393-7010
Hours: Mon-Thurs, 10-9; Fri-Sat, 10-6;
Oct 16-Apr 30, Sun, 1:30-5
Accessible to Public: Yes
Accessible to Scholars: Yes
Special Considerations: Some materials
used under staff supervision

Arthur Conan Doyle Collection: Consists of 4,200 books, 635 bound periodical volumes, 267 records and tapes, 750
file folders, and newspaper clippings, periodical articles, and other materials pertaining to the life and work of Arthur
Conan Doyle and Sherlock Holmes; includes some memorabilia and manuscripts. Collection housed separately; for
hours and information, call 393-7008.

Estelle Fox Collection: Consists of
about 1,200 volumes of detective fiction
from 1900-1970; emphasis is on first
books of detective story writers. Also 24
scrapbooks of clippings, reviews, and letters of crime writers of the era.

Cookbook Collection: Consists of 250
cookbooks in 40 languages.

649. Metropolitan Toronto Reference Library, Regional Multilanguage Services of Language and Literature Department
789 Yonge St
Toronto, Ontario M4W 2G8

Contact: Ms Jaswinder Gundara
(416) 393-7075
Hours: Mon-Fri, 9-5
Special Considerations: Collections only
accessible to public on a rotating basis
through public library systems in
Metro Toronto area, not through
Metro Toronto Reference Library

Deposit Language Collections: Consist of materials in 16 languages on a
variety of popular topics.

650. Metropolitan Toronto Reference Library, Science and Technology Department
789 Yonge St
Toronto, Ontario M4W 2G8

Contact: Ms J Forde
(416) 393-7080
Hours: Mon-Thurs, 10-9; Fri-Sat, 10-6;
Oct 16-Apr 30, Sun, 1:30-5
Accessible to Public: Yes
Accessible to Scholars: Yes
Special Considerations: Materials do not
circulate; ID required

Automotive Collection: Consists of
about 25,000 shop repair manuals and
over 500 books and periodicals on automobile history and collecting; both technical and popular works.

Cookbook Collection: Consists of
about 1,000 cookbooks with emphasis on
ethnic and regional cooking; includes
food history.

Sports Collection: Includes approximately 3,000 books and periodicals covering all sports, plus history and tech-
niques; also a sports newspaper index
(1981-present) and a Canadian sports biography index.

651. Metropolitan Toronto Reference Library, Theater Department of Arts Department
789 Yonge St
Toronto, Ontario M4W 2G8

Contact: Ms Heather McCallum
(416) 393-7116
Hours: Special Collections: Mon, Wed, 1-
9; Tues, Thurs, 12-4
Accessible to Public: Yes
Accessible to Scholars: Yes
Special Considerations: Restricted hours;
some restricted photocopying

Playbills Collection: Includes playbills
and souvenir/house programs for professional theatre and dance productions in
Canada, 1840-present.

Poster Collection: Consists of 30,500
theatre, dance, film, and circus posters,
primarily 20th century.

Photographs Collection: Consists of
about 72,000 photographs of performing
arts personalities (Canadian, American,
and British), film stills, and Canadian
theatre/dance productions; all 20th century.

Also available are about 150 Japanese
woodblock prints from the 19th century
depicting Kabuki and Noh theatre.

652. Ontario Film Institute
770 Don Mills Rd—Don Mills
Toronto, Ontario M3C 1T3

Contact: Sherie Brethour
(416) 429-4100
Hours: Mon-Fri, 9-5
Accessible to Public: Yes
Accessible to Scholars: Yes
Special Considerations: Materials do not
circulate

Ontario Film Institute incorporates the
Ontario Film Theatre and Ontario Film
Archive for a reference library and research centre with 15,000 books on the
cinema, 4,000 posters, 5,000 stills, 60,000
individual files on film/biography/sub-
ject, 2,000 videotapes, 4,000 soundtrack
scores, and 200 16mm films.

653. Spaced Out Library, Toronto Public Library Special Collections
40 St George St
Toronto, Ontario M5S 2E4

Contact: Lorna Toolis, Collection Head
(416) 593-5351
Hours: Mon-Fri, 10-6; Sat, 9-5; closed
Sun and statutory holidays
Accessible to Public: Yes
Accessible to Scholars: Yes

Special Considerations: Materials do not
circulate, with the exception of the
Campus Collection

Spaced Out Library: Collections include 18,348 science fiction and fantasy
novels, short story collections, and related nonfiction, with complete collection
of Arkham House and Ace doubles. Also
13,574 science fiction/fantasy periodicals,
including pulps and over 1,000 fanzine
titles, plus 303 records and audiotapes;
1.5 linear feet of manuscript boxes, 13
linear feet of French-language materials;
15 linear feet of materials in Japanese,
German, Dutch, Chinese, and Finnish.

Jules Verne Collection: Includes 15
linear feet of materials in both French
and English.

Campus Collection: About 6,000 current paperbacks, circulating.

654. St. Vladimir Institute Library and Resource Centre for Ukrainian Studies
620 Spadina Ave
Toronto, Ontario M5S 2H4

Contact: Mrs Donna Wilk, Librarian
(416) 923-3318
Hours: Mon, Tues, Fri, 10-6; Wed, 12-8;
Sat, 9-5
Accessible to Public: Yes
Accessible to Scholars: Yes

Ukrainian Poster Collection: Over
1,000 posters depicting Ukrainian events
for the last 15 years.

Ukrainian Folk Arts Collection: Includes books, postcards, and pamphlets
in English and Ukrainian on the subject
of Ukrainian folk arts; about 200 items.

655. University of Toronto, Thomas Fisher Rare Book Library
120 St George St
Toronto, Ontario M5S 1A5

Contact: Richard Landon, Head
(416) 978-6107
Hours: Mon-Fri, 9-4:45; closed on
statutory and University holidays
Accessible to Public: Yes
Accessible to Scholars: Yes

**Latin American Chapbooks Collec-
tion:** Consists of about 300 titles of con-

temporary chapbooks of Brazilian *literatura de cordel.*

Yellow-back Collection: Includes 400 novels, mostly from 1880s and 1890s, in the "yellow-back" format.

Juvenile Drama Collection: Consists of about 6,000 sheets, colored and uncolored, cut and uncut engravings and lithographs illustrating characters and scenery of contemporary drama, primarily British, from 1810-1940; includes two model theaters with sets and characters mounted.

Mark Gayn Collections: Consists of artifacts, posters, and other ephemera, primarily from China, many from the Cultural Revolution; and a collection of 1,215 Harlequin Romances from 1950s-1980s.

656. Victoria University Library
71 Queen's Park Crescent
Toronto, Ontario M5S 1K7

Contact: Librarian
Hours: Hours vary

Canadiana Collection: Consists of historical and geographical works, especially strong in 19th and early 20th century poetry and fiction.

Victoriana Collection: Includes materials and documents relating to the history and activities of Victoria University.

Weslyana Collection: Consists of works of John and Charles Wesley; also contains biographical and critical material on the Wesley family.

Waterloo

657. Seagram Museum
57 Erb St W
Waterloo, Ontario N2L 6C2

Contact: David Nasby, Assoc Dir
(519) 885-1857
Hours: Tues-Sat, 12-8; Sun and most
   holidays, 12-5
Accessible to Public: Yes
Accessible to Scholars: Yes
Special Considerations: Research and
   reference by advance appointment

Joseph E. Seagram and Sons Ltd. Collection: Includes photographs of plant, operations, employees, and events, 1895-1980, plus miscellaneous papers, ads, labels, receipts from 1878-1930s.

Kitchener-Waterloo Collection: Consists of photographs of sports teams, 1897-1947, including curling, rugby, hockey, and softball.

Bottle Archives: Over 5,000 examples of corporate brands, including an 1887 Scotch Malt Whiskey produced by Joseph E. Seagram and Sons, Waterloo.

Other collections relate to the business of Seagrams Ltd., including advertising, label collections, and photographs.

658. University of Waterloo Library, Doris Lewis Rare Book Room
200 University Ave
Waterloo, Ontario N2L 3G1

Contact: S Bellingham
(519) 885-1211
Hours: Mon-Fri, 9-12, 1-4
Accessible to Public: Yes
Accessible to Scholars: Yes

British Women's Periodicals Collection: Consists of 106 titles including many popular items from 1893-1977; 35,000 individual issues bound in 1825 volumes.

Kitchener Waterloo Photo Collection: Archive of all photos taken by staff of the local newspaper, the *Kitchener Waterloo Record,* from 1939-1982; 800,000 black-and-white and color negatives document all local activities. No wire service photos.

Willowdale

659. Ontario Puppetry Association Puppet Centre
171 Avondale Ave
Willowdale, Ontario M2N 2V4

Contact: Mrs Nancy Kyle
(416) 222-9029
Hours: Mon-Fri, 9-4; some Sat and Sun
   hours
Accessible to Public: Yes
Accessible to Scholars: Yes
Special Considerations: Some materials
   limited to members

Collections include 500 puppets from around the world, 325 books (available to members only), 275 slides (members only), and an ever-changing loan collection for display.

QUEBEC

Montreal

660. Bell Canada, Historical Section

1050 Beaver Hall Hill, Rm 820
Montreal, Quebec H2Z 1S4

Contact: Stephanie Sykes, Dir of
Historical/Information Res Cen
(514) 870-7088
Hours: Mon-Fri, 8:15-4:45
Accessible to Public: Yes
Accessible to Scholars: Yes
Special Considerations: Researchers
should contact office in advance
concerning intent

Collections pertain to the history of Bell Canada and the telephone, and include 650 postcards, 1900-1920s, with telephone themes; 40 pieces of sheet music with telephone themes; 5,000 advertisements from 1880-present of Bell Canada, Northern Telecom, and Telecom Canada; 5,000 biographical files of employees, 1880-present; about 1,000 employees' anecdotes, 1880-present; and telephone directories for most of Ontario and Quebec and parts of the Northwest Territories, 1880-present.

661. Fraser-Hickson Institute—Montreal

4855 Kensington Ave
Montreal, Quebec H3X 3S6

Contact: Mrs Jeanne Randle
(514) 489-5301
Hours: Mon-Tues, 10-9; Wed-Fri, 10-6;
Sat, 10-4:30; Sun, 1-4:30
Accessible to Public: Yes
Accessible to Scholars: Yes

Collections include materials on the Institut Canadien, as well as a children's library.

Sainte-Foy

662. Universite Laval, Cite universitaire, Archives de folklore/Division des archives

5172 Pavillon Charles De Koninck
Sainte-Foy, Quebec G1K 7P4

Contact: Carole Saulnier, Archivist
(418) 656-5892
Hours: Mon-Fri, 8:30-12, 1:30-5;
Summer: Mon-Fri, 8:30-12, 1:30-4:30
Accessible to Public: Yes
Accessible to Scholars: Yes

Folklore collections include over 1,400 items on folklore and oral history of North America (Quebec, Maritime provinces, Ontario, Manitoba, New England, and Louisiana); about 12,000 slides and photographs are also available. Subjects include music, dance, legends, tales, customs, costume, material culture, handicrafts, popular art, religion, and other topics related to past and present culture of the French people in North America.

Sherbrooke

663. College de Sherbrooke, Documentation Center in Comic Art and Narrative

475 rue Parc
Sherbrooke, Quebec J1H 5M7

Contact: Richard Langlois
(819) 564-0150
Hours: Mon-Fri, 8:30-5
Accessible to Public: Yes
Accessible to Scholars: Yes
Special Considerations: Specific research
approved in advance

Collections include the largest and most complete collection of European comics in North America, with over 5,000 items; some American comic books and strips, but collections are mainly European and Canadian publications in French.

SASKATCHEWAN

Battleford

664. Battleford National Historic Park
Box 70
Battleford, Saskatchewan S0M 0E0

Contact: Ginny Gendall, Asst Supt
(306) 937-2621
Hours: May-Oct; contact for hours
Accessible to Public: Yes
Accessible to Scholars: Yes
Special Considerations: Library by
   appointment only

Collection deals mainly with Northwest
Mounted Police, 1876-1924; includes
artifacts, maps, books, and other ephemera.

Saskatoon

665. Frances Morrison Library, Fine and Performing Arts Department
311 23rd St E
Saskatoon, Saskatchewan S7K 0J6

Contact: Frances Bergles, Dept Head
(306) 664-9579
Hours: Mon-Fri, 9am-9:30pm; Sat, 9-6;
   Sept-May, Sun, 1-5:30
Accessible to Public: Yes
Accessible to Scholars: Yes

Book Collection: Consists of 20,000
books on the fine and performing arts,
including material on antiques, collectibles, crafts, television, photography, motion pictures, art, and music.

Record Collection: Includes 20,000
records featuring jazz, ethnic, classical,
rock, sound effects, musicals, movie
soundtracks, plays, radio shows, comedy,
and language recordings.

Also 200 periodicals on the fine and performing arts.

Weyburn

666. Turner's Curling Museum
417 Woodlawn Crescent
Weyburn, Saskatchewan S4H 0X5

Contact: Don or Elva Turner
(306) 842-3604
Hours: Daily, 9-9
Accessible to Public: Yes
Accessible to Scholars: Yes
Special Considerations: Call in advance
   to verify hours

Collections consist of items relating to
the sport of curling, including pins,
badges, stones, irons, pictures, ribbons,
medals, flags, books, blazers, trophies,
trays, and brooms.

YUKON TERRITORY

Whitehorse

667. Yukon Archives
Box 2703
Whitehorse, Yukon Territory Y1A 2C6

Contact: Lynn McPherson
(403) 667-5625
Hours: Tues-Fri, 9-5
Accessible to Public: Yes
Accessible to Scholars: Yes
Special Considerations: After hours
   research by appointment

Yukon Archives: Contains materials
on Yukon history, cultures, and development. Collections include sound recordings of native history and traditions;
26,000 photographs; over 300 posters;
postcards; a fiction collection of works
dealing with the Yukon; and comic
books, with 22 issues of *Sergeant Preston of the Yukon* and 8 issues of *Klondike Kit Library.*

Subject Index

All references are to entry numbers, not page numbers.

Film festivals, 45
Film magazines, 279
Film music, 68, 118, 130, 137, 148, 237, 366, 423, 513, 537, 613, 652, 665
Film ratings, 28
Film scripts, 27, 30, 43, 45, 62, 70, 149, 158, 181, 241, 383, 409, 424, 461, 518, 548, 566
Filmstrips, 147
Fine arts, 76, 163, 337, 665. *See also* Art; Dance; Decorative arts; Folk arts; Music; Theater arts
Finn, Francis J., 433
Finnish language materials, 653
Firefighting, 9, 403
Fisheries, 231
Fishing, 407, 483, 569, 623
Fitch, John, 197
Fitzgerald, John D., 101
Fitzhugh, Percy Keese, 43
Fix, Paul, 566
Flags, 505
Flagship News, 192
Floating Bear, 621
Floods, 485
Florida, 108-10, 113, 115
Florida fiction, 110
Florida folklore, 116
Florida history, 110, 112, 114-15
Flowers, 317
Folk arts, 77, 99, 116, 127, 193, 196, 199, 348, 473, 499, 585, 654
Folk beliefs, 48
Folk dance, 495
Folk medicine, 48, 88, 116, 181, 420, 624
Folklore, 48, 50, 102, 110, 131, 149, 157, 160, 181, 192-93, 198-99, 210, 287, 323, 332, 362, 411, 453, 605, 607, 626
  Acadian, 624
  Appalachia, 533
  Arizona, 12
  Canada, 219, 624, 639, 662
  Connecticut, 98
  Florida, 116
  Ireland, 520
  Italy, 379
  Louisiana, 211, 662
  Maine, 219, 624
  Michigan, 269, 277
  Midwest, 195
  Minnesota, 420
  Missouri, 304
  New England, 662
  North Dakota, 420
  Ozark, 315
  Pacific Northwest, 473
  South, 5, 301
  West, 11, 48, 470
  Wyoming, 611

Folksongs, 48, 50, 79, 88, 93, 102, 116, 148, 154, 181, 193, 199, 211, 219, 237, 266-67, 277, 315, 383, 415, 423, 473, 486, 501-02, 537, 573, 613, 624, 639, 662
  California, 26
  Colorado, 74
  South, 5
Food, 85, 125, 429, 650. *See also* Cookbooks; Menus
Food containers, 76
Foot races, 310
Football, 54, 71, 447, 519, 524
Ford, Gerald, 575
Ford, Henry, 272
Ford, John, 62, 158
Ford Motor Company, 272
Ford News, 192
Foreign language materials, 110
Foreign languages, 415, 649, 665. *See also* names of specific languages, such as Spanish language materials
Forestry Service, 83
Fort Robinson, Nebraska, 320
Foster, Hal, 158
Foster, Stephen, 412
Foundations, 278
Fowler, Frank, 342
Fowlie, William, 50
Fox, Fontaine, 158
Fox, Jay, 592
France, 158, 170, 208, 242, 271, 332, 590
Franklin, Benjamin, 91
Fraternal organizations. *See* Clubs and societies
Freas, Frank Kelly, 233
Frederick, Pauline, 101
French Americans, 332, 662
French fiction, 158
French folklore, 211
French language materials, 50, 110, 250, 639, 653, 663
French music, 211
Friedan, Betty, 247
Friends of Irish Freedom, 371
Frontier, 17, 468
Frost, Robert, 63, 241
Fundamentalists, 507
Funerals, 139
Fur trade, 311
Furniture, 22, 85, 99, 168, 192, 196, 309, 397, 406, 475, 581, 640
Galaxy, 213
Gambling, 327
Games, 20, 51, 99, 181, 199, 202, 208, 285, 335-36, 378, 381, 453, 520, 567, 624, 626
Garages, 183
Garber, Jan, 538
Garden and flower shows, 52

Index of Collections

All references are to entry numbers, not page numbers. This index accesses both main institutions and collections as well as sub-collections contained within the main institution or collection and mentioned only in the entry annotation.

Finn, Father Francis J., Collection,
Xavier University, 433
Fitzpatrick Short Subjects Collection,
Sherman Grinberg Film Libraries, 40
Flexner Slide Collection, University of
Louisville, 207
Flickinger Foundation for American
Studies, Inc., 224
Flint Public Library, Children's
Department, 280
Florida Collection, Miami-Dade Public
Library System, 110
Florida Folk Festivals Collection, Bureau
of Florida Folklife Programs, 116
Florida Folklife Archives, Bureau of
Florida Folklife Programs, 116
Florida State University, Robert
Manning Strozier Library, 113
Folger, Raymond H., Library, Special
Collections Department, 218
Folk Medicine Archive, UCLA, 48
Folklore Archive, Universite de
Moncton, New Brunswick, 624
Folklore Archives, Western Kentucky
University, 199
Folklore Cassette Collection, University
of North Carolina at Chapel Hill, 411
Ford, Arthur Y., Albums, University of
Louisville, 207
Foundation for Research on the Nature
of Man/Institute for Parapsychology,
413
Fox, Estelle, Collection, Metropolitan
Toronto Reference Library, 648
Fox Films, 1920-1970, 20th Century Fox
Film Corporation, 28
Fox, George M., Collection of Early
Children's Books, San Francisco Public
Library, 63
Franklin and Marshall College, Shadek-
Fackenthal Library, Archives and
Special Collections Department, 486
Franklin Furnace Archive Inc, 377
Fraser-Hickson Institute—Montreal, 661
French Library in Boston, Inc., 242
Frentz, Suzanne, Collection of Television
Soap Opera Scripts, 194
Friends Historical Library of
Swarthmore College, 508
Friends of the Cabildo Oral History
Collection, Tulane University, 213
Friends of the Third World, Inc., 164
Fuller Gun Museum, Chickamauga and
Chattanooga National Military Park,
121
Furness Memorial Library of
Shakespeariana, Pennsylvania
University, 502
Gaming Collection, University of
Nevada-Las Vegas, 327

Gardner Lincolniana Collection,
Lafayette College, Pennsylvania, 483
Gardner-Webb College, Thomas Dixon
Room, 409
Gayn, Mark, Collections, Toronto
University, Ontario, 655
Geerhold, Niles C., Popular Music
Collection, University of Pennsylvania,
501
The Gem Village Museum, 73
Genealogical and Historical Collection,
Birmingham Public Library, 3
General Literature Collection, San
Francisco Academy of Comic Art, 62
Georgia Southern College, Zach S.
Henderson Library, 122
Georgia State University Library, Special
Collections Department, 118
Gerard Photo Collection, Western
Kentucky University, 200
Gerhardt Library of Musical
Information, Towson State University,
Maryland, 229
Gerhardt Marimba Xylophone
Collection, Towson State University,
Maryland, 229
Germans from Russia Collection,
Colorado State University, 80
Getz, Oscar, Museum of Whiskey
History and Bardstown Historical
Museum, 197
Gildersleeve Collection, Connecticut
College, 93
Gillette, William H., Collection, Stowe-
Day Foundation and Library, 87
Girls Books in Series Collection,
University of North Carolina at
Greensboro, 416
Goldstein, Kenneth, Folklore Collection,
University of Mississippi, 301
Gonzaga University, Crosby Library, 592
Goodman, Benny, Archives, Yale
University, 89
Goodrich, S. G./Peter Parley, Collection,
Amherst College, 238
Gordon, Robert, Collection, University of
Oregon, 473
Gornick Slavic Heritage Collection,
University of Southern Colorado
Library, 82
Gospel Songbooks, 1891-1973, University
of Arkansas Libraries, 20
Goucher College, Julia Rogers Library,
237
Graham, Bill, Cartoon Collection,
University of Arkansas at Little Rock,
21
Grandview College Library, Danish
Immigrant Archives, 179

Queens College, Ethnic Materials
Information Exchange, 365
Queen's University, Douglas Library,
Special Collections, 632
Quinn, Anthony, Collection of Film
Scripts, California State University at
Los Angeles, 43
Rackham Collection, Wright State
University, Ohio, 444
Radcliffe College, Arthur and Elizabeth
Schlesinger Library on the History of
Women in America, 247
Radical Pamphlets Collection, Ball State
University, 170
Radio Pioneers Project, Columbia
University, 376
Railroad Model Collection, Southern
Methodist University, 552
The Rakow Library, Corning Museum of
Glass, 363
Ramsey, Eloise, Collection of Literature
for Young People, Wayne State
University, 276
Randolph, Vance, Collection, Pittsburg
State University, Kansas, 192
Rare Book Collection, University of
Alabama, 5
Rare Book Collection, University of
North Carolina at Charlotte, 412
Rare Book Room, International
Swimming Hall of Fame Library, 105
Rare Books and Manuscripts, Ball State
University, 170
Rare Books Collection, University of
California at Berkeley, 25
Rather Political Americana Collection,
Western Kentucky University, 200
Ravalli County Museum, 317
Record Auction Lists, Keesing Musical
Archives, Maryland, 235
Recorded Sound Reference Center,
Motion Pictures, Broadcasting, and
Recorded Sound Division, Library of
Congress, 102
Recorded South Collection, Tulane
University, 214
Records and Tapes, Keesing Musical
Archives, Maryland, 235
Regional History Collection, Southeast
Missouri State University, 302
Regional Oral History Office, University
of California at Berkeley, 25
Reid, Albert, Collection, University of
Kansas, 191
Research Foundation for Jewish
Immigration, 386
Reynolds, Harriet Dickson, Collection,
Houston Public Library, 556

Rhode Island Football Officials'
Association Collection, Providence
College, 519
Rhode Island Historical Society Library,
521
RI Textile Workers: Oral History
Memories, 522
Richmond Oral History Association and
Related Oral History Collections,
Virginia Commonwealth University,
583
Ringling Museum Theatre Collection,
University of Florida, 108
Robertson Music Collection, Warren
Library Association, Pennsylvania, 513
Robichaux Collection, Tulane University,
214
Rockefeller, Abby Aldrich, Folk Art
Center, The Colonial Williamsburg
Foundation, 585
Rockwell, Norman, Museum, 570
Rogers, Lauren, Museum of Art Library,
300
Rogers, Will, Collection, Will Rogers
Memorial, Oklahoma, 465
Rogersville Card and Label Company,
Archives of Appalachia, Tennessee, 533
Romaine Trade Catalog Collection,
University of California at Santa
Barbara, 68
Romer Photograph Collection, Miami-
Dade Public Library System, 110
Roosevelt, Franklin D., Library and
Museum, 368
Roper, L. V., Collection, Pittsburg State
University, Kansas, 192
Rose, Al, Collection, Tulane University,
214
Rose, Billy, Theater Collection, New
York Public Library at Lincoln Center,
383
Rose Music Collection, Tennessee State
Library and Archives, 543
Rosenfeld, Azriel, Science Fiction
Research Collection, University of
Maryland Baltimore County, 233
Royal Photo Company Collection,
University of Louisville, 207
Rush County Historical Society, Inc.,
189
Russell, William, Collection, Tulane
University, 214
Rutgers University, Institute of Jazz
Studies, 338
Sacramento Museum and History
Division, 56
Sadleir, Michael, London Low Life
Collection, Indiana University, 158

Questionnaire

NATIONAL FINDING LIST OF POPULAR CULTURE HOLDINGS AND SPECIAL COLLECTIONS

We need your assistance to help us locate additional Popular Culture Collections for subsequent editions of our guide. We hope that you will use this form to report your own holdings and to notify others who might have collections that relate to our project. Please feel free to xerox and distribute this questionnaire!

Mail completed questionnaires to Editors, *DIRECTORY OF POPULAR CULTURE COLLECTIONS*, Department of Popular Culture, Bowling Green State University, Bowling Green, Ohio 43402. You may also wish to phone us at (419) 372-2981.

Name of Organization/Institution: _____

_____

Complete Mailing Address: _____

_____

_____

Contact Person: _____

Phone: Area Code (   ) _____

Hours and Days of Operation (Include seasonal variations): _____

_____

Accessible To General Public?   YES _____ NO _____

Accessible To Scholars?   YES _____ NO _____

Describe Special Conditions For Access: _____

_____

_____

Please describe in detail your Popular Culture Holdings or Related Special Collections. It would be most useful if you could provide a copy of any brochure or other publicity materials relating to these collections. Use the entries within this volume as a general guide to format and scope. Attach additional sheets if necessary.

Author Biographies

CHRISTOPHER D. GEIST holds an M.A. in Popular Culture from the program at Bowling Green State University and a Ph.D. in American Studies from the University of Maryland, where he studied southern history, folklore, and Popular Culture. He has published more than 20 essays on such topics as popular literature, high school mascots, television, slavery among the American Indians, radio, mass media, popular architecture, and Popular Culture in the American South. His three edited books include a text in Popular Culture, which is used in college courses throughout the United States and Canada. He is currently working on two books, a guide to historic villages in the United States and a history of entertainment in Colonial America.

RAY B. BROWNE is founder and secretary-treasurer of the international Popular Culture Association. Dr. Browne is one of only eight individuals to hold the title of University Professor, the highest academic rank at Bowling Green State University. After studies at the University of Alabama and at Birmingham and Nottingham in England, Dr. Browne received degrees from Columbia University and UCLA. His bibliography, which is extensive, includes more than 20 books and scores of articles. His research interests span the field of Popular Culture studies, with works in popular literature, humor, television, popular rituals and heroes, theory and methodology, and many other areas. He is also widely known for his work in folklore and is an important Melville scholar. He is also founder and chair of the Department of Popular Culture at Bowling Green State University, the only such department in the nation.

MICHAEL T. MARSDEN is Professor of Popular Culture and Associate Dean of Arts and Sciences at Bowling Green State University, and holds degrees from DePaul University, Purdue University, and Bowling Green State University. Dr. Marsden has published widely in Popular Culture studies, and his special research interests include popular western novels, festivals, television, mass media studies, Canadian studies, and film studies. He is cofounder and coeditor of *The Journal of Popular Film and Television,* which is one of the most respected journals in film studies. He has been awarded several major grants, including a National Humanities Institute Fellowship and several awards from the Canadian government to facilitate Canadian studies in the United States.

CAROLE PALMER is a graduate student in the Popular Culture M.A. program at Bowling Green State University. Her special interests include the study of television and of popular rituals such as garage sales. She has presented papers to national and regional meetings of the Popular Culture Association. Ms. Palmer is currently working on her M.A. thesis, a cultural analysis of the *Amerika* television miniseries.

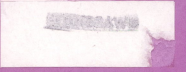